ELOQUENCE AND THE
PROCLAMATION OF THE GOSPEL
IN CORINTH

SOCIETY OF BIBLICAL LITERATURE

DISSERTATION SERIES

Michael V. Fox, Old Testament Editor
E. Elizabeth Johnson, New Testament Editor

Number 163

ELOQUENCE AND THE
PROCLAMATION OF THE GOSPEL
IN CORINTH

by
Brian K. Peterson

Brian K. Peterson

ELOQUENCE AND THE PROCLAMATION OF THE GOSPEL IN CORINTH

Society of Biblical Literature
Dissertation Series

Scholars Press
Atlanta, Georgia

Eloquence and the Proclamation of the Gospel in Corinth

by
Brian K. Peterson

Ph. D., 1997, Union Theological Seminary in Virginia
Dr. Paul Achtemeier, Advisor

Library of Congress Cataloging in Publication Data
Peterson, Brian K.
    Eloquence and the proclamation of the gospel in Corinth / Brian K.
Peterson.
        p.   cm. — (Dissertation series ; Society of Biblical
Literature ; no. 163)
    Includes bibliographical references.
    ISBN 0-7885-0445-2 (hardcover : alk. paper)
    1. Bible. N.T. Corinthians, 2nd, X-XIII—Criticism,
interpretation, etc. 2. Rhetoric in the Bible. 3. Rhetoric,
Ancient. 4. Eloquence. I. Title. II. Series: Dissertation series
(Society of Biblical Literature) ; no. 163.
BS2675.6.R54P47   1998
227'.3066—dc21   98-17374
                                                  CIP

Printed in the United States of America
on acid-free paper

To Aaron, Joel, and Sarah,
who have endured such foolishness

TABLE OF CONTENTS

LIST OF ABBREVIATIONS

BIBLICAL TRANSLATIONS

JB	Jerusalem Bible
KJV	King James Version
NEB	New English Bible
NIV	New International Version
NRSV	New Revised Standard Version
TEV	Today's English Version

BIBLICAL BOOKS

A. Old Testament

Gen	Genesis
Ex	Exodus
Num	Numbers
Deut	Deuteronomy
1 Sam	1 Samuel
2 Chr	2 Chronicles
Esth	Esther
Ps	Psalms
Prov	Proverbs
Eccl	Ecclesiastes
Is	Isaiah
Jer	Jeremiah
Ezek	Ezekiel
Dan	Daniel
Hos	Hosea
Mic	Micah
Zeph	Zephaniah
Zech	Zechariah

B. New Testament

Matt	Matthew
Mk	Mark

Lk	Luke
Rom	Romans
1 Cor	1 Corinthians
2 Cor	2 Corinthians
Gal	Galatians
Eph	Ephesians
Phil	Philippians
Col	Colossians
1 Thess	1 Thessalonians
1 Tim	1 Timothy
2 Tim	2 Timothy
Tit	Titus
Phlm	Philemon
Heb	Hebrews
1 Pet	1 Peter
Rev	Revelation

C. Apocrypha

2 Esd	2 Esdras
Wis	Wisdom of Solomon
Sir	Ecclesiasticus, or the Wisdom of Jesus the Son of Sirach
Bar	Baruch
1 Macc	1 Maccabees
2 Macc	2 Maccabees
3 Macc	3 Maccabees
4 Macc	4 Maccabees

OTHER ANCIENT LITERATURE

Ad Her.	[Cicero] *Ad Herennium*
Apoc. Abraham	Apocalypse of Abraham
Apoc. Moses	Apocalypse of Moses
Aristotle *Nich. Eth.*	Aristotle *Nichomachean Ethics*
Aristotle *Pol.*	Aristotle *Politics*
Barn.	Epistle of Barnabas
Cicero *Ad Fam.*	Cicero *Letters to his Friends*
Cicero *Ad Att.*	Cicero *Letters to Atticus*
Cicero *De Inv.*	Cicero *De Inventione*

Cicero *De Or.*	Cicero *De Oratore*
1 Clem.	1 Clement
Demosthenes *Ep.*	Demosthenes *Letters*
Demosthenes *Or.*	Demosthenes *Orations*
Did.	Didache
Dio Chrysostom *Or.*	Dio Chrysostom *Orations*
Diog.	Epistle to Diognetus
Epictetus *Disc.*	Epictetus *Discourses*
Epictetus *Enchr.*	Epictetus *Enchiridion*
IEph.	Epistle of Ignatius to the Ephesians
IPhil.	Epistle of Ignatius to the Philadelphians
Isocrates *Or.*	Isocrates *Orations*
Josephus *Ant.*	Josephus *Antiquitates Judaicae*
Josephus *Bell.*	Josephus *Bellum Judaicum*
Jub.	Jubilees
LXX	Septuagint
Philo *Agr.*	Philo *De Agricultura*
Philo *De Conf. Ling.*	Philo *De Confusione Linguarum*
Philo *Det. Pot. Ins.*	Philo *Quod Deterius Potiori Insidiari Soleat*
Philo *Leg. All.*	Philo *Legum Allegoriae*
Philo *Legat. ad Gaium*	Philo *De Virtutibus Prima Pars, Quod Est De Legatione Ad Gaium*
Philo *Op. Mund.*	Philo *De Opificio Mundi*
Philo *Praem.*	Philo *De Praemiis et Poenis*
Philo *Som.*	Philo *De Somniis*
Philo *Spec. Leg.*	Philo *De Specialibus Legibus*
Philo *Rer. Div. Her.*	Philo *Quis Rerum Divinarum Heres*
Philo *Virt.*	Philo *De Virtutibus*
Philo *Vit. Mos.*	Philo *De Vita Mosis*
Plato *Leg.*	Plato *Laws*
Plutarch *Pericl.*	Plutarch *Pericles*
Plutarch *Sert.*	Plutarch *Sertorius*
POxy	The Oxyrhynchus Papyri
Quintilian	Quintilian *Institutio Oratoria*
Seneca *Ep.*	Seneca *Ad Lucilium Epistulae Morales*
Seneca *Prov.*	Seneca *De Providentia*
Xenophon *Ag.*	Xenophon *Agesilaus*
Xenophon *Anab.*	Xenophon *Anabasis*
Xenophon *Resp. Lac.*	Xenophon *About the Lacedaemonians*

MODERN LITERATURE

AusBR	*Australian Biblical Review*
ATR	*Anglican Theological Review*
BDF	*A Greek Grammar of the New Testament and Other Early Christian Literature*, eds. Blass, Debrunner, and Funk.
Bib	*Biblica*
BT	*The Bible Translator*
CBQ	*Catholic Biblical Quarterly*
ETR	*Etudes théologiques et religieuses*
EvQ	*Evangelical Quarterly*
EvT	*Evangelische Theologie*
ExpTim	*Expository Times*
GBS	Guides to Biblical Scholarship
GRBS	*Greek, Roman, and Byzantine Studies*
HTR	*Harvard Theological Review*
HUCA	*Hebrew Union College Annual*
ICC	International Critical Commentary
Int	*Interpretation*
JAC	*Jahrbuch für Antike und Christentum*
JBL	*Journal of Biblical Literature*
JRH	*Journal of Religious History*
JSNT	*Journal for the Study of the New Testament*
JSOT	*Journal for the Study of the Old Testament*
LQ	*Lutheran Quarterly*
NedTTs	*Nederlands theologisch tijdschrift*
Neot	*Neotestamentica*
NICNT	New International Commentary on the New Testament
NovT	*Novum Testamentum*
NovTSup	Novum Testamentum Supplements
NTS	*New Testament Studies*
RB	*Revue Biblique*
RevExp	*Review and Expositor*
RHPR	*Revue d'histoire et de philosophie religieuses*
RSPT	*Revue des sciences philosophiques et théologiques*
SBLDS	Society of Biblical Literature Dissertation Series
TAPA	*Transactions of the American Philological Association*
TDNT	*Theological Dictionary of the New Testament*
TSK	*Theologische Studien und Kritiken*

TynB	*Tyndale Bulletin*
TZ	*Theologische Zeitschrift*
ZNW	*Zeitschrift für die neutestamentliche Wissenschaft*
ZTK	*Zeitschrift für Theologie und Kirche*

INTRODUCTION

With the Corinthian correspondence, we find the most extensive interaction that has survived between the apostle Paul and one of his congregations. The Corinthian letters offer a unique opportunity to investigate Paul's continuing interaction with a congregation, and to compare and contrast Paul's statements and positions made to the same group under different circumstances. This kind of longitudinal study cannot be ignored when dealing with the Corinthian letters; we cannot responsibly deal with a portion or an issue from these letters, pretending that we don't know anything else about this congregation or Paul's involvement with it.[1]

Other studies have recognized the ways in which Paul's tactics have changed during the course of the Corinthian correspondence. Jeffrey Crafton has recently published such a study in which he explores how Paul's "ethos" changes as the rhetorical situation changes throughout 2 Corinthians.[2] Others have noted changes that occur between 1 and 2 Corinthians:

> On Paul's side, too, there is a notable change which we should not overlook. When the question of parties and loyalties first raised its head he dealt with it by way of eloquent appeal against taking sides. . . . His appeal, we may suppose, had the effect that gestures of appeasement so often have—of cooling the enthusiasm of his own supporters and encouraging his opponents. The result was to precipitate a crisis in which he found himself unable to cope with the opposition for lack of support in the community . . . . As a result appeasement was dropped and the severe letter was written.[3]

Hans Dieter Betz has recognized that the nature of the issue regarding rhetoric has changed in the relationship between Paul and Corinth, and so had to be addressed differently in 1 Corinthians and 2 Corinthians –

---

[1]Jerome Murphy-O'Connor, *The Theology of the Second Letter to the Corinthians* (Cambridge: Cambridge University, 1991), 13 n. 15.

[2]Jeffrey Crafton, *The Agency of the Apostle: A Dramatistic Analysis of Paul's Response to Conflict in 2 Corinthians*, JSNT Sup. 51 (Sheffield: JSOT Press, 1991).

[3]T. W. Manson, "The Corinthian Correspondence," in *Studies in the Gospels and Epistles* (Manchester: Manchester University, 1962), 219.

namely, that in 1 Corinthians Paul could criticize the Corinthians for the kind of rhetoric they valued and point to himself as a model, but in 2 Corinthians it is Paul's own rhetoric that is under attack.[4]

The present study finds its beginning in a tension between the positions which Paul takes in 1 Corinthians 1-4 and 2 Corinthians 10-13 regarding the relationship of the Corinthian congregation to their spiritual leaders, particularly to Paul, and the possibility of their evaluating apostolic ministry. In 1 Corinthians 4:1-5, Paul argues that the evaluation and judgment of the apostles (not only of Paul!) is not for the Corinthians to make; that decision belongs to the Lord alone, and must await the final Day: "Therefore do not pronounce judgment before the time, before the Lord comes, who will bring to light the things now hidden in darkness and will disclose the purposes of the heart. Then each one will receive commendation from God" (1 Cor 4:5).[5] However, in 2 Corinthians 10-13, Paul obviously expects the Corinthians to make a judgment here and now, and to reject the "false apostles, deceitful workers" as apostles of Satan (2 Cor 11:12-13).

The tension between these two positions is often overlooked. For example, David A. Black notes that in 1 Cor 4 Paul insists that judgment of apostles is not the right of the Corinthians:

> The Corinthians are admonished to have the proper attitude toward apostles and teachers and to leave the estimation of their value and service to God.[6]

However, Black fails to relate this to Paul's insistence that the Corinthians judge and reject the "false apostles" in 2 Corinthians. Black is not alone here. Others have likewise emphasized Paul's rejection of apostolic evaluation by the Corinthians in 1 Cor 1-4, without mentioning that in 2 Cor 10-13 Paul urges the Corinthians to evaluate those who claim to be apostles, to reject his rivals, and to reaffirm their allegiance to him.

---

[4]Hans Dieter Betz, "The Problem of Rhetoric According to the Apostle Paul," in *L'Apôtre Paul: Personalité, style et conception du ministère*, ed. A. Vanhoye (Leuven: Leuven University, 1986), 44.

[5]Unless otherwise indicated, all English translations of biblical texts are from NRSV.

[6]David Allen Black, *Paul, Apostle of Weakness* (New York: Lang, 1984), 104.

At Corinth Paul deals with Christians who assume that judgment day
has already arrived and that they are the judges. As their judgment then
falls on Paul, he finds it necessary to insist that they withhold
judgment.[7]

Others have noted that Paul does allow the Corinthians a role in apostolic
evaluation in 2 Cor 10-13, but they fail to note that this is a shift from
Paul's emphatic position in 1 Cor 1-4:

The Corinthians were right to raise the question [of whether or not Paul
speaks on behalf of Christ] . . . , wrong only in the criteria they appear
to have applied in answering it.[8]

Paul does not deny the right of the Corinthians to evaluate the
legitimacy of his apostolate but he satirizes their criteria *ad absurdum.*[9]

Paul has conceded to the church the right to examine his work. In fact,
he welcomes this opportunity. . . .Paul is inviting them to scrutinize his
capabilities and credentials as an apostle.[10]

Is Paul being erratic in his statements to the Corinthians regarding
apostolic evaluation? Is he abandoning his principles in a desperate effort
to gain control of the situation in Corinth? If not, then what is it that
gives his arguments consistency and prevents the Corinthians from simply
concluding that Paul is both confused and confusing at this point? Why,
and perhaps more importantly, how does Paul make these shifts in his
argumentation? These are the questions that this dissertation proposes to
explore.

This investigation will involve us with rhetoric at two levels. First,
rhetorical eloquence has become a topic in Corinth's evaluation of Paul,

---

[7]Kenneth Rogahn, "The Function of Future-Eschatological Statements in the
Pauline Epistles" (Ph.D. diss., Princeton, 1975), 134.

[8]C. K. Barrett, *The Second Epistle to the Corinthians* (New York: Harper &
Row, 1973; reprint, Peabody, Mass.: Hendrickson, 1987), 335 (page references
are to reprint edition). See also C. K. Barrett, "Paul's Opponents in 2
Corinthians," *NTS* 17 (1971): 69.

[9]Jerry W. McCant, "Paul's Thorn of Rejected Apostleship," *NTS* 34 (1988):
563.

[10]Ralph P. Martin, *2 Corinthians*, Word Biblical Commentary (Waco, TX.:
Word, 1986), 473, 480.

and thus it also becomes an issue as Paul seeks to lead them to a more adequate understanding of apostolic ministry. Secondly, to inquire into how Paul makes shifts in his position and arguments, and whether he finds a way to be consistent, involves us in a rhetorical analysis of Paul's argumentation. This study will give attention both to rhetoric as an issue between Paul and the Corinthians, and to the rhetoric of Paul's own argument.

This study will find that Paul seeks to challenge the Corinthians' culturally accepted and supported view of rhetoric along with the social status and methods of evaluation connected with it. The Corinthians can continue in their present infatuation with rhetorical evaluations (especially evaluations of Paul!) only because they have not yet grasped the eschatological nature of the cross which has brought an end to the patterns of the old age. Paul's argument, however, is complicated by the shifting support for Paul himself in Corinth, and by his changing ability or inability to argue from his own premises; that is, at times Paul is forced to play on their field. As Paul moves through this argument the rhetorical situation will change, and so will Paul's argumentative strategy.

This study will argue that key to understanding Paul's rhetorical strategy is an issue that has been neglected by rhetorical criticism: the *stasis* of an argument. We will find that the *stasis* of Paul's argument changes as he meets new obstacles and as new opportunities become open to him. Specifically, we will find that in 2 Cor 10:1-18, Paul argues on the *stasis* of jurisdiction, not granting the Corinthians the right to pass judgment on him. This position is consistent with that taken in 1 Cor 1-4. However, for reasons discussed later in this study, Paul decides to argue on a different *stasis* beginning in chapter 11. There, Paul argues on the *stasis* of quality, admitting that the accusations made against him are true, but that such actions are not objectionable but in fact are necessary and honorable. This argument is grounded in the cross of Christ. It is the cross which determines the character of all legitimate apostolic ministry, and which has shaped Paul's own practices. With that, Paul has removed the criteria chosen by the Corinthians, and in fact removed their whole enterprise of competition and evaluation. Paul then returns at 12:19 to the *stasis* of jurisdiction. He now becomes the judge; through him the crucified and risen Christ speaks, and when Paul comes to Corinth, he will bring an anticipation of eschatological judgment. The Corinthians will not be judge over him or his ministry.

In all of this argumentation, it is the cross as the eschatological event of God which has unmasked, judged, and dismissed the world's ways which forms the stable center of Paul's arguments. It is the eschatological nature of the cross, and the proclamation of the cross which Paul brings, that leads Paul to deny the Corinthians' right to apply worldly standards to himself and his ministry. It is the eschatological event of the cross as the only adequate criterion to shape the church's present existence that becomes the basis for his arguments in defense of his apostolic ministry when the Corinthians insist on such evaluation. It is the eschatological judgment which the cross has brought upon the world that Paul himself will bring to Corinth when he arrives. Thus, though Paul is forced to change his argumentative tactics and the *stasis* on which he argues, the centrality of the cross remains consistent.

CHAPTER ONE

RHETORICAL CRITICISM

This study will approach 2 Corinthians 10-13 using rhetorical analysis, which has been experiencing a renaissance during the past thirty years.[1]

FROM THE ANCIENT CHURCH THROUGH THE REFORMATION

Reading Paul's letters as rhetorical works is hardly a new idea. Origen (185-254), Gregory of Nyssa (330-395), John Chrysostom (347-407), Jerome (342-420), and Theodore of Mopsuestia (350-428) all refer to the established practices and standards of rhetoric as they read and interpret Paul's letters. They may at times find Paul's grammar, clarity or style falling short of the ideals of rhetoric, but there is never any doubt that the letters are to be read in the context of rhetorical practice.[2] Augustine (354-430) taught rhetoric, and in his *De Doctrina Christiana* he analyzes

---

[1]For excellent reviews of this resurgence, on which the following discussion is largely dependent, see Burton L. Mack, *Rhetoric and the New Testament*, GBS (Minneapolis: Fortress, 1990), 9-17; R. Meynet, "Histoire de 'l'analyse rhétorique' en exégèse biblique," *Rhetorica* 8 (1990): 291-312; Margaret Mitchell, *Paul and the Rhetoric of Reconciliation: An Exegetical Investigation of the Language and Composition of 1 Corinthians* (Tübingen: Mohr, 1991), chap. 1; C. J. Classen, "St. Paul's Epistles and Ancient Greek and Roman Rhetoric," *Rhetorica* 10 (1992): 319-334; Stephen M. Pogoloff, *Logos and Sophia: The Rhetorical Situation of 1 Corinthians*, SBLDS 134 (Atlanta: Scholars, 1992), chap. 1; Duane F. Watson & A. J. Hauser, *Rhetorical Criticism of the Bible: A Comprehensive Bibliography With Notes on History and Method* (Leiden: Brill, 1994), 101-125.

[2]E. A. Judge, "The Reaction Against Classical Education in the New Testament," *Evangelical Review of Theology* 9 (1985): 170-171; Maurice F. Wiles, *The Divine Apostle: The Interpretation of St. Paul's Epistles in the Early Church* (Cambridge: Cambridge University, 1967), 16-17. For Gregory of Nyssa, see *Migne, Patrologia Graeca* 44, p. 1304 A-B, cited by H. D. Betz in "The Problem of Rhetoric," 17 n. 2.

biblical writings according to rhetorical principles, especially those espoused by Cicero.[3]

The Reformers also read Paul's letters in the light of Greco-Roman rhetoric. Luther, in his 1535 commentary on Galatians, "shows great interest in compositional and rhetorical matters."[4] Philipp Melanchthon writes his commentary on Romans as a rhetorical analysis; the letter is understood as an example of judicial rhetoric, and Melanchthon identifies the *exordium, narratio,* and *confirmatio.*[5]   Likewise, "Calvin's commentary on Romans has a thoroughgoing rhetorical analysis of the letter."[6] Erasmus' study of 1 and 2 Corinthians, *Paraphrasis in duas epistolas Pauli ad Corinthios,* is also a rhetorical analysis of those letters.[7]

EIGHTEENTH AND NINETEENTH CENTURIES

While "conscientious study of the history of biblical exegesis shows that the application of rhetorical categories never ceased entirely,"[8] it is in the eighteenth and nineteenth centuries that we again find a number of

---

[3]*On Christian Doctrine,* trans. D. W. Robertson, Jr. (Indianapolis: Bobbs Merrill, 1958), chap. 4. See also E. A. Judge, "Paul's Boasting in Relation to Contemporary Professional Practice," *AusBR* 16 (1968): 48-50; George A. Kennedy, *Classical Rhetoric and Its Christian and Secular Tradition from Ancient to Modern Times* (Chapel Hill: University of North Carolina, 1980), 149-160.

[4]H. D. Betz, *Galatians,* Hermeneia Commentary (Philadelphia: Fortress Press, 1979), 14 n. 97. For instance, on Gal 4:7 Luther writes "This is a rhetorical exclamation" (epiphonema); *Luther's Works* Vol. 26 (St. Louis: Concordia, 1963), 389.

[5]Philipp Melanchthon, *Commentarii in epistolam ad Romanos* (Wittenberg, 1532), ed. Rolf Schäfer, in *Melanchthons Werke in Auswahl 5* (Gütersloh: Mohn, 1965), esp. 373-78, (noted in Betz, *Galatians,* 14 n. 97); Karl-Heinz zur Muehlen's response to William J. Bouwsma in *Calvinism as Theologica Rhetorica,* ed. Wilhelm Wuellner (Berkeley: University of California, 1987), 55. Melanchthon's attention to rhetoric was not limited to his work on Romans; see the excellent discussion in Classen, "St. Paul's Epistles," 324-332.

[6]Betz, "The Problem of Rhetoric," 17. See also Bouwsma, "Calvinism," 7-9 on Calvin's rhetorical approach to the Bible in general.

[7]Cited by Betz, "Problem of Rhetoric," 17.

[8]Classen, "St. Paul's Epistles," 332.

scholars examining the writings of the New Testament as rhetorical works. In the eighteenth century, Johann Jacob Wettstein, Siegmund Jakob Baumgarten, and Johann Salomo Semler all paid careful attention to rhetorical aspects of Paul's writings.[9] Karl Ludwig Bauer produced his study of Paul's rhetorical technique, entitled *Rhetoricae Paulinae, vel Quid oratorium sit in oratione Pauli.*[10] Christian Gottlob Wilke wrote his *Die neutestamentliche Rhetorik: Ein Seitenstück zur Grammatik des neutestamentlichen Sprachidioms.*[11] In his dissertation, Hermannus Joannes Royaards includes a section discussing Paul's rhetoric.[12]

THE DECLINE OF RHETORIC

However, despite the appearance in the early twentieth century of such works as Friedrich Wilhelm Blass' *Die Rhythmen der asianischen und römischen Kunstprosa,*[13] Johannes Weiss' "Beiträge zur paulinischen Rhetorik,"[14] Rudolf Bultmann's dissertation *Der Stil der paulinischen Predigt und die kynisch-stoische Diatribe,*[15] and Hans Windisch's

---

[9]Johann Jacob Wettstein, Η ΚΑΙΝΗ ΔΙΑΘΗΚΗ. *Novum Testamentum Graecum*, 2 vols. (Amsterdam: Ex officina Dommeriana 1751, 1752); Siegmund Jakob Baumgarten, *Auslegung der beiden Briefe St. Pauli an die Corinthier; mit Anmerkungen und einer Paraphrase M. Johann August Nösselts, nebst einer Vorrede herausgeven von Johann Salomo Semler* (Halle: Gebauer, 1761) (these cited by Betz, "Problem of Rhetoric," 18); Johann Salomo Semler, *Paraphrasis II. Epistolae ad Corinthos* (Halle, 1776).

[10]2 vols. (Halae: Impensis Orphanotrophei, 1782).

[11](Dresden & Leipzig: Arnold, 1843).

[12]*Disputatio inauguralis de altera Pauli ad Corinthios epistola, et observanda in illa apostoli indole et oratione,* (Trajecti ad Rhenum: J. Altheer, 1818), 99-152. Cited by Betz, "Problem of Rhetoric," 18.

[13](Leipzig: Deichert, 1905).

[14]In *Theologische Studien, Bernhard Weiss zu seinem 70 Geburtstag dargebracht* (Göttingen: Vandenhoeck & Ruprecht, 1897), 165-247. Weiss argues that since the letters were intended for public reading, they must include oratorical aspects and can be evaluated accordingly.

[15](Göttingen: Vandenhoeck & Ruprecht, 1910). Bultmann's argument is that Paul functioned like a Cynic street preacher, and that his letters are thus from a lower level of rhetorical culture. The first aspect of this argument has been countered by Stanley K. Stowers, *The Diatribe and Paul's Letter to the Romans,* SBLDS 57 (Chico: Scholars Press, 1981); the second aspect has continued to influence pauline scholarship (see below).

rhetorical analysis in *Der zweite Korintherbrief*,[16] consideration of rhetorical categories and techniques had begun to fall into disrepute by the end of the nineteenth century. This trend can be seen in Eduard Norden's blistering attack against this approach in his *Die antike Kunstprosa vom IV. Jahrhundert vor Christus bis in die Zeit der Renaissance.*[17] Norden criticizes Wilke and Blass for using rhetorical categories from classical studies to examine the writings of the New Testament; he felt that biblical scholars had here overstepped their bounds, and that measured by the standards of classical rhetoric, the letters of Paul fell short, despite their rhetorical impact that even Norden had to admit. He also attacked Carl Friedrich Georg Heinrici for his use of classical Greek and Latin authors in his commentary on 2 Corinthians.[18] Heinrici responded to the attack in an appendix in the second edition of his commentary,[19] and Norden in his own second edition retracted much of his original criticism.[20] However, the scholarly world seems to have paid little attention to this retraction.

Rhetoric appeared to be on its way out, not only in biblical studies but in education in general. Schools began dropping rhetoric from their curricula, and what little attention was paid to rhetoric tended to be limited to matters of style or ornamentation; i.e., the forms had been separated from their content and purpose in the whole work.[21] In addition, currents within New Testament scholarship itself tended to keep rhetorical considerations separate from the core of study. Adolf Deissmann's influential (though sentimentalized) assessment was that the writings of the New Testament are closer to the simple papyri than to formal literary works; thus Paul's letters need to be seen as non-literary, connected with the life of the common people rather than a product of the literary elite.

> The New Testament was not a product of the colorless refinement of an upper class. On the contrary, it was, humanly speaking, a product of the force that came unimpaired, and strengthened by the Divine Presence,

---

[16](Göttingen: Vandenhoeck & Ruprecht, 1924).

[17](Leipzig: B. G. Teubner, 1898).

[18]Carl F. G. Heinrici, *Das zweite Sendschreiben des Apostels Paulus an die Korinthier* (Berlin: Hertz, 1887). Eduard Norden, *Die antike Kunstprosa*, 2.474-75, 493ff.

[19]"Zum Hellenismus des Paulus," in *Der zweite Brief an die Korinther, mit einem Anhang* (Göttingen: Vandenhoeck & Ruprecht, 1900), 436-58.

[20]Vol. 2 (1915), "Nachträge," 3-4.

[21]Watson and Hauser, *Rhetorical Criticism*, 105.

from the lower class. This reason alone enabled it to become the book of all mankind. . . . The New Testament has become the Book of the People because it began by being the Book of the People.[22]

New Testament scholarship was becoming occupied with apocalyptic in Jesus' teaching and with the history of religions approach, with renewed interest in the myth and ritual of early Christianity but little time for classical rhetoric. The theological movements of Dialectic and Existentialism had little interest in anything so rooted in human history and culture as classical rhetoric as a tool in New Testament interpretation. The focus was shifting from concerns of history to concerns of hermeneutics.[23] The result has been that while sociologists, psychologists, and philosophers of language and communication were paying renewed attention to issues of rhetoric, such concerns became strangely separated from biblical studies. What studies did appear in the first half of the twentieth century that paid attention to rhetoric tended to treat it as limited to aspects of style or devices,[24] and often these were seen as an unfortunate influence of the wider hellenistic culture. In fact, "denouncing rhetoric became fashionable."[25] Thus F. C. Grant can claim that in the writings of the New Testament, "there are echoes of oratory and of orators here and there, but no studied imitation." Grant assures us that "Paul was no Greek rhetorician," and he takes at face value Paul's claim to have "positively rejected the artful literary and rhetorical devices of the 'wise man of this age' (see his defense in I Cor. 1-4, II Cor. 10-13)."[26]

---

[22]Adolf Deissmann, *Paul: A Study in Social and Religious History*, 2d ed., trans. W. Wilson (London: Hodder & Stoughton, 1926), 144-45; see also his *Light From the Ancient East: The New Testament Illustrated by Recently Discovered Texts of the Graeco-Roman World* (London: Hodder & Stoughton, 1910).

[23]For these trends, see Mack, *Rhetoric*, p. 12; Betz, "Problem of Rhetoric," 19-21; Pogoloff, *Logos and Sophia*, 15-22.

[24]Thus N. Lund, *Chiasmus in the New Testament* (Chapel Hill: University of North Carolina, 1942).

[25]Betz, "Problem of Rhetoric," 20.

[26]"Rhetoric and Oratory," *Interpreter's Dictionary of the Bible* (Nashville: Abingdon, 1962), 4:76-77; note that the only connection Grant allows for rhetoric and Paul's writing is the model of the Cynic-Stoic diatribe (clearly with dependence here on Bultmann, though Grant mentions Bultmann's study only in his bibliography), which he sees as a less lofty kind of rhetoric used by "street preachers." Note also his rather prejudiced remark on page 77: "It was in a late

RENAISSANCE OF RHETORIC

Yet Grant's remarks dismissing the importance or even the appropriateness of rhetorical issues for New Testament interpretation were made on the eve of the modern revival of rhetorical study of the New Testament.[27] The beginning of this rebirth is often traced to James Muilenburg's 1968 SBL presidential address, published as "Form Criticism and Beyond."[28] Muilenburg recognized that form criticism had been able to move biblical scholarship beyond the limits reached by source criticism; but now he claimed form criticism had also reached its limits. Muilenburg issued a call to move beyond form criticism to other literary features of the texts, features often ignored by form criticism. By its very nature, form criticism laid emphasis on what was typical in a text, and paid little attention to what was unique. Form criticism was bound to generalize and miss the particularity of texts, and to treat texts as authorless examples of genres. To get at the particularity, Muilenburg proposed rhetorical criticism. It was a limited call, and one that has been outgrown by the interest it helped to spark. Muilenburg limited his remarks to the study of the Old Testament, his area of expertise. He also continued the tendency of equating rhetoric with stylistic devices.[29]

---

period, in the second century and afterward, that the artificial and florid popular rhetoric of the time began to influence Christian preaching and writing, especially sermons."

[27]For reviews of the current state of rhetorical criticism in biblical studies, see Martin Kessler, "An Introduction to Rhetorical Criticism," *Semitics* 7 (1980): 1-27; Wilhelm Wuellner, "Where is Rhetorical Criticism Taking Us?," *CBQ* 49 (1987): 448-63; C. Clifton Black, "Keeping Up With Recent Studies: Rhetorical Criticism and Biblical Interpretation," *ExpT* 100 (1989): 252-58.

[28]*JBL* 88 (1969): 1-18.

[29]This has, in fact, resulted in some confusion over just what is meant when biblical scholars speak of "rhetorical criticism;" see Paul J. Achtemeier, "Omne Verbum Sonat: The New Testament and the Oral Environment of Late Western Antiquity," *JBL* 109 (1990): 8. Dale Patrick, *Rhetoric and Biblical Interpretation* (Sheffield: Almond, 1990) follows Muilenburg's lead in treating rhetoric as limited to matters of style or devices used. Note also Yegoshua Gitay, *Prophecy and Persuasion: A Study of Isaiah 40-48*, Forum Theologiae Linguisticae, no. 14, ed. Erhardt Güttgemanns (Bonn: Linguistica Biblica, 1981), 27: "Muilenburg's definition and use of the term rhetoric does not understand rhetoric as the art of persuasion. That is to say, both Muilenburg and his followers are concerned with style as a functional device for determining the literary unit and its structure, but

Nevertheless, Muilenburg's call heralded a shift in paradigms for biblical scholarship.

There were other developments under way in biblical studies that aided this renewed appreciation for rhetoric. The old dichotomy between Hebrew and hellenistic culture that had seemed to separate Paul from the Greco-Roman rhetorical tradition was coming to be seen as false; there was in fact much more contact and influence between the two.[30] Furthermore, Deissmann's distinctions between literary epistles (Episteln) and non-literary letters (Briefe) was coming to be seen as too simplistic.

> Deissmann's antithesis between the natural and the conventional was typical of nineteenth- and early twentieth-century Romanticism. . . . Now, however, theorists of literature and culture are widely agreed that there is a conventional dimension to all intelligible human behavior. Thus Deissmann's dictum that 'the letter is a piece of life, the epistle is a product of literary art' (*Light from the Ancient East*, p. 230) is a misguided contrast. All letters are literature in the broadest sense. Even the common papyrus letters follow highly stylized letter-writing conventions.[31]

As Stowers indicates, recent studies have focused on the ways in which Paul has used and modified hellenistic epistolary conventions rather than on how Paul might be separated from hellenistic culture.[32]

---

their analysis is not oriented towards rhetoric as the pragmatic art of persuasion." Hans Conzelmann's Hermeneia Commentary *1 Corinthians* (Philadelphia: Fortress, 1975) is an example of the approach limited to issues of style (see esp. p. 5). See also BDF #485-96.

[30]Martin Hengel, *Judaism and Hellenism: Studies in Their Encounter in Palestine During the Hellenistic Period*, trans. J. Bowden (Philadelphia: Fortress, 1974). On the connections between the language of the New Testament and hellenistic culture see James Voelz, "The Language of the New Testament," *Aufstieg und Niedergang der Römischen Welt* 2.25.2, ed. H. Temorini & W. Haase (Berlin: Walter de Gruyter, 1984), 893-977, esp. 928.

[31]Stanley K. Stowers, *Letter Writing in Greco-Roman Antiquity* (Philadelphia: Westminster, 1986), 19-20. A more balanced approach to the typology of letters than that offered by Deissmann was given by William G. Doty, "The Classification of Epistolary Literature," *CBQ* 31 (1969): 183-99.

[32]Paul Schubert, *Form and Function of the Pauline Thanksgivings* (Berlin: Töpelmann, 1939); William G. Doty, *Letters in Primitive Christianity* (Philadelphia: Fortress, 1973); Peter Thomas O'Brien, *Introductory Thanksgivings in the Letters of Paul* (Leiden: Brill, 1977); John L. White, *Light from Ancient*

Deissmann's romantic identification of early Christianity with the simple, lower classes was also being challenged. Sociological studies of the New Testament were showing that the early church was a much richer social and economic mix.[33] The literary level that Deissmann found in the papyri of Egypt was not necessarily reflective of the literary or educational level that Paul would have found in the urban centers of the Greek world. There were members of the early church who belonged to the educated class; even apart from the question of Paul's own education, he was writing to congregations that included educated members, and his letters would be read and judged according to those standards.

The rise of sociological study of the New Testament also added interest to rhetorical analysis. Rhetoric treats speech as a social event, as an attempt to reshape the social realities which it addresses. Ancient rhetoricians emphasized that a speech could never be separated from its situation. That new appreciation for rhetoric as purposeful argumentation, rather than as simply ornamentation, found expression in the highly influential work by Chaim Perelman and L. Olbrechts-Tyteca, *La Nouvelle rhétorique: Traité l'argumentation.*[34] Besides their emphasis on rhetoric as argumentation, the authors also stress the importance of the context or social situation when analyzing the persuasive power of an argument.

Three other authors whose works predate Muilenburg's address also helped to fuel a renewed interest in rhetoric within biblical studies. The first is Amos Wilder's book *The Language of the Gospel: Early Christian Rhetoric.*[35] Wilder recognized that literary works have rhetorical characteristics, and that these characteristics can be used to investigate the

---

Letters (Fortress, Philadelphia, 1986); David E. Aune, *The New Testament in Its Literary Environment* (Philadelphia: Westminster, 1987).

[33] E. A. Judge, *The Social Pattern of Christian Groups in the First Century* (London: Tyndale, 1960); idem, "The Early Christians as a Scholastic Community," *JRH* 1 (1960-61): 125-137; Gerd Theissen, *The Social Setting of Pauline Christianity* (Philadelphia: Fortress, 1982); Abraham J. Malherbe, *Social Aspects of Early Christianity* (Philadelphia: Fortress, 1983); Wayne Meeks, *The First Urban Christians: The Social World of the Apostle Paul* (New Haven: Yale University, 1983).

[34] (Paris: Presses Universitaires de France, 1958); translation: *A Treatise on Argumentation*, trans. J. Wilkinson and P. Weaver (Notre Dame: Notre Dame University, 1969).

[35] (New York: Harper and Row, 1964).

social-historical situation that evoked them. The second author is Robert Funk, whose *Language, Hermeneutic, and Word of God*[36] argued that there is a similarity between letters and oral communication, and that letters can be understood and studied as structured speech. About this same time, E. A. Judge wrote an article entitled "Paul's Boasting in Relation to Contemporary Professional Practice"[37] that raised the question of Paul's possible rhetorical training, and called for an analysis of the rhetoric of the New Testament as well as the social context and implications of Paul's stance regarding rhetoric.

> Such is the subtlety of the lost rhetorical art, that until we have it back under control we can hardly think we know how to read passages which both by style and content belong to Paul's struggle with rhetorically trained opponents for the support of his rhetorically fastidious converts.[38]

This new appreciation for rhetoric as argumentation and its respect for the shape and integrity of a speech (or letter) as a whole also came at a time when form and redaction criticism were giving way to narrative criticism and its appreciation of the writers (particularly of the gospels) as creative and purposeful authors.[39] Rhetorical analysis was seen to hold the promise of drawing together the concerns of literary criticism and social history.

Application: Hans Dieter Betz

Hans Dieter Betz's 1979 Hermeneia commentary *Galatians* was the first modern study of a New Testament book according to Greco-Roman rhetoric. "What distinguishes Betz's work from previous examinations of Pauline rhetoric is his focus on the invention and arrangement of arguments in a letter discourse, whereas previous studies were mostly

---

[36](New York: Harper and Row, 1966).

[37]*AusBR* 16 (1968): 37-50.

[38]Judge, "Boasting," 48.

[39]Norman R. Petersen, *Literary Criticism for New Testament Critics* (Philadelphia: Fortress, 1978); David M. Rhoads and Donald Michie, *Mark as Story: An Introduction to the Narrative of a Gospel* (Philadelphia: Fortress, 1983); R. Alan Culpepper, *Anatomy of the Fourth Gospel: A Study in Literary Design* (Philadelphia: Fortress, 1983).

confined to style."[40] Betz's work has been criticized at several points.[41] Though his aim is to analyze the letter according to ancient rhetorical theory, one of the major sections of the letter (5:1-6:10) he labels as *exhortatio*[42] although no such element of arrangement is discussed by the ancient rhetorical handbooks. Betz himself recognizes this situation: "It is rather puzzling to see that parenesis plays only a marginal role in the ancient rhetorical handbooks, if not in rhetoric itself."[43] Betz also notes that neither Aristotle nor Quintilian mentions *exhortatio*, although "pare-nesis was characteristic of the philosophical literature," and "the philo-sophical letters . . . very often have at the end a parenetical section."[44]

Rhetoric and Ancient Epistolary Theory

Betz's use of an apparently non-rhetorical term in his rhetorical analysis of a letter[45] exposes an issue with which scholarship is still wrestling:

---

[40]Mitchell, *Rhetoric of Reconciliation*, 5-6.

[41]H. Räisänen, *Paul and the Law* (Tübingen: Mohr, 1987), 267 n. 17 criticizes the whole attempt at rhetorical analysis: "to interpret [Paul's] letters as carefully planned rhetorical products which follow the set rules of the time" reverses "Paul's own judgment of his rhetorical skill (1 Cor 2:1-5)." Yet Räisänen has made more than one error here. It is in 2 Corinthians 10:10, 11:6 that Paul addresses the issue of his rhetorical skill; in 1 Cor 2:1-5, Paul is talking about a conscious decision not to use rhetorical skill in his early proclamation in Corinth. That does not mean that Paul could not or even did not use rhetorical techniques in writing his letters; Räisänen also fails to consider that Paul may be joining a long philosophical tradition of using rhetorical techniques to attack many of the assumptions and claims of the rhetorical tradition. We will discuss both of these issues later in this study.

[42]Betz, *Galatians*, 5.

[43]Ibid., 254. Quintilian 9.2.103 mentions *exhortatio,* or παραινετικόν as a "figure," but not as a major division in a rhetorical work. "Obviously Betz has taken a feature of Paul's letter that would not be a normal feature in a forensic speech and given it a rhetorical label" (James D. Hester, "The Rhetorical Structure of Galatians 1:11-2:14," *JBL* 103 (1984): 223-33, here p. 224 n. 6). For a similar criticism of Betz, see Stanley E. Porter, "The Theoretical Justification for Application of Rhetorical Categories to Pauline Epistolary Literature," in *Rhetoric and the New Testament: Essays From the 1992 Heidelberg Conference*, ed. Stanley E. Porter and Thomas H. Olbricht, JSNT Sup. 90 (Sheffield: JSOT, 1993), 104.

[44]Betz, *Galatians*, 254.

[45]Betz also introduces into his analysis of 2 Corinthians 8 terms not found in

Since epistolary theory was not integrated into rhetorical theory,[46] or at least not addressed in the rhetorical handbooks, how closely to those handbooks must or can a rhetorical analysis of letters remain?[47]

Cicero, Seneca and Quintilian all have casual remarks in their works regarding the oral nature of letters and the application of rhetorical principles,[48] but there is no indication that there is an overall rhetorical theory governing the way in which letters were to be written, or that any of these rhetoricians had integrated letters into their rhetorical theories. For example,

> Cicero did know rhetorical prescriptions on letters and was probably familiar with handbooks on letter writing . . . but his comments on the types of letters are not a basis for an epistolographic system, nor are they part of such a system. They are rather practical, conventional means of finding an appropriate form for important situations to which letters are addressed. . . . In the first century A.D., Seneca, too, reflects

---

the ancient rhetorical handbooks: between *probatio* (8:9-15) and *peroratio* (8:24), Betz labels verses 16-22 as "commendation" and verse 23 as "authorization," terms which may be descriptive of their function but are not parts of ancient rhetorical arrangement. *2 Corinthians 8 & 9. A Commentary on Two Administrative Letters of the Apostle Paul,* Hermeneia Commentary (Philadelphia: Fortress, 1985), 38-41.

[46] Abraham J. Malherbe, *Ancient Epistolary Theorists* (Atlanta: Scholars Press, 1988), 3-6; S. K. Stowers, *Letter Writing,* 51-52; C. J. Classen, "St. Paul's Epistles," 323-24.

[47] Classen, "St. Paul's Epistles," 323 charges that Betz has not paid enough attention to the difference between rhetoric and epistolography. The question is also raised by C. Clifton Black, "Rhetorical Questions: The New Testament, Classical Rhetoric, and Current Interpretation," *Dialog* 29 (1990): 69; Porter, "Theoretical Justification," also warns against assuming that members of hellenistic culture would have expected rhetorical categories to be applied to letters. Only slightly more open to the possibility of ancient rhetorical traditions being expressed in epistolary works is Jeffrey T. Reed, "Using Ancient Rhetorical Categories to Interpret Paul's Letters: A Question of Genre," in *Rhetoric and the New Testament: Essays From the 1992 Heidelberg Conference,* ed. S. Porter and T. Olbricht, JSNT Sup. 90 (Sheffield: JSOT, 1993), 292-324.

[48] Quintilian 9.4.19-20; Cicero *Ad Fam.* 15.21.4; *Ad Att.* 8.14, 9.10; Seneca *Ep.* 75.1-2. When available and unless otherwise noted, all references and translations of classical Greek and Latin texts are from the appropriate volume in the Loeb Classical Library.

an awareness of descriptions of letters which had become traditional without his betraying any knowledge of an entire theoretical system.[49]

The handbooks on letters that survive are probably late: Pseudo Demetrius' "ΤΥΠΟΙ ΕΠΙΣΤΟΛΙΚΟΙ" (second century B.C. - third century A.D. in its surviving form, though Malherbe suggests its origins may in fact be pre-Christian), and Pseudo Libanius' "ΕΠΙΣΤΟΛΙΜΑΙΟΙ ΧΑΡΑΚΤΗΡΕΣ" (fourth century - sixth century A.D.).[50] These handbooks are little more than a listing of various functions of letters, with some short examples. Pseudo-Libanius includes some brief comments on general style and language. Neither is an application of rhetorical principles to the writing of letters. The first rhetorician to discuss letter-writing as a part of an *ars rhetorica* is Julius Victor in the 4th century.[51] Even his comments are brief, mainly discussing the appropriate style for official and personal letters.

However, there are indications that letters were thought of in rhetorical terms. It is Demetrius' *On Style* which has the first attempted systematic discussion of letter writing.[52] There, the author says that the style of a letter should be between the "plain" and the "graceful," using rhetorical terms applied to letters.[53] Cicero and Seneca both speak of letters as being oral in character, speech in written form.[54] Julius Victor begins his chapter "De Epistolis" with "Many directives which pertain to oral discourse also apply to letters," and includes "all the rules of oratory" as characteristic of official letters.[55] Furthermore, Cicero presents the following discussion on the value of rhetoric beyond the contexts stressed in the handbooks, including situations that seem likely to involve the writing of letters:

---

[49]Malherbe, *Ancient Epistolary Theorists*, 3.
[50]Ibid., 4-5.
[51]Ibid., 3. For the text, see 63-65.
[52]In *Aristotle, Poetics; Longinus, On the Sublime; Demetrius, On Style*, Loeb Classical Library, trans. W. Hamilton Fyfe (Cambridge: Harvard University, 1932), 257-487. The editor dates the writing to the end of the first century A.D. Malherbe, *Ancient Epistolary Theorists* p. 2, suggests that the sources for Demetrius go back to at least the first century B.C.
[53]Demetrius *On Style* 235.
[54]Cicero *Ad Att.* 8.14; 9.10; 12.53. Seneca *Ep.* 75.1.
[55]Malherbe, *Ancient Epistolary Theorists*, 63.

"And what if (as often happens to the most exalted personages) messages have to be communicated from a general at a meeting of the Senate, or conveyed from the Senate to a general or to any prince or nation? Because, on occasions of this sort, a style of diction more elaborate than the ordinary has to be employed, does it therefore seem to follow that this type of speaking should be accounted a distinct department of oratorical activity, or should be fitted out with its own peculiar rules?" "Why of course not," returned Catulus, "since the ability acquired by a ready speaker, from the treatment of his other subjects and topics, will not fail him in situations of that description."

"And so," continued Antonius, "those matters which often demand fluent expression, and which just now, in my praise of eloquence, I asserted to be within the part of the orator, have no special place in the formal classification of the branches of rhetoric, nor any particular code of rules, and yet they must be handled quite as skilfully as arguments at the Bar . . . .[56]

Thus, although letters were not incorporated into the ancient rhetorical handbooks, there is evidence that writers and readers of letters in late western antiquity would have viewed them according to principles of oral rhetoric.[57] "The formal line between the literary oration and the epistle is often a narrow one. . . . even when classical literature was written it was often orally published."[58]

This has raised a related question: What are the dangers of ignoring the possible changes as communication moves from one medium to another (from oration to letter)?

The relationship between written and oral communication, however, can be exaggerated. While there were many similarities between written

---

[56]Cicero *De Or.* 2.11.49-50. This passage is noted by F. W. Hughes, *Early Christian Rhetoric and 2 Thessalonians*, JSNT Sup. 30 (Sheffield: JSOT, 1989), 26. The importance of this discussion is too quickly dismissed by Porter, "Rhetorical Categories," 115-16 n. 40.

[57]John L. White, "St. Paul and the Apostolic Letter Tradition," *CBQ* 45 (1983): 435-6. Mack, *Rhetoric and the New Testament*, 30 notes that the classics of Greek literature (Homer, Hesiod, the poets, historians and tragedians) were studied according to the rhetorical techniques used in them, and that literary forms other than speeches showed attention to rhetorical issues (Plutarch's "Lives," the commentaries of Philo, the discourses of Dio Chrysostom and the letters of Seneca).

[58]Kennedy, *Classical Rhetoric*, 111.

letters and oral communication, there are also significant differences in language, style, and structure. We do not write the way we speak. Neither did the ancients. Oral communication, for example, tends to be linear or sequential. The immediate context for a statement is the preceding statement and the "interpretive" paralinguistic features of gesture, tempo, inflection, rhythm, and voice quality. While written texts can also be linear, the reader has the advantage of being able to reread earlier sections of a document not completely understood or fully appreciated on the first reading. Yet since written texts must do without the paralinguistic features of speech, they must be written in a special way to function without an interpreter.[59]

While Aune's cautions are well-taken, that should not be taken to imply that rhetorical categories cannot be used to analyze ancient letters.[60] Aristotle notes "that (i.e., the style) of written compositions is not the same as that of debate; . . . The style of written compositions is most precise, that of debate is most suitable for delivery."[61] Demetrius (*On Style* 4.224), Seneca (*Ep.* 75.1), Quintilian (9.4.19) and Pseudo-Libanius (47) all mention the difference between letters on the one hand and either formal oratory or friendly discourse on the other. However, these differences are mainly in terms of general style and elevation of language.[62] For example, Demetrius advises that letters be "a little more

---

[59]Aune, *Literary Environment*, 159.

[60]Aune himself, of course, does not assume this either. "Though primarily connected with oral delivery, rhetoric had a profound effect on all genres of literature including letters. A knowledge of ancient rhetorical theory, therefore, can contribute to understanding letters written by ancients (like Paul and Ignatius) who had more than a basic education" (p. 158). Mitchell, *Paul and the Rhetoric of Reconciliation*, 22 n. 5 also criticizes those who forget that the genre of 1 Corinthians is a letter, not a speech. Her point is not that rhetorical categories are inappropriate in the analysis of Pauline letters, but that such structures should not be imposed in a way that ignores epistolary conventions such as the salutation and thanksgiving, but should concentrate on the argument of the body of the letter (see also p. 10 n. 33; Troy Martin, "Apostasy to Paganism: The Rhetorical Stasis of the Galatian Controversy," *JBL* 114 (1995): 460 n. 11).

[61]Aristotle *The Art of Rhetoric* 3.12.2, Loeb Classical Library, trans. John Henry Freese (Cambridge: Harvard University, 1926).

[62]Porter, "Theoretical Justification," 111-116 argues that the differences in style between orations and letters which the ancient sources mention, along with the lack of discussion about rhetorical arrangement in letters, indicates the inappropriateness of applying ancient rhetorical categories to letters (similarly,

studied than the dialog," and Pseudo-Libanius (quoting Philostratus of Lemnos) says "Epistolary style should be more Attic than everyday speech, but more ordinary than Atticism, and it should be neither excessively elevated nor mean, but somewhere between the two."[63] Julius Victor says that all the rules of oratory govern the writing of official letters, "with one exception, that we prune away some of its great size and let an appropriate familiar style govern the discourse."[64] Thus, while recognizing a difference between formal oratory and letters in general style, these ancient writers did not see them as completely separate activities.[65] Quintilian can also say "My own view is that there is absolutely no difference between writing well and speaking well, and that a written speech is merely a record of one that has actually been delivered."[66] In fact, the great Athenian "orator" Isocrates was too nervous to address the assembly, instead writing his "speeches" for publication or sending them as "open letters."[67] In response to Aune's cautions about applying oral methods to written works, "the rhetorical qualities inherent in the text were originally intended to have an impact on

---

Reed, "Using Rhetorical Categories," 308-314). However, while the evidence cited by Porter shows that rhetorical theory does not appear applied to letters in the ancient handbooks until relatively late, and that ancient speakers and writers recognized differing occasions and possibilities in speeches and letters, it does not show that rhetorical concerns had no influence on the writing of letters. In fact, the remarks about the need for differentiating the appropriate styles for each is an indication that the two were seen as closely enough related that the line was easily crossed.

[63]Translation from Malherbe, *Ancient Epistolary Theorists*, 73.

[64]Ibid., 63.

[65]Classen, "St. Paul's Epistles," 335-6: "It is certainly advisable at this stage to remember that St. Paul is not making a speech, and that rules for speeches and other types of compositions cannot be expected always to be easily applicable to letters, especially as ancient theorists seem to have been aware of the very particular nature of letters." As with Aune's comments, these are well-taken, but the distinctions seen by classical rhetoricians should not be exaggerated.

[66]Quintilian 12.10.51.

[67]George Law Cawkwell, "Isocrates," *The Oxford Classical Dictionary* 2d Edition, ed. N. G. L. Hammond and H. H. Scullard (Oxford: Oxford University, 1970), 554-555; Kennedy, *New Testament Interpretation*, 86. Note also White, "St. Paul," 435, "Because of the letter's affinity to oral address and because of the democratization of knowledge in the Hellenistic period, it was adopted by the rhetorical schools for wider ends than the ordinary situational purposes of private and official correspondence."

the first hearing and to be heard by a group."[68] There is no evidence that, although letters could of course be reread and previous discussions rechecked as one read through the letter, Paul wrote with the assumption this would happen. The letter had to be rhetorically effective at the first reading, just as with oratory. "The NT must be understood as speech."[69]

However, there is a caution here. Since letter-writing was never incorporated into rhetorical theory, the rhetorical categories of "judicial," "deliberative," and "epideictic" may fit letters only loosely. In fact, most of the letter types listed by Pseudo-Demetrius' and Pseudo-Libanius' handbooks would appear to fall into the epideictic category.[70] Since the rhetorical handbooks give their major attention to judicial rhetoric, care must be taken not to impose on our analysis of Paul's letters expectations that are both too rigid[71] and skewed in the direction of judicial rhetoric.[72]

---

[68]Kennedy, *New Testament Interpretation*, 6.

[69]Achtemeier, "Omne," 19. For another helpful review of the oral nature of writing and reading in antiquity, see Pieter J. J. Botha, "The Verbal Art of the Pauline Letters: Rhetoric, Performance and Presence," in *Rhetoric and the New Testament: Essays From the 1992 Heidelberg Conference*, ed. S. Porter and T. Olbricht, JSNT Sup. 90 (Sheffield: JSOT, 1993), 409-428. So also James D. Hester, "The Use and Influence of Rhetoric in Galatians," *TZ* 42 (1986): 389: "If one accepts the notion that Paul's letters are rife with oral expressions or style . . . one had better begin to take seriously the possibility that Paul saw his letters as speeches."

[70]Aune, *Literary Environment*, 161, points out that the types of letters listed by Pseudo-Demetrius and Pseudo-Libanius conform quite closely to the types of epideictic oratory listed by Quintilian 3.4.3.

[71]One of Demetrius' guidelines for writing letters is that the letter needs to have some freedom in its structure; it should not be labored or elaborate (*On Style* 4.229). The needs and purposes of Paul in writing a letter would seldom, if ever, be simple enough to be covered by a single rhetorical identification.

[72]This is one more area in which Betz's work, as important as it is, has been rightly criticized. Betz has identified Galatians as judicial rhetoric, but this identification has been widely rejected. James D. Hester ("Placing the Blame: The Presence of Epideictic in Galatians," in *Persuasive Artistry: Studies In New Testament Rhetoric in Honor of George A. Kennedy* [Sheffield: Sheffield Academic Press, 1991], 281-307, esp. 288-291) sees Galatians as primarily epideictic. C. Clifton Black, "Rhetorical Questions," 66 makes a similar criticism of Betz's identification of Galatians as judicial rhetoric, though Black identifies it as deliberative. Aune, *Literary Environment*, 206-208 says Galatians is best understood as deliberative rhetoric with some apologetic features.

Early Christian letters tend to resist rigid classification, either in terms of the three main types of oratory or in terms of the many categories listed by the epistolary theorists. Most early Christian letters are multifunctional and have a "mixed" character, combining elements from two or more epistolary types. . . . Attempts to classify one or another of Paul's letters as *either* judicial *or* deliberative *or* epideictic (or one of their subtypes) run the risk of imposing external categories on Paul and thereby obscuring the real purpose and structure of his letters. Paul in particular was both a creative and eclectic letter writer. The epistolary situations he faced were often more complex than the ordinary rhetorical situations faced by most rhetoricians.[73]

Methodology: George A. Kennedy

While Betz's work on Galatians marked an important advance in modern application of rhetorical analysis of New Testament texts, he did not describe a methodology for such a task. That need was picked up by George Kennedy in his 1984 book *New Testament Interpretation Through Rhetorical Criticism*.[74] Kennedy sets out to use the developed rhetorical traditions of ancient Greece and Rome in his analysis of New Testament texts. Kennedy sees his task as one rooted in historical matters, as opposed to literary criticism, which Kennedy sees as reading ancient texts through modern eyes. Instead, Kennedy's goal for rhetorical criticism is to help us to read and hear the texts as they would have been read and heard by a member of Greco-Roman society. For Kennedy, the historical situation impinging on the author and the audience, and the author's intent, remain concerns in the study of the texts.

It [literary criticism] is distinct from my goal, which is the more historical one of reading the Bible as it would be read by an early Christian, by an inhabitant of the Greek-speaking world in which rhetoric was the core subject of formal education and in which even those without formal education necessarily developed cultural preconceptions about appropriate discourse.[75]

---

[73]Aune, *Literary Environment*, 203.

[74]George A. Kennedy, *New Testament Interpretation Through Rhetorical Criticism* (Chapel Hill: University of North Carolina, 1984).

[75]Kennedy, *New Testament Interpretation*, 5. Wuellner reflects a similar distinction between literary criticism and rhetorical criticism in "Where is Rhetorical Criticism . . . ?," 450, where he says that rhetorical criticism is shaped by the conviction that "a text must reveal its context," not simply in terms of

The methodology that Kennedy lays out has five parts (pp. 33-38):

1. Determine the rhetorical unit. The most basic consideration here is that the unit must be a complete persuasive unit, and may vary from a single pericope to an entire book.

2. Define the rhetorical situation that prompted this verbal response; that is, what are the people, events and relationships to which the writer is responding. Here, Kennedy draws upon the work of Lloyd Bitzer.[76] This will often lead to the identification of the rhetorical problem that is being faced: for example, prejudice against the writer, lack of authority, or difference in expectations.

3. Determine the "stasis" and "species" of the rhetorical unit. The "stasis" is the main ground on which the argument is waged. Is this a question of what has happened or is happening (fact), are the facts admitted but the meanings of particular terms in question (definition), are the actions justified or not justified based on other criteria (quality), or is it a question of whether or not the audience actually has any right to decide this issue (jurisdiction)?[77]   One also needs to determine the "species" of the rhetoric, whether judicial (dealing primarily with what has happened in the past, dealing with accusation and defense, the rhetoric of the courtroom), deliberative (dealing with what should happen in the future, its aim being persuasion or dissuasion, the rhetoric of the political assembly), or epideictic (praise or blame, aimed at increasing or decreasing assent to some value, the rhetoric of public ceremony).

4. Analyze the composition of the argument in terms of invention, arrangement and style. Invention is the composition of argumentation by *ethos*, *pathos* or *logos*. Arrangement is the ordering of structural elements, such as the *exordium* (an introduction and preparation of the audience), the *narratio* (setting forth the case briefly), the *probatio* (proving the case), and the *peroratio* (summing up). Style includes how various figures of speech are utilized. The question here is how these pieces work together to form a persuasive whole, and Kennedy is concerned to

---

historical situation or literary genre, but also in terms of a "rhetorical situation."
    [76]Lloyd Bitzer, "The Rhetorical Situation," *Philosophy and Rhetoric* 1 (1968): 1-14.
    [77]The classical theory of "stasis" was laid out by Hermagoras in the 2nd century B.C., and was influential on later rhetoricians, especially on Cicero and the writer of *Ad Herennium*; his influence shows up as well in a long discussion in Quintilian 3.6. We will have more to say regarding "stasis" later in this chapter.

remember that even letters are basically oral and linear in the nature of their writing and hearing.

5. Finally, evaluate how this particular argument has met (or not met) the rhetorical situation.

Rhetorical Criticism as a Synchronic Approach

Since the early work of Betz and Kennedy, the use of rhetorical criticism in New Testament studies has become more firmly established.[78] However, the numerous studies applying rhetorical criticism fall into two broad categories, each with a distinctive understanding of its task and of what is meant by "rhetorical criticism." First, there are those who have approached rhetorical analysis of New Testament texts using modern rhetorical theory. Such an approach "is a philosophical reconceptualization of Greco-Roman rhetoric, a synchronic approach to argumentation which does not suit purely historical investigation."[79] The basis for this approach is stated by Classen:

> When one turns to the categories of rhetoric as tools for a more adequate and thorough appreciation of texts, their general structure and their details, one should not hesitate to use the most developed and sophisticated form, as it will offer more help than any other. For there is no good reason to assume that a text could or should be examined only according to the categories known (or possibly known) to the author concerned. For rhetoric provides a system for the interpretation of all texts (as well as of oral utterances and even of other forms of communication), irrespective of time and circumstances (except, of course, for the fact that some rules of rhetoric immediately concern the external circumstances).[80]

Among studies which have adopted this approach we can mention Karl Plank's study of irony in Paul,[81] which not only draws on the "new rhetoric" of Perelman, but also uses reader-response criticism and structural linguistics to construct a literary-rhetorical paradigm which he

---

[78]The first full-scale analysis of a New Testament work along the lines laid out by Kennedy was Duane F. Watson's *Invention, Arrangement and Style: Rhetorical Criticism of Jude and 2 Peter*, SBLDS 104 (Atlanta: Scholars Press, 1988).

[79]Watson & Hauser, *Rhetorical Criticism*, 113.

[80]Classen, "St. Paul's Epistles," 322.

[81]Karl Plank, *Paul and the Irony of Affliction* (Atlanta: Scholars Press, 1987).

then uses to read 1 Corinthians 1-4. Raymond Humphries' study of 1 Corinthians 1-4[82] uses only "new rhetoric," since any speaker or writer who attempts to persuade an audience is acting rhetorically, regardless of the author's knowledge of or contact with any particular rhetorical tradition. Antoinette Clark Wire, charging that rhetorical analysis which relies on ancient rhetorical handbooks risks imposing the structure of the handbooks onto what Paul actually wrote, argues that using modern theories of rhetoric avoid this danger, are the most adequate approach, and are in fact viewing the classical topics of rhetoric primarily as argumentation.[83] She then proceeds to build from her rhetorical analysis of 1 Corinthians a picture of the social setting that has prompted this response from Paul.[84] Jeffrey Crafton's analysis of 2 Corinthians uses Kenneth Burke's dramatistic model, which analyzes a rhetorical event according to five elements: act, scene, agent, agency, and purpose. For Crafton, ancient rhetoric's self-understanding as intentional persuasion is insufficient; with Burke, Crafton sees the key term is not "persuasion" but "identification," and may include even factors of which the author was unconscious.[85] With particular attention to *ethos*, Crafton claims that Paul tries to move the Corinthians to view him as God's agency, rather than engaging in debates about Paul and other preachers as agents. However, Crafton's study illustrates the danger of this approach. Despite Wire's protestations, using modern theories of rhetoric to analyze New Testament texts runs a double risk: the danger of imposing a foreign structure onto Paul's writing, and the danger that this structure is anachronistic. "Crafton's distinction between the orientations of agency and co-agent with respect to these letters seems to reflect Burke's categories more than Paul's argument."[86] Far too often, such studies seem to mention classical rhetoric, but abandon concern for the historical nature and setting of the

---

[82]Raymond Humphries, "Paul's Rhetoric of Argumentation in 1 Corinthians 1-4" (Ph.D. diss., Graduate Theological Union, 1979).

[83]Antoinette Clark Wire, *Corinthian Women Prophets: A Reconstruction Through Paul's Rhetoric* (Minneapolis: Fortress, 1990), 197-98.

[84]Wire's study, though creative and provocative in its attempt to use rhetorical analysis to reconstruct the rhetorical situation (and in this case, also the historical situation), relies too much on mirror-reading of the texts and stretches the evidence by assuming that whatever Paul says in 1 Corinthians is composed with the women prophets in mind.

[85]Crafton, *Agency*, 19.

[86]Review of Crafton's book by J. L. Sumney in *JBL* 112 (1993): 168.

texts in favor of a "synchronic investigation of human communication and argumentation."[87]

Others who have been willing to use modern rhetorical theory to analyze New Testament texts have been more cautious, combining modern theory with more attention to the classical rhetorical sources. First among these is Wilhelm Wuellner, who has combined attention to ancient rhetoric and more modern rhetorical analysis, especially along the lines of Chaim Perelman and L. Olbrechts-Tyteca, with special attention paid to determining the social situation that prompted these particular rhetorical responses.[88]

Another scholar who has been cautious in his use of modern rhetorical theory and has thoughtfully defended such an approach is Stephen Pogoloff. Pogoloff criticizes those who have abandoned historical concerns in their rhetorical study of New Testament texts:

> However, even the recent enthusiasm for "rhetorical criticism" as a new method often tends to be socio-literary, not an historical, discipline; i.e., critics restrict themselves to modern theories of rhetoric. For example, Raymond Humphries, *Paul's Rhetoric of Argumentation in 1 Corinthians 1-4* (Ann Arbor: University Microfilms, 1980) and Karl Plank, *Paul and the Irony of Affliction* (Atlanta: Scholars Press, 1987).[89]

By contrast, Pogoloff claims to rely primarily on classical rhetorical theory, while supplementing it with modern rhetorical theory:

> In this work, I shall rely predominantly on classical rhetorical theory, but also bolster this with some modern theory in the manner of Kennedy. I hope to do so in a way that avoids both confusing admixture and illegitimate historical purism.[90]

---

[87]Mitchell, *Rhetoric of Reconciliation*, 7.

[88]Wilhelm Wuellner, "Greek Rhetoric and Pauline Argumentation," in *Early Christian Literature and the Classical Intellectual Tradition: In Honorem Robert M. Grant* (Paris: Beauchesne, 1979), 177-88; "Paul as Pastor: The Function of Rhetorical Questions in First Corinthians," in *L'Apôtre Paul: Personnalité, style et conception du ministère* (Leuven: Leuven University, 1986), 49-77; "Where is Rhetorical Criticism Taking Us?," *CBQ* 49 (1987): 448-63; "Paul's Rhetoric of Argumentation in Romans: An Alternative to the Donfried-Karris Debate," in *The Romans Debate*, rev. and exp. ed. (Peabody, Mass.: Hendrickson, 1991), 128-46.

[89]Pogoloff, *Logos and Sophia*, 12 n. 10.

[90]Ibid., 26.

Pogoloff claims that his task remains an historical one, but that modern theories of rhetoric are needed because "ancient rhetorical theories are simply inadequate for certain hermeneutical tasks."[91] He further claims that the pitfalls of using modern rhetorical theory can be avoided if scholars "clarify their rationale for importing modern theories and carefully distinguish between modern and ancient."[92]

Rhetorical Criticism as an Historical Approach

The second major group in the rhetorical study of New Testament texts has been those who are more insistent even than Pogoloff that the study remain an historical enterprise, and who reject the use of modern rhetorical theory in the study of ancient texts. This is the approach Pogoloff identifies as "historical purism." Most vocal in defense of such "purism" has been Margaret M. Mitchell.[93] Mitchell charges that to use new rhetoric in the analysis of New Testament texts is to confuse historical work with synchronic concerns.

> This is not to say that all such investigations are invalid in their own right, but they should not be confused or intertwined with historical arguments about Paul's rhetoric in the light of Greco-Roman rhetorical tradition, the sources for which are ancient texts.[94]

Contrary to Classen's view, for Mitchell rhetorical analysis must be done "in the light of the Greco-Roman rhetorical tradition which was operative and pervasive at the time of the letter's composition."[95] Mitchell finds that the new rhetoric is inadequate for investigation of New Testament texts because such an approach dismisses interest in authorial intent and the historical reader as important for our present study of the

---

[91]Ibid., 25.
[92]Ibid., 26.
[93]Perhaps less extreme in stance but certainly within this same group are the works of Duane F. Watson: *Invention, Arrangement, and Style*; "1 Corinthians 10:23-11:1 in the Light of Greco-Roman Rhetoric: The Role of Rhetorical Questions," *JBL* 108 (1989): 301-18; "1 John 2:12-14 as *Distributio, Conduplicatio,* and *Expolitio*: A Rhetorical Understanding," *JSNT* 35 (1989): 97-110.
[94]Mitchell, *Rhetoric of Reconciliation,* 7.
[95]Ibid., 6.

texts.[96]   The ways in which the approach of Perelman and Olbrechts-Tyteca skew rhetorical analysis of New Testament texts come under special criticism, especially since in large measure their rejection of the usefulness of the classical three "species" of rhetoric, and their redefinition that makes nearly all rhetoric sound "deliberative,"[97] have led to the anachronistic descriptions of rhetorical genre that are appropriate for the system of Perelman and Olbrechts-Tyteca, but would not fit the ancient understanding of those genres.[98]   Indeed,

> it must be emphasized that the "New Rhetoric," an important philosophical work . . . , does not claim to be a handbook of ancient rhetoric, but rather a revision and reappropriation of it to modern philosophical problems, particularly that of epistemology. Its intention is at basic points contrary to that of these New Testament scholars— it aims at *expanding* the realm of argumentation rather than classifying particular texts according to genre or arrangement.[99]

---

[96]Ibid., 8 n. 24.

[97]"We will consider argumentation above all in its practical effects: oriented toward the future, it sets out to bring about some action or to prepare for it by acting, by discursive methods, on the minds of the hearers." Perelman, *The New Rhetoric and the Humanities.   Essays on Rhetoric and Its Applications* (Dordrecht: Reidel, 1979), 47; cited by M. Mitchell, *Rhetoric of Reconciliation*, 8 n. 23.

[98]See especially Mitchell's critique of Wuellner's analysis of 1 Corinthians as epideictic, based not on the ancient understanding of that genre but on Perelman and Olbrechts-Tyteca's redefinition, *Rhetoric and Reconciliation*, 7 n. 23. Though B. Mack's appreciation for Perelman & Olbrechts-Tyteca's contribution to the rehabilitation of rhetoric from ornamentation to argumentation is fitting, it is not quite accurate to state so simply that "the new rhetoric is actually a rediscovery of the old" (*Rhetoric and the New Testament*, 16). In fact, contrary to the concerns of new rhetoric but in agreement with this writer, Mack goes on to speak of rhetorical criticism as a "new historiography" (17), and one that is properly concerned with "the culture of context within which the literature under investigation was written" (16).

[99]Mitchell, *Rhetoric of Reconciliation*, 7 n. 19. Note also the remark by Antoine Braet in "The Classical Doctrine of *status* and the Rhetorical Theory of Argumentation," *Philosophy and Rhetoric* 20 (1987): 79-93 which charges that Perelman & Olbrechts-Tyteca's understanding of stasis theory is more "monological" than classical rhetoric (79, 90), and "the fact that Perelman and Olbrechts-Tyteca build on classical rhetoric need not imply that these features may also be attributed to the classical precursor" (79). Roy Harrisville, "A Critique of Current Biblical Criticism," *Word and World* 15 (1995): 206-213 says that,

Mitchell also criticizes those rhetorical approaches that remain historical but limit themselves to what ancient rhetorical handbooks say, without drawing on actual ancient speeches.

> In reconstructing the Greco-Roman rhetorical tradition for comparison with the New Testament texts it is imperative that the ancient rhetorical handbooks not be the sole source. These handbooks present us with one type of evidence for what is *prescribed* for rhetorical discourse, and they put forth a far more regular, strict and almost mechanical view of rhetorical composition than actual speeches and letters embody. . . . The directions which the rhetorical handbooks provide must always be tempered and compared with actual speeches and other rhetorical compositions from the Greco-Roman world . . . .[100]

Mitchell then proceeds to do just that, showing by comparison with other ancient works how 1 Corinthians would be understood as deliberative rhetoric. Though she may be criticized for relying too much on similarity of form without enough attention to the situation[101] (including her failure to attempt a description of the historical situation at Corinth),[102] her insistence on a broader base of ancient texts is cogent and persuasive. She is joined in this endeavor to draw on actual ancient speeches by Frederick Danker, whose investigations of 2 Corinthians have drawn especially on Demosthenes' *De Corona*.[103] D. Watson and A. Hauser also support this move:

> Ancient theory was descriptive, not prescriptive; an abstraction from previous rhetoric and its situations. . . . The methodology as currently practiced does need to broaden its primary source base. The practices reflected in the extant letters and speeches composed by orators of

---

ironically, attention to rhetoric has done much to diminish the influence of New Criticism: "Return to a path earlier abandoned, return to Aristotle, for example, for whom rhetoric spelled persuasion, is doing the 'new criticism' in with its scorn for the 'intentional fallacy.' For if a text is ultimately 'intentional,' it surrenders isolation" (210).

[100]Mitchell, *Rhetoric of Reconciliation*, 8-9.

[101]Pogoloff, *Logos and Sophia*, 25-26.

[102]See review by Antoinette Clark Wire in *JBL* 112 (1993): 538-40.

[103]Frederick Danker, *II Corinthians*, Augsburg Commentary on the New Testament (Minneapolis: Augsburg, 1989); "Paul's Debt to the 'De Corona' of Demosthenes: A Study of Rhetorical Techniques in Second Corinthians," in *Persuasive Artistry: Essays in New Testament Rhetoric in Honor of George A. Kennedy* (Sheffield: Sheffield Academic Press, 1991), 262-80.

Greece and Rome must be brought to bear in analysis. Using actual speeches and letters gives the rhetorical critical art greater flexibility, credibility, and comprehensiveness. Since ancient rhetoric fully recognized the need to adapt to the needs of the rhetorical situation, the ancient rhetor could, and often did, veer from conventional theory and practice. Study of the actual products of rhetorical art helps recognize this flexibility in the New Testament works as well.[104]

Finally, Ben Witherington III has recently published his analysis of the Corinthian letters which also follows this more historical approach to rhetorical criticism.[105] Following the basic approach of Watson and Mitchell, Witherington expresses his goal: "If one wishes to understand *Paul's* use of rhetoric, and not merely appropriate Paul for some modern cause or agenda, it is critical that his works be evaluated in light of ancient Greco-Roman rhetoric."[106]

Rhetorical Criticism in This Study

It is in this latter approach, along the lines of Kennedy, Mitchell, Danker, and Witherington, that this study will place itself. The study of these ancient texts is first of all an historical task, and for most scholars who study these texts it does matter what Paul intended to communicate and accomplish with those original hearers. Rhetorical analysis of these texts requires a referent within the world of Paul and his churches, and the Greco-Roman rhetorical tradition, embodied both in the handbooks and speeches, provides that referent. However, some of Mitchell's concerns appear to be too rigid, and some of Pogoloff's points about the value of some careful use of modern rhetoric are cogent. For example, even Kennedy, who certainly sees rhetorical criticism as an historical undertaking rooted in Greco-Roman tradition, imports modern terms for elements which, though in principle present in ancient rhetoric, do not seem to have been discussed by ancient theorists. For instance, with

---

[104] Watson & Hauser, *Rhetorical Criticism of the Bible*, 112. Also Classen, "St. Paul's Epistles," 343: "Perhaps the most useful aspect which practical oratory can illustrate is that the best orator disguises his knowledge of the theory, that he alters accepted patterns and adjusts them to the particular case and his special intention. Thus, not what conforms to the rules, but what seems at variance with them often proves the most instructive for interpretation."

[105] Ben Witherington III, *Conflict & Community in Corinth: A Socio-Rhetorical Commentary on 1 and 2 Corinthians* (Grand Rapids: Eerdmans, 1995).

[106] Ibid., 58.

Kennedy we will need to talk about "rhetorical unit"[107] and "exigence"[108] (or rhetorical situation), though these terms are not used or discussed in ancient handbooks.[109] However, it is to the Greco-Roman tradition of rhetoric that we will pay closest attention, since "knowledge of ancient rhetorical convention helps us place the New Testament amidst its Greco-Roman oral and written culture, and to appreciate the role this placement can play in interpretation."[110] There is in particular one aspect of ancient rhetoric that will receive special attention in this study, and that is the issue of *stasis*. It is to this topic that we now turn our attention.

STASIS THEORY

Ancient Theory

The term στάσις[111] is difficult to translate. It describes the "state" or "standing" of the rhetorical work; depending on one's perspective, it may be described as the "starting point" (i.e., of the *inventio*), or as the "main issue" (i.e., of the argument), or as the "point of decision" (i.e., as far as the judge is concerned).[112] The στάσις is that point in the matter where the dispute between the parties centers, and where the questions arise.[113] It is largely determined by the "defendant,"[114] and at what point the

---

[107]Kennedy, *New Testament Interpretation*, 33.

[108]Ibid., 34-35.

[109]Though this does not mean that such things were not part of the consideration even of the ancient rhetoricians. Bitzer, "Rhetorical Situation," 2: "Those rhetoricians who discuss situation do so indirectly— as does Aristotle, for example, who is led to consider situation when he treats types of discourse."

[110]Watson & Hauser, *Rhetorical Criticism*, 109-110.

[111]Usually rendered as *status*. This is the term, for example, used by Quintilian, though at other times he renders it with *basis*. Cicero, in *De Inventione*, uses the term *constitutio* to describe the same concept.

[112]Antoine Braet, "The Classical Doctrine of *status*," 89-90.

[113]Quintilian 3.6.4, 7.1.6.

[114]The description of the *stases* in the handbooks is given from the perspective of a defendant, i.e. in terms of refuting a charge (Quintilian 3.6.83); however, a prosecutor would have to deal with the same four *stases* (3.6.85). On στάσις viewed by ancient rhetoricians primarily from the perspective of the defendant, see Braet, "Status," 82. It should also be noted that although the handbooks describe these *stases* in terms of forensic rhetoric, the same *stases* would be at work in deliberative or epideictic rhetoric as well (Quintilian 3.6.1, 81).

defendant decides to disagree with the adversary and raise objections. "The *stasis* of a case is its basic issue. It comes to light not in the charges made against the defendant but in the issue raised by the defendant's response to the charge."[115] It was the στάσις of the argument which was to steer the *inventio*,[116] and the importance of στάσις for the rhetorical work can be seen in Quintilian's description of it as "the point which the orator sees to be the most important for him to make,"[117] and as the "most important point on which the whole matter turns."[118]

It appears that Hermagoras of Temnos (fl. 150 B.C.) was the first to present a systematic description of στάσις. Hermagoras' work has not survived, but it became so influential[119] that its main aspects can be reconstructed through the reports of later rhetoricians, principally Cicero, Quintilian and Hermogenes. There are four possible *stases* on which an argument can be based:[120]

1. Denial (*constitutio coniecturalis*, στοχασμός)—Here the issue is a matter of bare fact, and the charge itself is denied: either the event never happened, or it did not involve the person accused.[121]

2. Definition (*constitutio definitiva* or *proprietas*, ὅρος)—Here, the bare facts are admitted, but their significance is disputed, i.e., it is denied that such an act involves the particular crime charged.[122]

3. Quality (*constitutio qualitas* or *generalis*, ποιότης or κατὰ συμβεβηκός)—Here, the parties agree on what was done and on how to describe it, but disagree on whether or not such an act should be punished

[115]James D. Hester, "The Rhetorical Structure of Galatians 1:11-2:14," *JBL* 103 (1984): 226. See also Braet, "Classical Doctrine," 81; Ray Nadeau, "Classical Systems of Stases in Greek: Hermagoras to Hermogenes," *GRBS* 2 (1959): 55.

[116]Braet, "Status," 81.

[117]Quintilian 3.6.9.

[118]Ibid. 3.6.21.

[119]Braet, "Status," 80 describes the position of Hermagoras' work among ancient rhetoricians as "canonical."

[120]The main discussion of *stases* can be found in Cicero *De Inv.* 1.8.10-11.16, 2.4.12-39.115; *Ad Herennium* 1.10.18-17.27; Quintilian 3.6.

[121]Cicero *De Inv.* 1.8.10; Quintilian 7.2. According to George A. Kennedy, *Art of Persuasion in Greece* (Princeton: Princeton University, 1963), 309, Hermagoras specified three aspects that needed to be proven with regard to "fact:" motive, ability and desire. For longer lists of the subjects under this *stasis*, see *De Inv.* 2.8.28-9.31.

[122]Cicero *De Inv.* 1.8.10, Quintilian 3.6.56, 7.3. For a fuller discussion of the specific issues to be addressed under "definition," see *De Inv.* 2.17.53-55.

under these circumstances; the defense argues that the action is justified by some criterion other than the bare letter of the law.[123]

4.   Jurisdiction (*constitutio translatio*, μετάληψις)—here, the legitimacy of the particular legal action is questioned.[124]

Though George Kennedy indicates that these four *stases* were coordinate until the system of Hermogenes, which made each one subordinate to the one which preceded it,[125] it seems clear that these four *stases* were viewed as a kind of hierarchy, moving from strongest to weakest position, at least as early as Quintilian.[126]

> . . . far the strongest method of self-defense is, if possible, to deny the charge. The second best is when it is possible to reply that the particular act with which you are charged was never committed. The third and most honourable is to maintain that the act was justifiable. If none of these lines of defense are feasible, there remains the last and only hope of safety: if it is impossible either to deny the charge or justify the act, we must evade the charge with the aid of some point of law, making it appear that the action has been brought against us illegally.[127]

Unlike the first three *stases*, the final one would not necessarily grant the ones preceding it. However, the quotation above indicates that Quintilian did not have great confidence in this as a basis for defense. In fact, elsewhere Quintilian says that he considers the first three *stases* sufficient.[128] "Evidently the ancients saw it as a formal refuge with which those who resorted to it heaped upon themselves the suspicion that they had no material defense."[129]

---

[123]Cicero *De Inv.* 1.8.10; Quintilian 3.6.56, 7.4.

[124]Cicero *De Inv.* 1.8.10; Quintilian 3.6.56, 7.5.

[125]G. Kennedy, *Classical Rhetoric*, 104.

[126]Braet, "Status," 83.

[127]Quintilian 3.6.83.

[128]See, for example, 3.6.67-82; for a similar view, see also Cicero *De Inv.* 1.6.8-11.16, *Orator* 14.45 (though Cicero, as Quintilian, does in the end follow Hermagoras in identifying four "bases" [*De Inv.* 1.8.10-11]). The teacher of the author of *Ad Herennium* (1.10.18) rejected jurisdiction as a fourth *stasis*, and made it part of the "legal" *stasis*, his equivalent for the *stasis* of definition (see G. Kennedy, *Art of Persuasion in Greece*, 307).

[129]Braet, "Status," 83-84. See also G. Kennedy, *Art of Persuasion in Greece*, 308, who points out that in fact this *stasis* can be a strong one, but that

Within these four *stases*, it is in the area of "quality" that Hermagoras' system becomes the most developed. Here, according to Quintilian,[130] Hermagoras discussed the *stasis* of quality in deliberative and epideictic oratory. In forensic oratory, Hermagoras outlined two major divisions for the *stasis* of quality. The first could be called "justification" (ἀντίληψις; Quintilian 7.4.4; *De Inv.* 1.15, 2.60), in which no wrong is admitted, but it is claimed that the action which is being prosecuted is in fact honorable.[131] The second major division within the *stasis* of quality can be called "defense"[132] (ἀντίθεσις; Quintilian 7.4.7; *De Inv.* 1.15, 2.69), in which the wrong is admitted but punishment is countered on some other grounds. This position is further broken down into four subtypes: 1) Counter-charge (ἀντέγκλημα; Quintilian 7.4.8), in which one accuses the person that the opposition is trying to vindicate; 2) Counter-plea (ἀντίστασις; Quintilian 7.4.12), which insists that some benefit was rendered by this act, or at least that it resulted in a lesser evil; 3) Shifting blame (μετάστασις; Quintilian 7.4.13), either blaming some other person or some thing (such as another law); 4) Plea for leniency (συγγνώμη; Quintilian 7.4.17), a "last resort" asking for mercy because the act resulted from ignorance, accident or over-riding necessity. Hermagoras was apparently the first to present an organized discussion of *stasis* theory; but the ideas certainly predate his work. The basic ideas are present already in Aristotle's *Rhetoric*,[133] and the basic outline of *stasis* theory remained remarkably consistent. Quintilian includes a survey of the various versions of *stasis* theory[134] which he begins in this way:

Hermagoras put it last because he regarded it as "a kind of petty legalism," and thus not very useful for the rhetorical exercises that interested Hermagoras.

[130]Quintilian 3.6.56.

[131]Quintilian 7.4.4: "By far the strongest line that can be taken in defense is to assert that the act which forms the subject of the charge is actually honourable."

[132]"Justification" and "Defense" come from Georg Thiele, *Hermagoras* (Strassburg: Trubner, 1893) diagramed in Nadeau, "Classical Systems," 56.

[133]For instance, 1.13.9-10 discusses arguments based on "definition," 3.15.10 discusses motive ("quality"), 3.16.6 and 3.17.1 briefly mention issues of "fact" and "quality," and 3.17.1 lists four possible points of dispute (fact, injury not done, issue not as important as asserted, or the act was just). See also Hermogenes *On Stases*, trans. with an introduction and notes by Ray Nadeau, *Speech Monographs* 31 (1964): 374.

[134]Quintilian 3.6.22-62.

> There is the greatest possible disagreement among writers about this as about everything else, but in this case as elsewhere they seem to me to have been misled by a passion for saying something different from their fellow-teachers. As a result there is still no agreement as to the number and names of the bases . . . .[135]

However, for all the variety that Quintilian notes, it is Hermagoras' system that remained the standard expression.[136] Braet expresses not only the importance of *stasis* theory for rhetoric, but the stability of it:

> The doctrine of *status* continued to dominate the later Greek and Roman doctrines of *inventio* and hence the entire rhetorical system. Later rhetoricians did try to reap glory for themselves by inventing all sorts of variants on Hermagoras's system. They met with little success, however, and Hermagoras's doctrine has continued to set the tone.[137]

Nadeau's study concludes that "the system of Hermagoras, which first appeared in the second century B.C., remained current for approximately three centuries in spite of revisions and the publication of rival systems."[138] Kennedy has shown that "stasis theory remained the heart of rhetorical invention until the end of the Renaissance."[139]

Stasis Theory in Biblical Study

Given the importance and stability of *stasis* theory in ancient rhetoric, it is surprising that the modern revival of rhetorical analysis in New Testament studies has not paid more attention to it. Kennedy's outline of methodology passes over *stasis* theory, which he notes is "useful," with a single sentence, and even that is buried in a longer discussion of identifying the species of rhetoric.[140] Betz's commentary on Galatians has

---

[135]Quintilian 3.6.22.

[136]Note the place afforded Hermagoras's position by Quintilian himself, for example in 3.6.59-60.

[137]Braet, "Status," 80.

[138]Nadeau, "Classical Systems," 71.

[139]Kennedy, *Classical Rhetoric*, 88. Kennedy traces discussion of στάσις through Tertullian (p. 135), commentaries written on Hermogenes in the 5th and 13th centuries (p. 165), the writings of Boethius and Isidore (p. 178-79), and up to Agricola (p. 209).

[140]Kennedy, *New Testament Interpretation*, 36. Kennedy does, however, include some remarks about *stasis* in most of his analyses of texts throughout the

some brief comments about the *stasis* of Galatians 3.[141] Duane Watson
has written a rhetorical analysis of Philippians which contains a
subheading "The Species of Rhetoric, the Question, and the Stasis," but
the discussion of *stasis* is limited to two sentences.[142] James D. Hester
has written an article that pays careful attention to the issue of *stasis* in
understanding the opening sections of Galatians.[143] Troy Martin is also
careful and explicit about his use of *stasis* theory to explore the rhetorical
situation addressed by Galatians.[144]

Ben Witherington's commentary on the Corinthian letters discusses
aspects of the text that would seem to describe *stasis*, but he fails to make
this identification explicit.[145] For instance, regarding 2 Corinthians
1:8-2:16:

> He does not deny the charge that he has said one thing and done
> another, but rather seeks to give reasons that it was necessary for him to
> do this. He did it to "spare" his converts more grief (1:23). He does not
> deny causing his converts sadness through the severe letter, but claims
> that he did it for the sake of the good end of producing repentance.[146]

This certainly seems to describe a *stasis* of quality rather than of fact. I
agree with Witherington's analysis here, but his failure to deal explicitly
with issues of *stasis* does detract from the clarity of his analysis,
especially when he seems to describe different *stases* as he moves through

---

rest of the book: regarding the Sermon on the Mount as *stasis* of fact (i.e., telling
what should be done and by whom; p. 46-47); 2 Corinthians 2 as *stasis* of quality
(Paul wrote the "letter of tears" for their own good, and to some extent he shifts
the blame for this away from himself; p. 88); Galatians as *stasis* of fact (what
gospel is true; p. 147). Kennedy also has scattered notes about the *stasis* of
several speeches in Acts (pp. 117-121, 123, 134, 136-137).

[141] Betz, *Galatians*, 129.

[142] Duane F. Watson, "A Rhetorical Analysis of Philippians and Its
Implications for the Unity Question," *NovT* 30 (1988): 60.

[143] Hester, "The Rhetorical Structure," 225-228.

[144] Martin, "Apostasy to Paganism."

[145] J. Paul Sampley, "Paul, His Opponents in 2 Corinthians 10-13, and the
Rhetorical Handbooks," in *The Social World of Formative Christianity and
Judaism*, ed. Jacob Neusner, Peder Borgen, Ernest S. Frerichs and Richard
Horsley (Philadelphia: Fortress, 1988), 162-77 includes a brief discussion of the
types of issues and responses in 2 Cor 10-13, but without explicitly mentioning
stasis theory (see 165-67). This work will be discussed in more detail in chap. 4.

[146] Witherington, *Conflict and Community*, 361.

later sections of 2 Corinthians. For instance, his discussion of 2:17 (which he identifies as a statement of the *propositio*) seems to indicate a new *stasis*, one of definition[147] (though Witherington's discussion of the argument here tends to blur the lines between issues of fact, definition and quality), and in discussing the same section, Witherington also speaks of issues that would properly be called issues of jurisdiction.[148] The problem here is not that the *stasis* of an argument cannot change. In fact, in a rhetorical work as long and as complicated as 2 Corinthians, the *stasis* may change as new stages in the argument are reached and new rhetorical possibilities are opened up to the author.[149] Yet by failing to be clear about the issue of *stasis*, Witherington has sacrificed clarity with regard to Paul's rhetorical strategy and with regard to what Paul sees as the major issues at stake. Attention to the *stasis* of the argument in the Pauline letters remains an area of rhetoric that has been largely neglected in recent study, which has concentrated far more on identifying the rhetorical species of the letters.[150] Yet surely more attention to the *stasis* of the argument, and the ways in which that *stasis* may change as Paul moves his audience along through the argument, is needed. This study will attempt to address that need.

---

[147]Ibid., 371.

[148]Ibid., 374: "What Paul suggests here he will state clearly at the end of his discourse, namely that God, not the Corinthians, is the real judge of his case, of the authenticity of his ministry, and thus he is laying his case before God."

[149]See Hester, "Placing the Blame," 283-85 where he discusses the changing nature of the argumentative situation, as earlier stages of the discussion influence the argumentative possibilities that are opened. A rhetorical situation is dynamic, with the author predicting the effect of his or her words on the hearers and judging where they are in the trajectory from their old position toward the change sought through this rhetorical work. Hester suggests an addition to Kennedy's methodology should be to look for signs (vocabulary, figures of speech, etc.) that the argumentative situation has changed and given Paul new possibilities. We agree with Hester, but would add the need to be aware that the *stasis* itself may change as the complex arguments proceed.

[150]The difficulty— and perhaps futility— of trying to fit one of Paul's letters into the category of any single species of rhetoric may be seen in the wide disagreement by scholars over such identifications (see chapter 4 regarding such decisions about 2 Corinthians). Paul's letters address problems that are complex and multiple, and so any single letter may contain aspects of different species (this is not limited to Paul; Demosthenes' *De Corona*, for example, is forensic in purpose, but in form consists largely of epideictic rhetoric). See Nadeau, "Classical Systems," 57.

CHAPTER TWO

RHETORICAL UNIT AND
RHETORICAL SITUATION

RHETORICAL UNIT

This study will treat 2 Corinthians 10-13 as a compositional unit, the identification of which is the first step in Kennedy's methodology. Such a decision will be no surprise, as this section has long been recognized as distinct for reasons discussed below. It is necessary at this point to include a brief description of the various theories about the composition and unity of 2 Corinthians, and to make clear the position of the present writer on those issues.

Compositional Unity Challenged

The challenge to the compositional unity of 2 Corinthians is generally traced to J. S. Semler's study in 1776.[1] Semler's suggestions, however, didn't gain much attention until the work of another scholar almost a century later, Adolf Hausrath.[2] Hausrath suggested that 2 Corinthians 10-13 was in fact a separate letter, that it preceded chapters 1-9, and that it should be identified with the "tearful letter" referred to in 2:3-4, 7:8-12. All three of these issues continue to occupy scholarship, and none has reached any apparent resolution.

Suggested reconstructions of the literary history of 2 Corinthians have specified up to 6 separate letters or letter fragments that make up canonical 2 Corinthians.[3] However, the more complicated the theory becomes, the more difficult it becomes to explain why anyone would have

---

[1] J. S. Semler, *Paraphrasis II. Epistolae ad Corinthos*. Halle, 1776.

[2] Adolf Hausrath, *Der Vier-Kapitalbrief des Paulus an die Korinther* (Heidelberg: Bassermann, 1870).

[3] The best summaries of the history of these issues can be found in Victor Paul Furnish, *II Corinthians*, Anchor Bible (Garden City: Doubleday, 1984), 30-48; Martin, *2 Corinthians*, xl-xlvi.

put the pieces together in this way.[4] As a result, the only compositional theories that have gained wide acceptance, and the only ones that will be discussed here, are those that find two separate letters in canonical 2 Corinthians: one made up of chapters 1-9, and the other of chapters 10-13. Though there are other supporting arguments,[5] the main reason for suggesting such a division is that "nothing in 2 Corinthians 1-9 prepares the reader for the rude shock administered by the opening words and sustained argument of 2 Corinthians 10-13."[6]

2 Corinthians 10-13 Subsequent to 1-9

Scholars who have concluded that chapters 10-13 were sent as a separate letter after chapters 1-9 include Semler (1776), Krenkel (1895), Drescher (1897), Windisch (1924), Munck (1954), Batey (1965), Bruce (1971), Barrett (1973), Furnish (1984), Martin (1986), and Best (1987). Those who hold this position have usually found the "conclusive"[7] evidence for this order in the remarks about Titus in 7:6-7, 13-15; 8:6, 16-24; 9:3-5; and 12:18.

As the argument is clearly presented by Furnish,[8] there are three main claims: 1) The visit of Titus and one brother in 12:18 refers to the same visit as the one in 8:16-24 where Paul mentions that two brothers accompanied Titus. The verb in 8:18 (συνεπέμψαμεν) is thus read as an epistolary aorist, while the verb in 12:18 (συναπέστειλα) must be taken

---

[4]One of the few to even wrestle with this issue is Günther Bornkamm, who identifies at least 5 and perhaps 6 fragments in his study "The History of the So-Called Second Letter to the Corinthians," *NTS* 8 (1962): 258-64. See the appreciation for this effort but critique of the specifics in Furnish, *II Corinthians*, 39-40. See also the comments of C. K. Barrett, *A Commentary on the Second Epistle to the Corinthians*, 23, "Such stupidity in a responsible editor is hard to credit," and 25, "It may be that no limit should be set to the stupidity of editors, and one cannot expect always to understand their motives; but it cannot be said that any good explanation of the process that led to the composition of 2 Corinthians out of disordered fragments has yet been given."

[5]See below.

[6]Bruce, *I & II Corinthians*, 166. In 2:3-4, 7:8-12 Paul needs to carefully explain that he did not take such a harsh tone in his previous letter to hurt the Corinthians. It seems unbelievable that he would follow this careful explanation with the unparalleled invective of 10-13.

[7]Ibid., 168-69.

[8]Furnish, *II Corinthians*, 38.

as a true past reference. 2) This past visit of 12:18 cannot refer to the visit of 7:6, 13-15 because the latter makes no reference to anyone accompanying Titus. 3) The visit of 12:18 cannot be prior to that referred to in chapter 7, since 7:14 implies that this was Titus' first visit to Corinth. On these bases it is argued that 12:18 must look back on 8:16-24, and thus the letter containing chapters 10-13 was written after chapters 1-9.

We will examine the soundness of each of these claims. It does seem most likely that the aorist verbs in 12:18 need to be understood as references to the past; in the latter part of the same verse, Paul uses Titus' and the brother's conduct as evidence that he is not out to defraud them. Such an appeal requires a somewhat extended experience with Titus and his companion, not just the necessarily short preliminaries by the bearer(s) of this letter. However, it is not clear that the previous visit referred to in 12:18 must be equated with the visit of 8:16-24. Most importantly, 12:18 mentions one brother that goes with Titus, while in chapter 8 there are two brothers that accompany Titus, one who is famous in the churches and appointed by them to this collection, and one who has been Paul's companion.[9] This objection has been countered by noting the distinction made between the two companions. In chapter 12, Paul's point is that his associates have behaved in an exemplary manner, and since only one of the companions in 8:16-24 was actually his associate, he only mentioned that one in chapter 12.[10]

While this explanation does save the theory from a quick demise, it does not mean that the visit referred to in chapter 12 must be the same visit as 8:16-24. We would agree that it is unlikely that the visit in chapter 12 can be equated with the visit of chapter 7, but not because there is no companion mentioned in chapter 7. Such an argument shares the weakness of all arguments from silence. It is puzzling that Furnish would dismiss the need for correspondence in the number of companions for equating the visits in chapters 12 and 8, but insist on it when looking at chapter 7. Yet there are other reasons against equating the visit of chapter 12 and chapter 7. The visit in chapter 12 seems to deal with the

---

[9]Charles H. Talbert, *Reading Corinthians: A Literary and Theological Commentary on 1 and 2 Corinthians* (New York: Crossroad, 1987), xix finds in this conclusive evidence that "these are not the same visit;" so also Martin, *2 Corinthians*, 447-48. This difficulty is simply ignored by Werner Georg Kümmel, *Introduction to the New Testament*, Rev. Ed. (Nashville: Abingdon, 1975), 290.

[10]Furnish, *II Corinthians*, 566; Bruce, *I & II Corinthians*, 251; Barrett, *Second Epistle to the Corinthians*, 325.

matter of the collection; Titus' visit in chapter 7 was either to deliver the "Painful Letter" or to check on its results. Either way, that would hardly have been the time to stay around and organize this offering.[11]

Finally, the claim that 7:14 implies that this was the first visit of Titus to Corinth will not stand. There is nothing in the context that makes it necessary that this be Titus' first visit to Corinth. In fact, we would not expect Paul to send someone unknown to those in Corinth at such a delicate time.[12] More importantly, chapter 8 implies that in fact Titus had been to Corinth before. 8:10 says that the Corinthians had begun the collection a year before, and that now they should complete it. This comes just after Paul has mentioned how Titus made a beginning among the Corinthians, and now has been encouraged by Paul to complete this offering (ἐπιτελέσῃ εἰς ὑμᾶς καὶ τὴν χάριν ταύτην-v. 6). These two verses share the same word for "began" (προενάρχομαι), a word which occurs only these two times in the entire NT. The beginning made by Titus is thus verbally linked with the beginning of the collection in Corinth. It seems most logical then to conclude that the "beginning"

---

[11]Barrett (*Second Epistle*, 20-21) disagrees, claiming that Titus did carry the "Painful Letter" and on the same visit organized the collection. To make such an event possible, Barrett must claim that the problems at Corinth that prompted the Painful Letter weren't all that serious, that Paul's apostolic authority was not challenged, and that Paul's desire to see Titus in 2:13 did not come from uncertainty about the Corinthians, but because Paul was worried about Titus' safety, as he might be carrying a considerable amount of money. Furnish (*II Corinthians*, 171) rightly criticizes Barrett on this last point. The context (see especially 1:12-14) indicates that Paul's eagerness to meet Titus is a part of his concern for the Corinthians, and that this relationship is under considerable strain. Yet Furnish (p. 397) unfortunately joins Barrett in claiming that the problem addressed by the Painful Letter is not all that serious; the people are not in revolt against their apostle. While the crisis has passed, 2 Cor 1-9 does have indications of its serious nature (1:12-14, 3:1-3, 7:2-4). To claim that the situation was not so bad is to make Paul's Painful Letter an over-reaction. Furnish's claim (p. 397) that the boasting to Titus which Paul mentions shows that the problem in Corinth wasn't serious fails to consider that Paul's expression of confidence here is intended to draw the Corinthians closer for healing of the relationship and prepare them for the work he has for them, and may not necessarily be an objective view of how Paul was feeling or exactly what he communicated to Titus. On the use of such expressions of confidence, see Stanley Olson, "Pauline Expressions of Confidence in his Addressees," *CBQ* 47 (1985): 282-95.

[12]A point also made by Francis Watson, "2 Corinthians 10-13 and Paul's Painful Letter to the Corinthians," *JTS* 35 (1984): 324-46.

made by Titus is the beginning of the collection a year before the writing of chapters 1-9.[13]

2 Corinthians 10-13 Preceding 1-9

Thus, while it remains possible to equate the visits in chapter 12 and chapter 8, it is not true that this is the only possibility. Nor is it clear that this argument can support the claim that chapters 10-13 must be written after chapters 1-9, especially in the face of contrary evidence. Those scholars who have found that evidence convincing include Hausrath (1870), J. H. Kennedy (1900), Plummer (1915), Lake (1927), Goguel (1926), Filson (1953), Hanson (1967), Watson (1984), Talbert (1987), and Taylor (1991). There have been three main arguments in favor of this position: 1) the apparent relationship between the insult Paul suffered during his painful visit and the crisis addressed in chapters 10-13; 2) likely relationships between statements regarding suspected fraud and the collection; 3) chapters 10-13 seem to look forward to many things that are already past in 1-9. These arguments also point to 10-13 being identified as the "Painful Letter," which most proponents of this arrangement also claim.[14]

Again, we will take each of the arguments and examine its merits. The first argument is a psychological guess at what Paul would likely do. If 10-13 is written after 1-9, then there is a repeated pattern of rebellion, harsh letter, reconciliation (at least possible reconciliation after 10-13). It seems hardly credible that the Corinthians, who are busy punishing the

---

[13]Witherington, *Conflict and Community*, 332. Johannes Weiss (*The History of Primitive Christianity*, ed. F. C. Grant [New York: Wilson-Erickson, 1937], 353) says that this beginning of the collection is in fact prior to the writing of 1 Corinthians. Barrett (*Second Epistle*, 19-20) rightly criticizes this suggestion: 1 Corinthians 16:1-4 does sound like initial instructions, and nothing is said there about any representatives from Paul already working with this collection. However, this doesn't mean that Titus could not have begun this collection work shortly after 1 Corinthians was written.

[14]To claim that 10-13 precede 1-9 but are NOT the Painful Letter would have to assume that Paul wrote two such letters within a short span of time without referring in 1-9 to the remarkable need to do this. We only hear there of one painful letter, and though argument from silence is seldom conclusive, it hardly seems credible that Paul could have let it pass with comment on only one of those letters.

offender and showing their renewed loyalty to Paul in chapters 1-9, would so quickly turn against him (again). Even less credible seems to be that Paul would pass by such a quick, repeated defection without comment in 10-13. "The assumption that 10-13 belongs to a letter written later than 1-9 is contradicted by the fact that 10-13 contains no allusions to Paul's knowing that the situation in Corinth has deteriorated following the writing of his letter (1-9), which could scarcely fail to be mentioned."[15] Though any argument that relies on reading the mind of Paul is risky, there seems to be no likely suggestion for why Paul would fail to comment on such a repeated betrayal.

The second argument deals with the relationship between collection efforts and charges of fraud. Furnish, arguing that 10-13 must follow 1-9, has said that the confidence regarding the collection in chapters 8-9 would be impossible if Paul has already had to face the kind of accusations answered in 12:14-18.[16] However, the careful arrangements made in 8:16-23 indicate that there has already been some concern over the collection (see v. 20). Furthermore, 2 Corinthians 4:2 mentions the same suspicion of "trickery" (πανουργία) as in 12:16 (πανουργός). Taylor argues that the more explicit and detailed discussion of this (the one in chapter 12) is likely to be prior to the mention of it which seems to assume the readers will recognize what Paul is talking about.[17] A similar argument could be made about the rather ambiguous reference to "blame" with regard to the collection in 8:20 and the more explicit discussion of 12:16. This argument, however, cannot carry the burden of proof here. Furnish cannot prove that Paul would be unable to express confidence in the collection (perhaps more for the effect it might have on the Corinthians than as an expression of his true feelings) once such charges have been leveled; and Taylor cannot prove that the "ambiguous" remarks

---

[15]Kümmel, *Introduction*, 290. Similar arguments are made by Bornkamm, "History," and by Watson, "2 Corinthians 10-13," 332.

[16]Furnish, *II Corinthians*, 38.

[17]N. H. Taylor, "The Composition and Chronology of Second Corinthians," *JSNT* 44 (1991): 67-87. This explanation is surely more likely than that offered by Witherington, *Conflict and Community*, 411-12, that the financial matters of chapters 8-9 are dealt with in order to improve Paul's credibility with the Corinthians, so that he can argue as he does in 10-13 in attacking his opponents; surely Witherington has gotten things backwards here—Paul's credibility with the Corinthians must already be intact for the collection to proceed.

about these charges in chapters 4 and 8 refer specifically to the charges of fraud discussed in chapter 12.

As for the third argument, there do seem to be references in 1-9 back to what Paul anticipates in 10-13.[18] For example:

> 12:11—Paul says he has acted like a fool, but the Corinthians forced him to it by not commending him themselves, as they should have done.
> 3:1—Paul asks if he is commending himself "again."[19]

> 13:2—When Paul comes again, he will not "spare" (φείδομαι).
> 1:23—Paul didn't come to Corinth as he had planned, because he wanted to spare them (φείδομαι).

> 13:10—Paul writes this letter so that when he comes, he will not have to act severely.
> 2:3,4,9—Paul wrote the Painful Letter so that he would not be grieved when he came, so that they would know his love for them.

> 10:6—Paul will punish the offenders when the community has proven its obedience.
> 2:9—Paul wrote the Painful Letter to test if the Corinthians were obedient.
> 7:15—Titus has seen their obedience.

Buck and Bruce[20] attempt to point out that there are verses in 1 Corinthians that present parallels for these statements in 2 Corinthians 1-9 "*almost* as impressive"[21] as those suggested in 10-13. Their caution is necessary; simple similarity in theme need not mean common reference. However, the apparent connections between a forward view in 10-13 and a past view of similar if not the same events in 1-9 are remarkable, and cannot be dismissed so easily.

---

[18]Bruce, *I & II Corinthians*, 167; Barrett, *Second Epistle*, 13; Talbert, *Reading Corinthians*, xix; so also Watson, "2 Corinthians 10-13," 326-27, and J. H. Kennedy, *The Second and Third Epistles of St. Paul to the Corinthians* (London: Methuen, 1900), 81-85.

[19]Taylor, "Composition," points out that if 10-13 doesn't precede this comment in chapter 3, then we must theorize another, lost letter of self-commendation.

[20]Bruce, *I & II Corinthians*, 168; C. H. Buck, "The Collection for the Saints," *HTR* 43 (1950): 1-29, here p. 6.

[21]Bruce, *I & II Corinthians*, 6 (emphasis mine).

The continuing disagreement over these issues probably indicates that we simply don't have enough information to be able to prove conclusively the order of these two letters. Barrett makes a good caution here: "The field is one in which theories are more numerous than facts, and clear distinctions between the two are not always made."[22] The literary and historical issues are intertwined, and one must make assumptions about the one in order to answer questions about the other. Those who argue that chapters 10-13 were written last must support that claim by the assumption that Titus did not visit Corinth before the visit referred to in chapter 7; those who argue that chapters 10-13 were written prior to 1-9 must rely at least in part on some assumptions about what Paul would have considered an appropriate response to the situation in Corinth. Thus we are left only with probabilities. Yet within that limit, we find that the arguments for understanding chapters 10-13 as prior to 1-9 carry enough weight to tip the scales in that direction.

2 Corinthians 10-13 as the Painful Letter

If that is the case, then we need to discuss a bit further the claim that 10-13 can be equated with the Painful Letter.[23] That claim has been strongly challenged. Besides the arguments above claiming that 10-13 must be written after 1-9 (and thus obviously not the Painful Letter), there are two substantial arguments raised against identifying 10-13 as the Painful Letter.[24] First, it is argued that the tone of 10-13 doesn't match the tone of the Painful Letter as that is described in 2:4. There, Paul says that he wrote the letter out of (ἐκ) great affliction and anguish of heart, and

---

[22]C. K. Barrett, *Second Epistle*, 5.

[23]Those scholars, in addition to the ones listed above in support of 10-13 as prior to 1-9, who claim 10-13 as the Painful Letter include Bornkamm (1962), Gilmour (1962), Bultmann (1976), and Georgi (1976).

[24]A third criticism, that 2 Cor 1:23, 2:1-4 indicates that the Painful Letter is written instead of a visit, while 10-13 (see 12:14, 13:1) is written in anticipation of a visit (see Furnish, *II Corinthians* 37-38, 160), will not hold. Paul's remarks in 2:3 indicate that the Painful Letter was not written with the intention that Paul would not come to Corinth (ἐλθών), but that the visit had only been delayed (οὐκέτι in 1:23 meaning "not yet") while the Painful Letter did its work. From Paul's remarks about the Painful Letter, his visit to Corinth was no more permanently canceled than indicated by the remark in 13:2, "when I come" (ἐὰν ἔλθω).

through (διά) many tears. Yet 10-13 does not sound tearful on Paul's part; instead, there Paul sounds ironic and angry.[25] This argument, however, does not carry as much weight as may at first appear. It is not necessarily the case that something written "with tears" will sound sad. Anger is often the way that "affliction, anguish, and tears" are expressed. One must interpret the comment in 2:4 along with Paul's further reflection on this Painful Letter in 7:8, where Paul wrestles with whether that letter might have been too strong.[26] Furthermore, in Philippians 3:18 Paul says that he is writing with weeping (κλαίων), but the comments that follow (as well as 3:2 which opens this section) sound more angry than sad. In 2 Corinthians 12:21 Paul looks ahead to the possibility that he will have to mourn (πενθήσω) over some in Corinth when he comes, but again there is little sorrow in his tone. Georgi is certainly correct when he points out that in 2:4 and 7:8, "only the emotional circumstances of the drafting are hinted at; no summary is given."[27] In fact, Paul may describe the writing of this letter after it has been received and done its work differently than was objectively true at the time of writing; to say that he wrote it with great anguish and tears may be a way of saying to these chastised and restored children, "it hurt me more than it hurt you."[28]

The second and more difficult objection to identifying 10-13 with the Painful Letter concerns the content of that letter as described in chapters 2 & 7. It is claimed that 10-13 focuses on the infatuation of the Corinthian community with false apostles who have come to Corinth, and that nothing is said about this issue when Paul discusses the effects of the Painful Letter in chapters 2 and 7;[29] furthermore, it is argued that the Painful Letter was written about disciplining an individual who had

---

[25]Bruce, *I & II Corinthians*, 167-68 (though he comes close to realizing that tears and anger are not mutually exclusive); Furnish, *II Corinthians*, 37; Witherington, *Conflict & Community*, 330 n. 6.

[26]Martin, *2 Corinthians*, 36.

[27]Dieter Georgi, "Corinthians, Second," *Interpreter's Dictionary of the Bible Supplement Volume* (Nashville: Abingdon, 1976), 183-186, here p. 184.

[28]Furnish, *II Corinthians*, 160: "One could argue that the tearful letter had actually been written out of pique, not love, and that only Titus' report of its good effect (7:6-8) allows Paul to describe it now as he does." We would agree with the general direction here, but would apply it more to the tone of the letter than to Paul's motive in writing.

[29]Kümmel, *Introduction*, 290.

offended Paul (2:5-6, 7:12), and that nothing is said about this in 10-13.[30]

As to the first criticism, when one looks carefully at the statements in chapters 2 and 7, it becomes clear that the issue addressed by the Painful Letter did not simply involve an individual; at least most of the community was involved, perhaps simply by not coming to Paul's defense (note that in 7:7-12 it is the community as a whole that has been led to repentance). Furthermore, there are indications in chapters 1-9 that an outside group has been active in Corinth and are on Paul's mind. In 2:17 Paul says that he does not peddle the Word of God like "the others" (οἱ λοιποί);[31] in 3:1 Paul says that he doesn't need letters of recommendation to or from the Corinthians, the way that "some people" (τινες) do; in 5:12 Paul indicates that he needs to give the Corinthians a way properly to boast about him to those who "boast in outward appearance." These other "boasters" are evidently not members of the Corinthian community, but have come in from the outside. These statements are allusions; the opponents are not brought to center stage. Betz suggests this is because by the time Paul writes 1-9, these outsiders have left, and Paul doesn't want to give them an excessive amount of attention.[32] Thus it is not quite true that there are no signs of the false apostles in 1-9, and the involvement of the whole community in this affair is seen both in 7:7-12 and in 10:1-11, 11:2-11.[33]

With regard to the second criticism, we need to note that chapters 10-13 are framed by references to punishment (10:6, 13:10). Furthermore, Watson has suggested that there are indications that an individual in Corinth is in view when Paul speaks of punishment in

---

[30]Bruce, *I & II Corinthians*, 168: "The main point of 'Corinthians C', the demand for discipline against 'you know who' (GK ho toioutos), is totally absent from 2 C. 10-13; it is not even hinted at." For evidence that this may not be the case, see below.

[31]This assumes that the reading of P46, D, F, G, et al. is correct. Bruce Metzger's remark rejecting this reading in *A Textual Commentary on the Greek New Testament* (United Bible Societies, 1971), 577, perhaps misses the point: "in any case, however, οἱ λοιποί seems to be too offensive an expression for Paul to have used in the context." Even with the reading οἱ πολλοί, we can hear Paul's perhaps less caustic reference to a group he assumes the Corinthians know about, and perhaps know by experience.

[32]Hans Dieter Betz, *Der Apostel Paulus und die sokratische Tradition. Eine exegetische Untersuchung zu seiner "Apologie" 2 Korinther 10-13*, Beiträge zur historischen Theologie 45 (Tübingen: Mohr, 1972), 7.

[33]Watson, "2 Corinthians 10-13," 340-42; Talbert, *Reading Corinthians*, xix.

chapter 10 as well as in chapter 2.[34] Watson points to how the offender dealt with in the Painful Letter is referred to ambiguously as "someone" (τις) and "such a person" (τοιοῦτος) in 2:5-6, and that these are the same terms that are used in Paul's discussion of the problem in Corinth in 10:7-11 (τις in v. 7, τοιοῦτος in v. 11). However, this correspondence is far from decisive. Such terms are too general and common[35] to provide any sure connection between these two texts. In fact, by this criterion one could also point back to the incestuous man in 1 Corinthians 5, thus making him the one who insulted Paul on the "painful visit" and making 1 Corinthians the "Painful Letter," an identification that most scholars today rightly reject.[36] Watson also points out that the charge against Paul is made with a singular verb φησίν in 10:10, claiming that this reflects the individual in chapter 2 who insulted Paul. However, again this is not conclusive. Though indefinite references are made more often with plural verbs ("they say," or "it is said"), the singular verb can be used in the

---

[34]Watson, "2 Corinthians 10-13," 345-46.

[35]Note the use of both these terms in 1 Corinthians 5:11, where the reference seems to be instruction in general and not directed at a specific individual.

[36]Note 1 Cor 5:5, where τοιοῦτος is used to describe the incestuous man. For the cogent reasons against identifying him with the one who insulted Paul on the painful visit, see Furnish, *2 Corinthians*, 164-66; Rudolf Bultmann, *The Second Letter to the Corinthians* (Minneapolis: Augsburg, 1985), 48. However, that identification between 2 Corinthians 2 & 7 and the man in 1 Corinthians 5 has been known from the early church (see Furnish, *II Corinthians*, 164), and is still not without its proponents: Francis Young and David F. Ford, *Meaning and Truth in Second Corinthians* (Grand Rapids: Eerdmans, 1988), 53, not only treat 2 Corinthians as a unity, but claim that 1 Corinthians is the former, Painful Letter. Similarly, C. G. Kruse, "The Relationship between the Opposition to Paul Reflected in 2 Corinthians 1-7 and 10-13," *EvQ* 61 (1989): 195-202, claims that the one finally punished in 2 Corinthians 2 & 7 is the incestuous man, who himself has used the intruders' complaints against Paul to rebuff him on the "painful visit." Such an identification will not stand, but there is probably some relationship between the punishment threatened in 1 Corinthians 5 and the indications in 2 Corinthians 10-13 that the Corinthians were doubting Paul's ability or resolve to carry through on punishment. It seems likely that for whatever reason, Paul was unable to carry out the punishment against this member the way he indicated that he would, and that this led to the accusation (by someone else in the community) that Paul was deficient (so also Talbert, *Reading Corinthians*, 112).

same way.[37] One such place this use shows up is in the "diatribe" style, where the imagined accusation of an opponent is given; such a use would seem appropriate here.[38]

Yet Barrett surely makes a good point by noting "But this does not fit the context well; Paul is not speaking of a possible reaction, but of one that has taken place, and to which he is now in turn reacting."[39] Furthermore, this would be the only time that Paul uses this kind of an indefinite 3d singular verb without any stated subject to indicate what is being, or might be said. The diatribe questions in Romans do not use this kind of construction at all (cf. Rom 6:1, 15; 7:7, 13); when Paul reports what some (τινες) are saying against him, he uses the more typical third plural verb (φασίν—Rom 3:8); and in 1 Corinthians 15:35, where Paul does use a third singular verb to give voice to a hypothetical question, the indefinite nature of the subject is indicated by τις. Thus it seems more likely that we should understand φησίν in 10:10 as a reference to what one specific individual in Corinth is saying. Though not all of Watson's arguments are convincing, these elements together lead us to conclude that Paul is referring to the "ringleader"[40] of the opposition in this section, and we should read the use of τις and τοιοῦτος as veiled references to him (as one must often do when criticizing a figure respected and powerful, as this man must have been to have swayed much of the Corinthian congregation).[41] "No one is named; the words used are

---

[37]Baur, Arndt, Gingrich & Danker, *A Greek-English Lexicon of the New Testament and Other Early Christian Literature*, 2d Edition (Chicago: University of Chicago, 1979), 856 (φημί 1.c); Blass, Debrunner & Funk, *A Greek Grammar of the New Testament and Other Early Christian Literature* (Chicago: University of Chicago, 1961), #130.3.

[38]This connection with the diatribe is made by C. F. D. Moule, *An Idiom Book of New Testament Greek*, 2d Edition (Cambridge: Cambridge University, 1959), 29; Bultmann, *Second Letter*, 190; Furnish, *2 Corinthians*, 468; Talbert, *Reading Corinthians*, 111 (though Talbert goes on to insist that this still gives voice to the accusation of a specific individual in Corinth). For such a use of φησίν, see Epictetus *Enchr.* 24.4; *Disc.* 3.9.15; 4.1.11, 151, 158; 4.9.6.

[39]Barrett, *Second Epistle*, 260.

[40]Martin, *2 Corinthians*, 311.

[41]Peter Lampe, "Theological Wisdom and the 'Word About the Cross:' The Rhetorical Scheme of 1 Corinthians 1-4," *Int* 44 (1990): 117-31, esp. 128-31. See also Quintilian 9.2.65-75.

capable of generalization; but the multiplication of references . . . adds to the probability that Paul has in mind a leader of the opposition."[42]

The arguments on both sides of this issue fail to be completely persuasive. Those who argue against 10-13 being the Painful Letter expect too much correspondence between the remarks in chapters 2 & 7 and the content of 10-13; they fail to recognize that there may be rhetorical reasons why Paul's description of what he wrote may not stress the same things as that Painful Letter did. Those who want to argue that 10-13 is the Painful Letter also assume that there should be more correspondence here than is realistic, and that leads them at times to stretch the connections beyond what the evidence warrents. However, this work will assume that 10-13 does represent at least the majority of the Painful Letter; we have seen that the concerns for an individual ringleader, the community and the outsiders do appear, though with different emphasis, in both the description of the Painful Letter and in 10-13; also, this position seems preferable to concluding that Paul must have written two harsh letters and either: a) doesn't mention a previous harsh letter in 10-13, assuming it is the second one, or b) wrote a letter even more harsh than 10-13, assuming it is the first one, and then only mentions that letter in chapters 2 and 7.

Traditional Arguments for Unity

We cannot, however, leave this discussion without noting that the unity of 2 Corinthians is not without supporters. Those in this century who have upheld the unity of 2 Corinthians include Menzies (1912), Goudge (1927), Tasker (1958), Guthrie (1961-70), Hughes (1962), Stephenson (1965), Bates (1965), Price (1967), Kümmel (1973), Hydahl (1973), and Harris (1976). The biggest problem for this position is explaining the drastic change in tone at chapter 10, and it is in the explanations that one can see how unlikely this position is.[43] Most desperate of all seems to be

---

[42]Barrett, *Second Epistle*, 260; see also p. 256.

[43]These studies have also tried to prove the unity of 2 Corinthians by tracing common themes and vocabulary throughout the letter (see especially James L. Price, "Aspects of Paul's Theology and Their Bearing on Literary Problems of Second Corinthians," in *Studies in the History and Text of the New Testament: Festschrift for K. W. Clark*, ed. B. D. Daniels and M. J. Suggs (Grand Rapids: Eerdmans, 1967), 95-106; Young & Ford, *Meaning and Truth*; Witherington, *Conflict & Communtiy*). Yet such studies often ignore that there are some

Lietzmann's suggestion that Paul had a bad night's sleep, and finished the letter in a more angry tone.[44] No better is the attempt to explain the difference in tone by suggesting that at 10:1 Paul takes over the writing from a secretary.[45] While it is certainly possible that Paul used a secretary in writing this letter as he did others,[46] it is scarcely possible that he would have approved and sent the work of a secretary that was so startlingly different from his own feelings.[47] Another explanation that has been offered in defense of the letter's unity is that Paul received fresh news after writing chapters 1-9, and learned either that Titus' report had been overly optimistic, or that things had taken a drastic turn for the worse in

---

differences in these themes and vocabulary between the two sections of 2 Corinthians (for instance, that the "boasting" in chapters 1-9 is always a positive idea, while in chapters 10-13 it is usually viewed negatively). Yet Furnish cogently points out, "the basic thematic coherence of these two sections is no guarantee of their literary unity. An underlying thematic coherence may also obtain in the case of two (or more) separate letters dispatched over a period of time, especially when they are addressed to the same congregation" (*II Corinthians*, 37).

[44]H. Lietzmann, *An die Korinther 1/2* (Tübingen: Mohr, 1969), 138.

[45]A. Deissmann, *Light*, 167 n. 7; A. M. G. Stephenson, "A Defence of the Integrity of 2 Corinthians," in *The Authorship and Integrity of the New Testament* (London: SPCK, 1965), 82-97; W. H. Bates, "The Integrity of 2 Corinthians," *NTS* 12 (1965-66): 50-69, here 67; Gordon J. Bahr, "The Subscriptions in the Pauline Letters," *JBL 87* (1968): 27-42, here 37-38. The use of a secretary with such a large role for the composition of the letters fails to account for the overall consistency in tone, terminology and argument that we do find in the Pauline letters. This does not, however, deny the partnership which biblical scholarship has largely neglected between Paul and those who undoubtedly helped him in the strenuous task of producing lengthy letters, not to mention the responsibility entrusted to them to deliver and appropriately perform these letters. See Botha, "Verbal Art," 415-17.

[46]See 1 Cor 16:21, Gal 6:11, Phlm 19, Rom 16:22. Dio Chrysostom (*Disc.* 18.18) recommends dictating to a secretary rather than writing yourself, because in dictating one is more like a person addressing an audience; Quintilian, however, cautions against the use of a secretary (10.3.19-21): a fast scribe will hurry you and make you reluctant to pause and think; a slow scribe will interrupt your thoughts and perhaps make you lose your temper! See also Achtemeier, "Omne Verbum Sonat," 12-15.

[47]Especially when ancient writers stressed that the letter should contain "glimpses of character" (Demetrius, *On Style* 4.227), and that in a letter people "reveal their real self" (Seneca *Ep.* 40.1, 75.1-2).

Corinth.[48]   Yet in this case, "he would probably have torn up his first draft and started over, writing a whole new letter in light of the new situation,"[49] or at least have reported at 10:1 that he had received new and disturbing reports from Corinth.[50]   Such arguments have, then, failed to account for the change in tone at 10:1 and have failed to persuade most scholars of the letter's unity.[51]

Rhetorical Arguments for Unity

More substantial are the recent claims for unity which arise from rhetorical analyses of 2 Corinthians.[52] Witherington's claim is that "part

---

[48]Martin, *2 Corinthians*, xliii, though Martin does not subscribe to this theory (p. xlvi).

[49]Witherington, *Conflict & Community*, 332.

[50]Best, *Second Corinthians*, 91.

[51]Kümmel's negative argument (*Introduction*, 290), that it is unlikely for 2 Corinthians to be a composite letter because one cannot account for why the end of 1-9 and the beginning of 10-13 would have been omitted, begs the question. Kümmel's arguments against such editorial activity perhaps have more validity against more elaborate composition theories, but not so when the question is about two letters simply placed side by side (cf. his discussion of this issue and the composite nature of Polycarp's letter to the Philippians on 261-62). In fact, collections of ancient letters show varying practice with regard to preserving the beginnings and endings of letters. Deissmann (*Light*, 236) mentions collections in which the prescript of the letter has been abbreviated and moved to the margin of the page. Philipp Vielhauer (*Geschichte der urchristlichen Literatur* [Berlin: de Gruyter, 1975], 154-55) notes that while the letters of Plato and Demosthenes were preserved with both beginning and ending intact, those of Isocrates have had most of their beginnings and endings omitted, those of Pliny the Elder have been preserved without their beginnings, and those of Apollonius of Tyana and of Pliny the Younger retain neither beginning nor ending. Thus even if we would wish for some ancient editor to have shown a bit more respect than it took to omit an opening or closing of Paul's letters, it would have certainly been in keeping with the way many letters were in fact preserved.

[52]Not strictly rhetorical is the suggestion by Stanley Olson, "Confidence Expressions in Paul: Epistolary Conventions and the Purpose of 2 Corinthians" (Ph.D. diss., Yale University, 1976), that chapters 10-13 are an extended "travel talk," common at the end of letters, which is here used as a motivating threat, and thus requiring a bold, harsh tone. In this way Olson would explain the difference between 1-9 and 10-13 as due to Paul's different purposes and strategies in different parts of the letter. Yet Olson's suggestion is not convincing: As an

of the reason for these [partition] theories is that most treatments of 2 Corinthians have not taken into account Paul's use of rhetorical conventions."[53] It has been claimed that the dramatic shift in tone that is found at 10:1 would not have been surprising to Paul's hearers; in fact, that this is precisely the kind of thing that would be expected by hearers, that was called for by rhetorical handbooks, and that is seen in extant speeches. Young and Ford[54] draw attention to the emotional shift near the end of Demosthenes' Second Epistle, comparing it with the shift between 2 Corinthians 9 and 10. They conclude that 2 Corinthians 10-13 should be understood as the *peroratio*, with its stronger emotional appeal.[55] Cicero *De Inv.* 1.52.98 says:

> The peroration is the end and conclusion of the whole speech; it has
> three parts, the summing-up, the *indignatio* or exciting of indignation
> of ill-will against the opponent, and the *conquestio* or the arousing of
> pity and sympathy.

It seems that only the second, and perhaps the third, of these elements could describe what is going on in 2 Cor 10-13; it seems unlikely that 10-13 can be thought of as summarizing the arguments in 1-9.

---

apologetic digression, this section seems overly long; the shift in tone at 10:1 still seems too drastic, especially considering the positive tone of the material that comes between it and the last mention of Paul's travel plans in 9:5; finally, as Furnish points out (*II Corinthians*, 37), in 5:20-9:15 there has already been an extended section of instructions and appeals in the context of Paul's (and his representatives'!) upcoming visit, and it is difficult to see how two sections of appeal based on this visit could stand in the same letter but be so radically different in tone and intent.

[53] Witherington, *Conflict & Community*, 329.

[54] F. Young and D. F. Ford, *Meaning and Truth*, 37-38.

[55] A similar argument is made by J. A. Loubser, "A New Look at Paradox and Irony in 2 Corinthians 10-13," *Neot* 26 (1992): 507-21. For the emotional appeal in the *peroratio*, see Aristotle *Rhetoric* 3.19.1-4; Cicero *De Inv.* 1.53.100-109; Quintilian 6.1.1, 9-55.

Witherington has also questioned this identification of 10-13 as *peroratio* because it seems far too long for this usually brief[56] rhetorical feature:

> It is difficult to maintain that all of 2 Corinthians 10-13 is a *peroratio*. I would suggest that the shift in tone is there not because we have arrived at a *peroratio* but because Paul now chooses to go on the counterattack by means of a rhetorical *synkrisis*, and this will include *pathos*, an appeal to the stronger emotions.[57]

Witherington compares this with a shift in tone that he finds in Galatians 5-6, where "the syntax becomes more abrupt, the style becomes more violent, and the *pathos* is in greater evidence than in Galatians 1-4."[58] It is true that the address in Gal 5:2 (ἴδε ἐγὼ Παῦλος λέγω ὑμῖν) is nearly as emphatic as 2 Cor 10:1 (αὐτὸς δὲ ἐγὼ Παῦλος παρακαλῶ ὑμᾶς); it is not true that this is a sudden or surprising turn toward more stern language or tone. After all, if the lack of thanksgiving at the beginning of the letter weren't enough to signal Paul's harsh mood here, Gal 3:1 had already addressed the readers as Ὦ ἀνόητοι Γαλάται.[59]

The parallels with Demosthenes' *De Corona* have been explored by Frederick Danker, who, though he expresses appropriate caution,[60] nonetheless finds chapters 10-13 a "rhetorically appropriate" climax to the arguments of chapters 1-9,[61] and further claims:

---

[56]Quintilian 6.1.2: "This final recapitulation must be as brief as possible . . . For if we devote too much time thereto, the peroration will cease to be an enumeration and will constitute something very like a second speech." See also 6.1.27-28; *De Inv.* 1.52.100.

[57]Witherington, *Conflict and Community*, 338.

[58]Ibid., n. 32.

[59]Note also the harsh tone that is evident in Gal 3:3; 4:11, 15-20.

[60]Danker, *II Corinthians*, 17: "it is probable that chaps. 10-13 were written after additional reports about Corinth had reached the apostle;" 18: "there are rhetorical traditions that help account for some of the data, but the probability is strong that 2 Corinthians was not written in its present form at one sitting, but consists of at least 2 letters;" on p. 19, Danker suggests that some of the argumentative consistency that is found throughout canonical 2 Corinthians may in fact be due to the post-Paul editors who gathered and circulated the letters to Corinth.

[61]Danker, "Paul's Debt," 290. Peter Marshall, *Enmity in Corinth: Social Conventions in Paul's Relations with the Corinthians* (Tübingen: Mohr, 1987),

Nor would Greco-Romans with but the slightest exposure to rhetorical tradition be in the least disconcerted by such an apparent shift in mood. Demosthenes' oration *On the Crown* (278) makes detailed commentary on the matter otiose:

> Citizens who are held in high repute ought not to expect a court that is in session for the common interest to gratify any tendency they might have to indulge themselves in anger or hatred or related feelings, nor should they go before you with such an end in mind. Indeed, it were best if such feelings were totally foreign to their disposition; but if that is not possible, they ought to moderate them carefully (proas kai metrios). But under what circumstances ought the politician and orator to be vehement? Of course, when the city is in any way imperiled and when the public is faced by adversaries. Such is the obligation of a noble and patriotic citizen.[62]

Yet it is hard to see how this quotation proves Danker's point; Demosthenes speaks of the appropriate use of vehemence in his speech, but this says nothing about the kind of sudden and unexpected shift that we find at 2 Corinthians 10:1.[63] There is no doubt that ancient orators found variety in tone and mood desirable in a speech, including the use of strong emotions,[64] but the shift in tone at 10:1 is surprisingly unexpected. This is what makes the parallels which Danker draws with *De Corona* less than convincing. In Demosthenes' speech, though he does turn to address his opponent directly and vehemently near the end (297-320), this is hardly the first time he has done such a thing, and we are not

---

392 likewise cautiously concludes that because of the comments of ancient rhetorical handbooks regarding variety of tone in a speech, we simply need to understand more about the practice of ancient rhetoric before we can conclude that because of the change in tone, 2 Corinthians cannot have been written as a single work. Witherington, *Conflict and Community*, 431 follows Danker by referring to *De Corona* as an illustration for why "a sudden change in tone and atmosphere was not unusual."

[62] *II Corinthians*, 149-50.

[63] Witherington's claim that "the tone of ch. 10 is much the same as what has preceded it; it is only when Paul gets to the Fool's Discourse at 11:1 that a notable change occurs in tone" (*Conflict and Community*, 432) ignores the emphatic shift from 1st plural to 1st singular, the intense self-reference, and the irony that is present from 10:1 on, as well as the threatening language of 10:2-6.

[64] Aristotle *Rhetoric* 3.1.4, 3.19.1-4; Cicero *De Or.* 3.57.215-58.219; Quintilian 12.10.71.

unprepared for it. Demosthenes has had bouts of such vituperation throughout his speech. For instance, early in the speech (50) Demosthenes says "My antagonist is to blame, for he has so bespattered me with the sour dregs of his own knavery and his own crimes, that I was obliged to clear myself . . . ." This is not an isolated remark, but is echoed throughout the speech: "You backbiter, who tell me to hold my tongue with a fee in my pocket, and cry aloud when I have spent it! That is not your habit; you cry aloud without ceasing, and nothing will ever stop your mouth" (82); "people like you, who make stupid pretensions to the culture of which they are utterly destitute, succeed in disgusting everybody whenever they open their lips" (128).[65]

It is these previous revelations of animosity that we find lacking in 2 Corinthians, which makes the emotional shift so unexpected and jarring, and makes it difficult to read chapters 10-13 as an emotional move parallel to the end of speeches such as *De Corona*.[66] We conclude then that neither the traditional defenses for the unity of 2 Corinthians nor the more recent rhetorical defenses of that unity are persuasive.

Conclusions

All seem to agree that chapters 10-13 are a marked change from what has preceded, and may be treated as a rhetorical unit. That is sufficient for this study to continue by focusing especially on chapters 10-13. Our investigation of the rhetorical strategy and the *stasis* of the argument in 2 Corinthians 10-13 does not depend upon chapters 10-13 being part of or separate from chapters 1-9, nor on the order of these letters if they are separate. Nonetheless, these issues will affect how the rhetorical situation behind the argumentation is understood, and so our position needs to be made clear before we proceed. Based on the arguments presented at length above, we conclude that chapters 10-13 are most likely a letter separate from and prior to chapters 1-9. There is also a strong possibility that it is the Painful Letter, but the evidence here is less convincing.

---

[65]One could note also sections 196-97, 209, 242, 257-66, 296.

[66]For the same reasons, Young's and Ford's suggestion of a parallel in Demosthenes' Second Epistle doesn't answer the problems created by the change in 2 Cor 10-13. Though the Second Epistle does contain heightened emotional appeal near the end, it is in keeping with the rest of the letter and not the kind of shocking turn toward anger that we find in 2 Corinthians 10-13.

RHETORICAL SITUATION

Lloyd Bitzer has provided the standard definition of "rhetorical situation:" "Let us regard rhetorical situation as the natural context of persons, events, objects, relations, and an exigence which strongly invites utterance."[67] Rhetorical analysis may then be described as criticism of "forms of activity inseparable from the wider social relationships between writers and readers."[68] Rhetorical activity takes place within social structures, group conflicts, and struggles for power.[69]

We now turn to consider the most important of the social structures and forces that make up the "exigence" that has prompted Paul's response in 2 Corinthians 10-13. Though it is clear that the relationship between Paul and this congregation has become strained and that there is dissatisfaction on both sides, the problem cannot be reduced to a single cause. There are three major aspects of Paul's relationship with the Corinthians that were already areas of contention when 1 Corinthians was written, and which have come to a point of crisis by the time of the writing of 2 Corinthians 10-13: questions regarding Paul's rhetorical performance (1 Cor 1:17, 2:1-5), questions regarding financial support of Paul (1 Cor 9:1-27), and a Corinthian tendency to compare and judge spiritual leaders (1 Cor 1:10-15, 3:1-15). We will examine each of these to gain some idea of the rhetorical situation for 2 Corinthians 10-13.[70]

---

[67]Bitzer, "Rhetorical Situation," 5. It is Bitzer's formulation which greatly influences the understanding of Kennedy, *New Testament Interpretation*, 34-36.

[68]T. Eagleton, *Literary Theory: An Introduction* (Minneapolis: University of Minnesota, 1983), 205-6.

[69]Dale B. Martin, *Slavery as Salvation: The Metaphor of Slavery in Pauline Christianity* (New Haven: Yale University, 1990), 147. Thus, while "rhetorical situation" may have much in common with form criticism's concern for the *Sitz im Leben*, rhetorical situation is distinguished by its explicit and emphatic concern for the interaction between the text and the audience in a setting where the text is seen as having the potential to change the audience's thoughts and/or actions.

[70]We do well to remember that rhetorical situation is not the same as historical situation. Any text presents a selected description or impression of the situation at hand, and that description itself is intended to be part of the persuasive strategy. See Wuellner, "Where is Rhetorical Criticism Taking Us?," 456. This distinction between rhetorical situation and historical situation is also emphasized by Martin, "Apostasy," 444 n. 32 and by Dennis L. Stamps, "Rethinking the Rhetorical Situation: The Entextualization of the Situation in New Testament Epistles," in *Rhetoric and the New Testament: Essays From the 1992 Heidelberg Conference,*

Rhetoric in Hellenistic Society

In Hellenistic society the practice and expectations of rhetorical eloquence were pervasive. Not only were political leaders expected to speak persuasively and eloquently, but so also those who claimed authority in philosophy or religion.[71] Among such people there was great competition, and success depended upon one's ability to express the power of the divine in his or her performance—not only through miracles, but also through rhetorical performance.[72]

Rhetorical training occupied the final stage of education; it was the crowning achievement in the education of Roman youth.[73] But awareness of the art of rhetoric was not limited to the elite or the highly educated.[74] The theater and gymnasium were traditional places of public speaking and discourse, and were a part of society across the Roman empire. Even those who had not received advanced education were aware of the rhetorical art, had heard the arguments of teachers and philosophers, and knew the speeches of temples, civic events and games.[75] Tacitus notes

---

ed. S. Porter and T. Olbricht, JSNT Sup. 90 (Sheffield: JSOT, 1993), 193-210, who prefers to use the label "literary-rhetorical situation" (p. 200). However, as helpful as this reminder is, it should not lead us to exclude historical concerns and issues from our discussion of rhetorical situation. The text was produced in response to certain historical and social conditions, and to be effective it had to correspond to a large degree with the view of those conditions held by the audience. Though the rhetorical situation presented in an argument is a product of the author, it is not simply a creation of the author's imagination.

[71] Andrew D. Clarke, *Secular & Christian Leadership in Corinth: A Socio-Historical and Exegetical Study of 1 Corinthians 1-4* (Leiden: Brill, 1993), 37.

[72] Georgi, *Opponents*, 155. Thus, even Lucian admits that Alexander's appearance and speech were flawless, and this accounts in part for Alexander's ability to gain a following; see Lucian *Alexander the False Prophet* 3, trans. A. M. Harmon, Loeb Classical Library (New York: G. P. Putnam's Sons, 1925) 4:173-253.

[73] It should not, however, be assumed that only those who reached advanced education studied rhetoric. Quintilian complains that the teaching of rhetoric *should* be left to the rhetoricians, and not taken up at the final stages of literary study under a *grammaticus* (Quintilian 2.1.1-6); the need for Quintilian to argue this shows that rhetoric was being taught at lower levels of education. See also Dale B. Martin, *The Corinthian Body* (New Haven: Yale University, 1995), 49.

[74] Cf. Achtemeier, "Omne," 19-20.

[75] D. A. Russell, *Greek Declamation* (Cambridge: Cambridge University,

that audiences in general were quite capable of evaluating the rhetorical skill of the speaker, and that almost everyone knew some rhetoric.[76] Dio says that good oratory was appreciated by the average listener, and that even women and children recognized good or bad rhetoric when they heard it.[77]

To be a part of hellenistic culture meant to have ears trained for the ways of persuasive speech. Rhetoric provided the rules for making critical judgments in all kinds of social settings. The importance of rhetorical eloquence can be seen in the advice given by Seneca:

> But do study eloquence. You can easily pass from this art to all others; it equips even those whom it does not train for its own ends.[78]

The Corinthian church appears to have transferred these standards and expectations from the rest of society into the church. The issue of rhetorical eloquence is evident in 1 Corinthians, where Paul calls into question the kind of rhetoric which the Corinthians were seeking (see 1 Cor 1:17; 2:1-4, 13; 3:1-4, where the factions may well have resulted from a desire to contrast one leader against another in competition similar to the competition between various philosophers and preachers in the larger society).[79] In 2 Corinthians 10-13, members of the church are still judging spiritual leaders by the criterion of rhetorical eloquence, but now that judgment has turned more sharply against Paul than was evident in 1 Corinthians (see 2 Corinthians 10:1, 10; 11:6; 13:3).

1983), 76.

[76]Tacitus *Dialogus* 19, in *Tacitus. Agricola, Germania, Dialogus*, trans. M. Hutton and W. Peterson, Loeb Classical Library (Cambridge: Harvard University, 1914; rev. ed. 1970), 231-347.

[77]Dio Chrysostom *Or.* 37.33. Cf. also Quintilian 1.1.6, who mentions a few women orators who, though not formally trained, learned rhetoric and whose lives brought them into public affairs in which they used their facility in speaking.

[78]Seneca *Controversies* 2, Preface 3, in *The Elder Seneca*, 2 vols., trans. M. Winterbottom, Loeb Classical Library (Cambridge: Harvard University, 1974).

[79]Neither Richard A. Horsley's suggestion ("Wisdom of Word and Words of Wisdom in Corinth," *CBQ* 39 [1977]: 224-39) that the σοφία λόγου discussed in 1 Corinthians 1:17 refers to Jewish wisdom traditions, nor Ulrich Wilckens' suggestion (*Weisheit und Torheit. Eine exegetisch-religionsgeschichtliche Untersuchung zu 1 Kor. 1 und 2* [Tübingen: Mohr, 1959]) that it refers to gnostic charismatic speech are persuasive. The phrase most likely does refer to rhetorical skill and eloquence. Note the discussion in Barrett, "Christianity at Corinth."

Though only a few members of the Corinthian church were among the social elite (1 Cor 1:26), most or all of them would have been familiar with the style and expectations of popular rhetoric.[80]   Proper rhetorical performance was a mark of status in society, and the Corinthians apparently expected their spiritual leader to perform in keeping with his position.

> The fundamental problem is the Corinthians' image of Christian leadership. At least some of them had created in their minds an image, largely shaped by the values of their culture, of a leader who had honor, power, spiritual gifts, rhetorical skills, and good references and who would accept patronage. They looked, that is, for a Sophist, or at least for a rhetorically adept philosophical teacher.[81]

Corinth itself seems to have been a city designed for those who were preoccupied with the marks of social status. Roman Corinth was a relatively new city, with little of the established aristocracy that would have occupied the pinnacle of society elsewhere.   It was largely a freedman's city,[82] a place where upward social mobility was possible for the socially ambitious and which offered "opportunities for merchants, bankers, and artisans to gain higher social status and accumulate a fortune in this city refounded by freed slaves."[83]

In such a setting, inability on Paul's part to live up to the accepted and expected standards would have been disturbing; for Paul to deliberately act in accordance with a lower social level would have been confusing, disgusting and provocative.[84]   The Corinthians were apparently operating

---

[80]A. D. Litfin, "St. Paul's Theology of Proclamation: An Investigation of 1 Corinthians 1-4 in the Light of Greco-Roman Rhetoric." (Ph.D. diss., Oxford University, 1983), 203. Thus it is not necessary or even likely that the expectation of rhetorical eloquence on the part of the spiritual leader was only held by the social elite among the congregation (as argued, for instance, by D. W. J. Gill, "In Search of the Social Elite in the Corinthian Church," *TynB* 44 [1993]: 331). For evidence that the "Second Sophistic" movement was already underway in Corinth during the mid-first century, see Kennedy, *Art of Rhetoric*, 513; idem, *Classical Rhetoric*, 37; Witherington, *Conflict & Community*, 348-50.

[81]Witherington, *Conflict & Community*, 348. Cf. also Judge, "Paul and Socrates," 107; idem, "Reaction," 172.

[82]Furnish, *II Corinthians*, 7.

[83]Witherington, *Conflict & Community*, 20.

[84]Ibid., 21.

within the church as though it were simply one more social group in which one could compete for and enjoy status according to the norms of society.[85] The members of the Corinthian church felt they had the right to judge Paul according to those standards by which orators and teachers were judged,[86] and the majority of the congregation appears to have found Paul lacking.

Though even Paul's opponents had to admit the power of his letters (2 Cor 10:10; an opinion Paul shares—cf. 2 Cor 13:10, 1 Cor 14:37, Rom 15:15-16), it was his performance in person that they found faulty (2 Cor 10:1, 10). That Paul lacked, or at least failed to practice, the niceties of rhetorical style among the Corinthians is confirmed by Paul himself (1 Cor 2:1-5, 2 Cor 11:6).

It may not have been only Paul's rhetorical style that the Corinthians found unacceptable. Physical "presence" and delivery were considered very important.[87] That Paul's physical presence was less than overwhelming is confirmed by 1 Cor 2:3 and 2 Cor 10:10.[88] The importance of delivery and physical appearance is discussed by Quintilian:

---

[85] Pogoloff, *Logos and Sophia*, 274.

[86] Clarke, *Secular & Christian Leadership*, 47.

[87] Cf. Witherington, *Conflict & Community*, 21 n. 54. Note also Lucian *The Ship, or The Wishes* 2, trans. K. Killburn, Loeb Classical Library (Cambridge: Harvard University, 1959), 433, where he describes one whose attractiveness and social status were called into question by his Greek: "He spoke in a slovenly manner, one long, continuous prattle; he spoke Greek, but his accent and intonation pointed to his native-land." It seems probable that part of the reason Paul's letters were admired more than his personal performances was that his letters were read by others, who did not exhibit those defects in speech, delivery, or physical characteristic that those at Corinth found disturbing in Paul.

[88] So also Gal 4:13, if this condition were chronic; but in Galatians, the disability that strikes Paul appears to be unexpected. Betz, *Der Apostel*, 44-57 rightly points out that the pairing of ἀσθένεια / ἀσθενής and λόγος in both 1 Cor 2:3-4 and 2 Cor 10:10 indicates that the problem here is not one of Paul's inner emotional state (such as discouragement after a failure in Athens, suggested by F. F. Bruce, *Paul, Apostle of the Heart Set Free* [Grand Rapids: Eerdmans, 1977], 248), but had to do with how Paul and his preaching were perceived by others; so too Ronald Hock, *The Social Context of Paul's Ministry: Tentmaking and Apostleship* (Philadelphia: Fortress, 1980), 59.

For a good delivery is undoubtedly impossible for one who cannot remember what he has written, or lacks the quick facility of speech required by sudden emergencies, or is hampered by incurable impediments of speech. Again, physical uncouthness may be such that no art can remedy it, while a weak voice is incompatible with first-rate excellence in delivery.[89]

It is not simply Paul's poor performance which the Corinthians have found disturbing, but the inconsistency between his written *persona* and his performance when with them.[90] Such inconsistency would make Paul vulnerable to the charge of being merely a "flatterer," a sham who would say or do whatever will serve himself at the time.[91] Such suspicions of

---

[89]Quintilian 11.3.12-13; cf. Epictetus *Disc.* 3.1.41. For other texts illustrating the importance of physical appearance for rhetorical excellence, see Danker, *II Corinthians*, 155. Martin, *Corinthian Body*, 25-29, 53-55, shows how a physical defect could be seen by a hellenistic audience not simply as an obstacle to effective rhetoric, but as a sign of a flaw in character.

One might also recall the earliest description of Paul's physical appearance, from The Acts of Paul and Thecla 3:

[Onesiphorus] saw Paul coming, a man small of stature, with a bald head and crooked legs, in a good state of body, with eyebrows meeting and nose somewhat hooked, full of friendliness . . . ." (Trans. from *New Testament Apocrypha*, ed. E. Hennecke, W. Schneemelcher, R. McL. Wilson [Philadelphia: Westminster 1963, 1965], II:353-54.)

(see also E. A. Judge, "St. Paul and Socrates," *Interchange: Papers on Biblical and Current Questions* 13 [1973]: 112). But note, beyond the questions regarding the historicity of such a description of Paul, that this text concludes that Paul, at times, appeared to have "the face of an angel;" cf. also Abraham J. Malherbe, "A Physical Description of Paul," in *Christians Among Jews and Gentiles*, ed. G. Nickelsburg and G. MacRae (Philadelphia: Fortress, 1986), 170-75, who points out that this description was not as unflattering as we might assume, and was in fact a typical way in which heroes, from Herakles to Augustus, were described.

[90]Henry Chadwick, *The Enigma of St. Paul* (London: Athlone, 1969), 13-14; Bultmann, *Second Letter*, 190; Marshall, *Enmity*, 341; A. T. Lincoln, "Paul the Visionary: The Setting and Significance of the Rapture to Paradise in 2 Corinthians 12:1-10," *NTS* 25 (1979): 207; Abraham J. Malherbe, "Seneca on Paul as Letter Writer," in *The Future of Early Christianity*, ed. B. A. Pearson (Minneapolis: Fortress, 1991), 416-17; Kennedy, *New Testament Interpretation*, 93-94. Similar arguments were made by David E. Fredrickson in an unpublished paper presented at the 1993 SBL, "Freedom of Speech in Pauline Letters."

[91]Marshall, *Enmity*, 251-57. Cf. also Gal 1:10. Note also Dio Chrysostom *Or.* 42.1: "For I have never given anyone to understand that I am an able speaker or

inconsistency and flattery may have been strengthened by Paul's own policy of being "all things to all people" (1 Cor 9:19-23).[92]

Some scholars have concluded that although Paul's letters exhibit rhetorical skill,[93] he was probably *unable* to follow through with an effective delivery. Barrett[94] suggests that Paul, in the excitement of preaching, would get himself into "grammatical knots" such as those that show up in the letters. Marshall[95] suggests that Paul's preaching was done passionately and without regard to propriety. In contrast, Allo says that Paul's preaching style must have differed little from his letters, that passages such as 2 Cor 11:6 which depreciate Paul's rhetorical skill in preaching must be read as ironic, and that Paul's eloquence should not be questioned.[96] While we may agree with Allo regarding Paul's rhetorical skill, it seems clear from 2 Cor 10:10 that his preaching style did in fact differ from the letters he wrote. Most modern scholars have been willing to admit that difference, and have found that Paul's letters, at least, possess considerable rhetorical quality.[97]

---

thinker or that I possess more knowledge than the average; . . . and many consider this very protest of mine to be ostentation."

[92]Stanley K. Stowers, "Paul on the Use and Abuse of Reason," in *Greeks, Romans and Christians: Essays in Honor of Abraham J. Malherbe* (Minneapolis: Fortress, 1990), 271, suggests that Paul's lack of dogmatic, unqualified answers in 1 Corinthians contributed to the suspicion that Paul was weak and inconsistent. A similar conclusion was reached by E. B. Allo, "Le defaut d'eloquence et de 'style oral' de Saint Paul," *RSPT* 23 (1934): 30.

[93]There has been growing appreciation for the rhetorical skill shown in Paul's letters, and many scholars have been willing to admit that Paul probably had some rhetorical training. This would not necessarily mean that Paul had attended a school with a rhetorician, since "all educated people would have been drilled in rhetoric; for Greco-Roman education *was* rhetorical education" (Martin, *Corinthian Body*, 50).

[94]Barrett, *Second Epistle*, 261. Best, *Second Corinthians*, 97 agrees.

[95]Marshall, *Enmity*, 332, 400.

[96]Allo, "Defaut," 30-31.

[97]Judge, "Early Christians," 136; Christopher Forbes, "Comparison, Self-Praise, & Irony: Paul's Boasting and the Conventions of Hellenistic Rhetoric," *NTS* 32 (1986): 23; Witherington, *Conflict & Community*, 433. However, there remains a question regarding by what standards Paul's rhetoric was or should be judged. The Church Fathers recognized that Paul's style didn't match the Attic standards held by their own time (cf. Judge, "Reaction," 170-71; Allo, "Defaut," 36), but that may well not have been the standard active in Corinth either (Marshall, *Enmity*, 390). Quintilian 12.10 discusses the arguments of his

Whether or not the complaints about Paul's physical presence (ἡ παρουσία τοῦ σώματος, 2 Cor 10:10) concerned anything over which Paul had a choice, the fact that he could write with effective force (αἱ ἐπιστολαὶ βαρεῖαι καὶ ἰσχυραί) but when with them his speech (λόγος) was contemptible (ἐξουθενημένος) must have seemed to the Corinthians to be due to a deliberate—and perverse—choice on Paul's part. Paul confirms that it is his decision not to use "lofty words or wisdom" in his proclamation, and that his speech (λόγος) would not be with persuasive words of wisdom (πειθοῖς σοφίας λόγοις, 1 Cor 2:1-4).[98]

That decision had serious consequences for Paul.[99] The culture of late western antiquity, despite the debates surrounding styles of rhetoric and the tension between philosophy and sophistry, was one dominated by the value of rhetorical skill. By deliberately choosing not to use the techniques expected from someone in a teaching, leadership position, Paul made a remarkable break with his culture, and with the values of education, wisdom and beauty which were connected with rhetoric. To have a leader who did not measure up to society's standards meant not

---

day regarding the two branches of rhetoric: the "Attic" (which Quintilian describes as "withered, sapless, anemic") and the "Asiatic" (which Quintilian describes as "bombastic, redundant, excessive, sensuous"). Though Hengel (*The Pre-Christian Paul* [London: SCM Press, 1991], 58) says that Paul's style was probably Asiatic, with its "sovereign contempt for beautiful form," most scholars have claimed that it is the Asiatic style (and thus not necessarily the value of rhetoric itself) that Paul is rejecting, and for which perhaps the Corinthians were looking (Judge, "Paul's Boasting," 41; Furnish, *II Corinthians*, 490; David E. Garland, "Paul's Apostolic Authority: The Power of Christ Sustaining Weakness [2 Corinthians 10-13]," *RevExp* 86 [1989]: 376; Pogoloff, *Logos and Sophia*, 183-90; Witherington, *Conflict & Community*, 21 n. 58, 46).

[98]The suggestion by Witherington (*Conflict & Community*, 46 n. 139) that 1 Cor 9:22 implies that Paul would use rhetoric to make a good first impression on rhetorically sophisticated audiences does not correspond with the complaints of the Corinthians.

[99]Those who conclude that Paul deliberately chose to avoid the adoption of rhetorical technique in his preaching include: Judge, "Reaction," 171-73; Black, *Apostle of Weakness*, 102; Marshall, *Enmity*, 390. George A. Kennedy ("Truth and Rhetoric in the Pauline Epistles," in *The Bible as Rhetoric*, ed. M. Warner [London: Routledge, 1990], 195-202) notes that Paul avoids using the language of rhetoric that was pervasive in his society, and Kennedy compares this to someone today with a fundamentalist stance avoiding scientific terminology.

only a decrease in Paul's own social status, but also in the social status of the congregation which followed him.[100] In the situation faced in 2 Corinthians 10-13, Paul finds himself forced to argue against rhetorically trained opponents to a rhetorically picky audience.[101]

Whatever his practice in preaching, Paul in this letter uses rhetorical technique while he attacks the value of rhetoric.[102] As we will see, one of the things Paul will do in this letter will be to show the Corinthians that his abandonment of eloquence in rhetoric is a deliberate choice on his part, and thus move them to grasp a different view of ministry, the gospel, and authority.[103]

Patronage and Paul's Self-Support

The issue over whether or not Paul would accept financial support from the Corinthian church, and just how Paul did find financial support, is likewise an issue of status:

> Gifts and benefactions in the ancient world were a recognized way of establishing social patronage. One's dependents might be classified as friends, but it was a friendship that was created from above and placed the privileged recipient under commitments. To refuse such a benefaction, on the other hand, constituted a breach of friendship, and one could slip into the exhausting rituals of formal enmity.[104]

The offer of financial support from Corinth has been interpreted in various ways: as an offer of benefaction;[105] more specifically, as an

---

[100]See Marshall, *Enmity*, 357; Arthur J. Dewey, "A Matter of Honor: A Socio-Historical Analysis of 2 Corinthians 10," *HTR* 78 (1985): 209-17.

[101]Judge, "Paul's Boasting," 48.

[102]Kennedy, *New Testament Interpretation*, 93-94; Pogoloff, *Logos and Sophia*, 120-21. In this respect, Paul's strategy recalls ancient admiration for Plato's *Gorgias*: "What impressed me most deeply about Plato in that book was that it was when making fun of orators that he himself seemed to be the consummate orator" (Cicero *De Or.* 1.47).

[103]Murphy-O'Connor, *Theology of 2 Corinthians*, 107-8. See also Judge, "Reaction," 171; John William Beaudean Jr., *Paul's Theology of Proclamation* (Macon, Ga.: Mercer University, 1938), 202-3.

[104]Judge, "Reaction," 172. See also Witherington, *Conflict & Community*, 22.

[105]Danker, *II Corinthians*, 166-68; idem, *Benefactor: Epigraphic Study of a*

attempt to establish a patron-client relationship with Paul;[106] or as an offer of "friendship."[107] Whichever was the intent of the Corinthians (and the three may not be mutually exclusive), the end result is the same: to accept the money could have placed Paul under unwanted obligations; to refuse the money apparently was perceived by the Corinthians as an insult which incurred enmity.[108]

Paul was certainly not alone in refusing financial support. There was a strong current in the philosophical tradition that likewise was wary of the dangers of accepting the role of a paid teacher, lecturer, or philosopher.[109] Philosophers should stay away from such arrangements that might obligate them to the wealthy.[110] Epictetus urges that the philosopher should be free from "private duties" and not become involved

---

Greco-Roman and New Testament Semantic Field (St. Louis: Clayton, 1982).

[106]Young and Ford, *Meaning and Truth*, 191; Furnish, *II Corinthians*, 507-8. The patron-client relationship was basic to the social and political structure of the Roman Empire, and was considered to be divinely ordained; see John T. Carroll and Joel B. Green, *The Death of Jesus in Early Christianity* (Peabody, Mass.: Hendrickson, 1995), 179-80. For further information on the patron-client relationship, see John Elliott, "Patronage and Clientism in Early Christian Society," *Forum* 3 (1987): 39-48. For evidence that the patron-client system was a common paradigm in Greek cities, see Judge, "Cultural Conformity," 16-20.

[107]The argument of Marshall, *Enmity in Corinth*. Patron-client relationships were euphemistically referred to as "friendship" (*amicitia*). Such "friendships" supposedly "were voluntary, but in practice social inferiors often had no choice but to engage in such relationships in order to be materially supported" (Witherington, *Conflict & Community*, 414).

[108]See E. A. Judge, "The Social Identity of the First Christians," *JRH* 11 (1980): 214; Witherington, *Conflict & Community*, 418. The Corinthians' anger toward Paul over this issue may have been furthered by the offering he was trying to collect for the church in Jerusalem, which the Corinthians apparently interpreted as an attempt at fraud, a scheme to get their money without any of the social obligations that would come from a gift given directly to Paul (2 Cor 12:14-18).

[109]For a discussion of how wealthy citizens became the patrons of philosophers, who then acted as household tutors, advisors, and chaplains, see Tacitus *Annals* 16.34, Dio Chrysostom *Or.* 77/78.34-35; cf. also A. D. Nock, *Conversion* (Oxford: Oxford University, 1933), 178. For evidence of similar arrangements in the New Testament, note Lk 10:5-7; Acts 16:15, 17:5-9, 18:3.

[110]See Lucian *On Salaried Posts in Great Houses*, trans. A. M. Harmon, Loeb Classical Library (New York: G. P. Putnam's Sons, 1921), 3:411-481.

in relationships that will prevent him from acting as "a good and excellent man."[111]

Yet it was not simply that in declining their offer of financial support Paul was denying the Corinthians the status of benefactors or patrons. This refusal on Paul's part also meant that he would have to work to support himself, which was a scandal to the Corinthians and a blow to Paul's perceived status as well as to their own.[112]   Though some philosophical traditions expressed appreciation for the value of work and self-support,[113] the majority opinion was that plying a trade was humiliating for someone with the assumed status of a philosopher.[114] Paul recognizes that this is an issue of status, and that his manual labor does bring humiliation (see 1 Cor 9:19, 2 Cor 11:7).[115] It will be Paul's task to

---

[111]Epictetus *Disc.* 3.22.69; see also 3.23.9-14, 22-23, 30-32. For similar criticisms of being paid as a philosopher, see Plato *Apology* 19 D-E, Aristotle *Nich. Eth.* 9.1.7, Philostratus *Life of Apollonius* 1.13, Dio Chrysostom *Or.* 77/78.34-35. See also Talbert, *Reading Corinthians*, 126-27.

[112]Stanley K. Stowers, "Social Status, Public Speaking and Private Teaching: The Circumstances of Paul's Preaching Activity," *NovT* 26 (1984): 70. See also Furnish, *II Corinthians*, 508.

[113]See Marcus Aurelius *Meditations* 1.5; Epictetus *Disc.* 3.12.7, 15.11; Lucian *The Dream or Lucian's Career* 1-2. The best example is perhaps Simon the shoemaker, who in the Cynic traditions is presented as a friend of Socrates who continues to work in his shop and carry on philosophical conversations there; Simon refused to accept an invitation from Pericles to become part of his court, in order that he might preserve his freedom of speech (παρρησία). See Ronald Hock, "Simon the Shoemaker as the Ideal Cynic," *GRBS* 17 (1976): 41-53.

[114]Cf. Lucian *The Dream or Lucian's Career* 9, idem *The Double Indictment* 6, idem *The Runaways* 12-13, Aristotle *Pol.* 8.2.1-2, Seneca *Ep.* 47.10. Witherington (*Conflict & Community*, 209) points out that it was mainly the upper social levels, who left the literary record and who wielded the social power, who tended to look down on manual labor. As shown by the funerary inscriptions, the artisans and merchants did not share such a low view of their own labors. Martin, *Slavery as Salvation*, 140 notes that Paul's employment was a self-identification with the lower social levels, an act of solidarity with them, but one that was interpreted as "flattery" by the elite at Corinth. While both these authors help us gain a fuller understanding of the social diversity and dynamics that may have been functioning at Corinth, it should not be assumed too quickly that the members of the Corinthian church from lower social levels appreciated Paul's employment; they may have valued their own work, and yet considered it inappropriate for their preacher.

[115]That Paul sees his work as a form of humiliation may be a sign that Paul

re-interpret his actions for the Corinthians so that they will see that he is not acting out of a lack of love for them (2 Cor 11:11) or a sense of inadequacy regarding his apostolic authority (2 Cor 11:20-21).

Judging Spiritual Leaders: Paul's Opponents

The problems encountered in trying to identify the opponents Paul faced in any particular situation are well-known, and certainly apply to the situation behind 2 Corinthians 10-13:[116]

1) Since the people whom Paul addresses in his letter know Paul's opponents, Paul does not need to identify or describe them; Paul's references to his opponents are mainly allusions.

2) Furthermore, one must be careful about assuming which positive statements by Paul about himself are in fact reactions to the opposite position, i.e., the position of his opponents. Such "mirror reading" has been seriously challenged.[117] Paul's polemical statements may owe as much to his rhetorical purposes as they do to the actual positions of his opponents.

3) We also cannot assume that there is a consistent and united front against Paul reflected in all his letters; one cannot assume that information from different letters can be combined for a more complete picture of the opponents.

4) We need to keep in mind that any statements which Paul makes about his opponents are no doubt partial and partisan. We hear only Paul's side of the discussion, and have no direct evidence for how the opponents would describe themselves.

5) Finally, we cannot even be certain that Paul is fully informed about the situation; it could be that at times Paul is misinformed about his opposition, or purposely ambiguous in order to cover more than one possibility.

---

comes from the upper levels of society; see Martin, *Slavery as Salvation*, 123; idem, *Corinthian Body*, xv-xvi.

[116] Jerry L. Sumney, *Identifying Paul's Opponents: The Question of Method in 2 Corinthians*, JSNT Sup. 40 (Sheffield: JSOT Press, 1990), esp. 85-125. See also Furnish, *II Corinthians*, 48-49; Best, *2 Corinthians*, 132-33; Witherington, *Conflict & Community*, 343-45.

[117] See especially George Lyons, *Pauline Autobiography: Toward a New Understanding*, SBLDS 73 (Atlanta: Scholars, 1985).

The attempt to identify Paul's opponents in 2 Corinthians has led to a multitude of suggestions, but they fall into three main categories:[118]

1) The opponents were Judaizers, emissaries of the Jerusalem church (or at least they claimed such authority) sent out to correct the Pauline congregations.[119] However, it is certainly unlikely that the opponents here were Judaizers, since Paul's arguments never mention the Law, circumcision or Sabbath.[120]

2) The opponents were Gnostics.[121] This theory, however, has lost support for two main reasons. First, the references to γνῶσις in 2 Corinthians are all positive; the issue is not fought around this topic.[122] Second, there has been growing dissatisfaction with theorizing that gnostics were present in the first century based on evidence from the second century and later.[123]

3) The opponents were Jewish-Christian missionaries who had adopted the methods of popular hellenistic propaganda.[124] One suggestion that gained significant support was that the opponents had adopted the

---

[118] See Furnish, *II Corinthians*, 48-49; Barrett, *Second Epistle*, 28-30.

[119] F. C. Baur, *Paul the Apostle of Jesus Christ* (London: Williams & Norgate, 1876); Windisch, *Der zweite Korintherbrief*; Ernst Käsemann, "Die Legitimatät des Apostels: Eine Untersuchung zu II Kor. 10-13," *ZNW* 41 (1942): 33-71; Derk William Oostendorp, *Another Jesus: A Gospel of Jewish-Christian Superiority in 2 Corinthians* (Kampen: J. H. Kok, 1967); Barrett, "Paul's Opponents;" John Gunther, *St. Paul's Opponents and Their Background: A Study of Apocalyptic and Jewish Sectarian Teachings*, NovTSup. 35 (Leiden: Brill, 1973); Gerd Theissen's suggestion ("Legitimation and Subsistence: An Essay on the Sociology of Early Christian Missionaries," in *The Social Setting of Pauline Christianity* [Philadelphia: Fortress, 1982], 27-67) that they are from Judea and the major difference is over how the mission is supported (i.e., differing models of ministry) is helpful in many ways, but fails to account for the Christological issue that Paul sees as being at stake (11:4; see Martin, *Second Corinthians*, 338).

[120] See Martin, *Second Corinthians*, 336.

[121] Rudolf Bultmann, *Exegetische Probleme des zweiten Korintherbriefes* (Darmstadt: Wissenschaftliche Buchgesellschaft, 1963); Walter Schmithals, *Gnosticism in Corinth* (Nashville: Abingdon, 1971).

[122] A major problem with Schmithals' study is that he takes 1 Corinthians and 2 Corinthians as though addressing the same opponents, surely a mistake; see also Bultmann, *Second Letter*, 203.

[123] Beginning with A. D. Nock, *St. Paul* (New York: Harper & Bros., 1938).

[124] Bornkamm, "History;" Betz, *Der Apostel*, while helpfully pointing out the parallels with Sophist propaganda and Cynic philosophy, has understated the importance of Jewish heritage for the opponents.

figure of the θεῖος ἀνήρ as their model.[125] However, this theory has suffered much the same fate as the gnostic theory.[126] Sources for the concept of θεῖος ἀνήρ before the second century are rare, and even then the diversity of figures that could be described as θεῖος ἀνήρ suggests that there was not a single, stable concept communicated by that term. At most, we could perhaps speak of a fluid expression or a cluster of ideas, since religions, philosophical schools and government all wanted to portray their leaders as "divine;" but the evidence doesn't support a definite, clear category recognized as θεῖος ἀνήρ in the first century.[127]

The evidence which we have is insufficient to prove any of the above theories regarding the opponents, and is likely insufficient ever to allow a definite identification. But for the purposes of understanding Paul's rhetoric in this letter, it will be sufficient to gain a general description of the opponents in Corinth; Paul does say enough about them in 2 Corinthians for such a description.[128]

---

[125]Gerhard Friedrich, "Die Gegner des Paulus im 2 Korintherbrief," in *Abraham unser Vater. Festschrift für Otto Michel*, ed. O. Betz, M. Hengel, and P. Schmidt (Leiden: Brill, 1963), 181-215; Dieter Georgi, *Die Gegner des Paulus im 2. Korintherbrief* (Neukirchen-Vluyn: Neukirchener Verlag, 1964); trans: *The Opponents of Paul in Second Corinthians* (Philadelphia: Fortress, 1986).

[126]See David Tiede, *The Charismatic Figure as Miracle Worker* (Missoula, Mont.: Scholars, 1972); E. A. Judge, "St. Paul and Socrates," *Interchange: Papers on Biblical and Current Questions* 13 (1973): 106-16; Carl Holladay, *Theios Aner in Hellenistic Judaism: A Critique of the Use of This Category in New Testament Christology*, SBLDS 40 (Missoula, Mont.: Scholars, 1977); Jack Kingsbury, "The 'Divine Man' as the Key to Mark's Christology—The End of an Era?," *Int* 35 (1981): 243-57; Witherington, *Conflict & Community*, 436.

[127]Morton Smith, "On the History of the 'Divine Man'," in *Paganisme, Judaisme, Christianisme*, ed. F. F. Bruce et al. (Paris: De Boccard, 1978), 335-45.

[128]It is likely that the same opponents are dealt with in 2 Cor 10-13 and 2 Cor 1-9. If the analysis of the relationship between these two letters given earlier in this chapter is accurate, then they are written within a short span of time, and to address the same crisis. Furthermore, the issues of recommendation (3:1, 10:12) and boasting (5:12, 11:18) appear as characteristics of the opponents in both letters (see Furnish, *II Corinthians*, 51; Susan R. Garrett, "The God of This World and the Affliction of Paul: 2 Cor 4:1-12," in *Greeks, Romans, and Christians: Essays in Honor of Abraham J. Malherbe*, ed. D. L. Balch, E. Ferguson, and W. A. Meeks (Minneapolis: Fortress, 1990), 99-117, here 102). To gain a picture of the opponents, it will be sufficient to draw from 2 Cor 10-13, supplemented and supported by remarks in 2 Cor 1-9.

From Paul's remarks in 2 Corinthians 10-13, the following characteristics of the opponents are clear:

—There is a group of opponents in Corinth (10:1, 12; 11:12-13, 15, 18-19, 22-23a), but there is no way to determine how large that group might be.

—There is an unnamed individual who appears to be a "ringleader" (10:10, 11) who claims to belong to Christ in some special way (10:7). It isn't clear whether this is one of the intruders, or one of the members of the Corinthian church who has supported them (perhaps the one who insulted Paul during the "painful visit" and whom the Corinthian church eventually punishes [2 Cor 2:6-8]).

—They have come into Corinth from the outside (11:3-4); in Paul's view, they are intruders (10:13-16).

—They present themselves as apostles of Christ, with at least a right to be in Corinth equal to Paul's. To Paul, this is clearly a misrepresentation and deception (11:12-15).

—They are skilled in rhetoric, and (perhaps at their own urging) have been compared with Paul in that regard by the Corinthians; in that comparison, Paul has been found lacking (10:9-10, 11:6).

—They engage in boasting (11:16-18) and comparison (10:12), which Paul labels as "foolishness."

—They demand monetary support from the Corinthians (11:7-11, 20). Paul questions their motives, calling them "peddlers of the word" (2:17) who bring a different Jesus, a different spirit, and a different gospel (11:4).

—They boast in their Jewish heritage (11:22). They are certainly not Judaizers in the way that Paul's opponents in Galatians were.[129] However, the relationship between these Jewish Christians and the church in Jerusalem remains unclear. If (as this study will show) there is no reason to suppose that the "super apostles" of 11:5, 12:11 refers to the apostles in Jerusalem, there is little evidence linking these intruders with the church leadership there. They come with letters of recommendation (3:1), and it has been argued that Jerusalem is the only logical source for such letters that would impress the Corinthians.[130] Yet Jerusalem is hardly the only possibility; Antioch is

---

[129]Not all Jewish missionaries required obedience to requirements such as circumcision; see Josephus *Ant.* 20.34-48.

[130]Bruce, *I & II Corinthians*, 173.

another center from which missionaries might go out with letters of recommendation.[131] Munck has suggested that it is unlikely that they are from Jerusalem, since then Paul would not call them "ministers of Satan" (11:14-15) while raising a collection to send to Jerusalem;[132] Munck is probably correct. Paul's remarks about missionary boundaries in 10:13-16 have been taken by some to be a reference to Paul's understanding of the agreement made with the Jerusalem leadership reported in Galatians 2,[133] but there is no clear evidence for this. As our exposition in the following chapter will show, Paul's reason for claiming that the opponents have overstepped their bounds is not based on an agreement with the leadership in Jerusalem, but on the fact that God brought Paul to Corinth first.

From wherever these opponents have come, it seems clear that they are Jewish Christian missionaries who have adopted the style, values and criteria current in hellenistic philosophical and religious propaganda,[134] and they have won over a sizable portion of the Corinthian congregation (10:6, 2:5, 7:8-12). They have impressed the Corinthians with their spiritual experiences and their eloquence, with their bold comparisons and boasting:

> Their standard, so to speak, was one of Greek respectability, comprising the norms of a cultured society. The rivals present themselves as the ideal products of education, beauty and action.[135]

---

[131]If, as seems likely, Paul lost the argument reported in Galatians 2, then Antioch may well have sent out people to "correct" Paul's gentile churches. See Theissen, *Social Setting*, 50; Ralph P. Martin, "The Setting of 2 Corinthians," *TynB* 37 (1986): 13; Witherington, *Conflict & Community*, 346.

[132]Johannes Munck, *Paul and the Salvation of Mankind*, trans. Frank Clarke (Richmond: John Knox, 1959), 178.

[133]Bruce, *I & II Corinthians*, 174; Ralph P. Martin, "The Opponents of Paul in 2 Corinthians: An Old Issue Revisited," in *Tradition and Interpretation in the New Testament* (Grand Rapids: Eerdmans, 1987), 279.

[134]Barrett, *Second Epistle*, 30; Furnish, *II Corinthians*, 53; Lincoln, "Paul the Visionary," 204 n. 3; Helmut Koester, *Introduction to the New Testament Volume Two: History and Literature of Early Christianity* (Philadelphia: Fortress, 1982), 127.

[135]Marshall, *Enmity*, 369.

It is not clear whether these opponents had appeared in Corinth before Paul made his "painful visit,"[136] but their success there was aided by other factors. It seems that Paul had failed to follow through with the kind of severe discipline that he promised in 1 Cor 4:18-21 (cf. 2 Cor 10:6; 13:2, 10).[137] Furthermore, and perhaps sparked by this, one member of the Corinthian church challenged Paul's authority (2 Cor 2:5-11, 7:11-12). Whether the comparisons between Paul and the intruders were a part of that challenge or simply were given an opportunity by it, they are both part of the situation which Paul must address in 2 Cor 10-13.

The issue in these chapters revolves around the "character and criteria of apostolic praxis"[138] and authority. The intruders (and their Corinthian supporters) assumed the standards and criteria that functioned in the rest of society; by those standards, the opponents' actions were impressive, even praiseworthy.[139] There is no doctrinal issue that becomes the focus of attention in Paul's argument.

Yet that does not mean that this is not a theological argument. Paul examines his rivals' practices and criteria in the light of the gospel, and concludes that they are contrary to the message of salvation through a crucified Christ. Christology is at the heart of this confrontation. Both sides would agree that the messenger should reflect the message. Yet where the intruders revel in accomplishments according to the standards of eloquence and power, Paul reveals God's power in weakness (2 Cor 12:9-10).

> Above all, the contrast is seen in the way the rival preachers overlooked, and Paul expounded, the truth that the "true apostle" not only is a proclaimer of the passion story; he also lives it out.[140]

Paul's task in this letter, then, is to dislodge the socially determined and supported criteria of his rivals in Corinth without joining in their attitude of boasting and self-commendation, and to give the Corinthians a view of apostolic ministry more consistent with the preaching of the cross.

---

[136]See Furnish, *II Corinthians*, 52.
[137]See Talbert, *Reading Corinthians*, xxii.
[138]Witherington, *Conflict & Community*, 348; see also Munck, *Salvation*, 176.
[139]See Munck, *Salvation*, 187.
[140]Martin, *2 Corinthians*, 341.

CHAPTER THREE

RHETORICAL ANALYSIS: INVENTION, ARRANGEMENT, AND STYLE OF 2 CORINTHIANS 10-13

We have laid the methodological groundwork for the application of rhetorical analysis to Paul's letters (chapter 1). We have also discussed 2 Corinthians 10-13 as a rhetorical unit, and have explored the rhetorical situation which this letter is intended to address (chapter 2). In this chapter, we will analyze the rhetorical structure of 2 Corinthians 10-13 with special attention to the guidelines of the hellenistic rhetorical handbooks.[1]

EXORDIUM: 10:1-6[2]

The *exordium* is designed to gain the attention of the hearers, and is especially important if one's opponent has already gained a favorable hearing. Paul begins with a remarkably bold self-reference: αὐτὸς δὲ ἐγὼ Παῦλος παρακαλῶ. This is the most emphatic self-reference in the Pauline corpus;[3] Paul calls attention to himself and draws on whatever

---

[1] Some scholars have included chaps. 10-13 in a rhetorical analysis of 2 Corinthians as a whole (Young and Ford, *Meaning and Truth*; Witherington, *Conflict & Community*). Others have examined a particular aspect of 2 Corinthians 10-13 from the perspective of hellenistic rhetoric (Judge, "Paul's Boasting;" H. D. Betz, *Paul's Apology: II Cor. 10-13 and the Socratic Tradition* [Berkeley: Center for Hermeneutical Studies, 1975]; Christopher Forbes, "Comparison;" J. Paul Sampley, "Paul, His Opponents"). The only rhetorical analysis of 2 Corinthians 10-13 as a separate work of which I am aware is the outline in Charles B. Puskas, Jr., *The Letters of Paul* (Collegeville, Minn.: Liturgical Press, 1993), 67-68. Puskas, however, offers no defense of his outline, and the outline offered in this study will disagree with Puskas at significant points.

[2] The discussions of the *exordium* in the ancient handbooks are found in Aristotle *Rhetoric* 3.14.1-12, *Ad Her.* 1.4.6-7.11, Cicero *De Inv.* 1.15.20-17.25, Quintilian 4.1.1-79.

[3] Similar constructions, without the emphatic αὐτὸς, occur in three places. In Gal 5:2 Paul uses an emphatic self-reference to bring the weight of his authority to a solemn declaration and warning to those churches that were in danger of

authority he still carries in Corinth. The emphatic self-reference in our passage, then, is intended to introduce the weight of Paul's apostolic authority, remind the Corinthians just who is addressing them, and, Paul hopes, get them to listen.

Paul needs to draw attention to himself and his apostolic authority here in the *exordium*, but he also needs to avoid being seen as arrogant at this early stage. The handbooks suggest gaining a favorable hearing "by praising our services without arrogance and revealing also our past conduct . . . ; likewise by setting forth our disabilities, need, loneliness, and misfortune, and pleading for our hearers' aid . . . ."[4] Paul will discuss his past service to this community as well as his disabilities later in this letter. Here at the opening, Paul guards against appearing arrogant by softening his opening through his choice of verbs. The use of παρακαλῶ may signal a more tactful approach to the Corinthians,[5] especially when linked with δέομαι in v. 2.

Paul further guards against the charge of arrogance by referring to the basis of his appeal as being grounded outside of himself: διὰ τῆς πραΰτητος καὶ ἐπιεικείας τοῦ Χριστοῦ. Why should Paul choose these particular attributes of Christ as the basis of his appeal? Some have claimed that here Paul is drawing on his knowledge of the earthly Jesus.[6]

---

abandoning Paul and his gospel, a concern not unlike Paul's concern in 2 Cor 10-13. In 1 Thess 2:18 the same kind of construction is used, not so much to bring the weight of Paul's authority to bear against a resistent or rebellious congregation, but to reassure them of his love and his desire (and attempts) to visit them again (these too are themes that we meet in 2 Corinthians 10-13, but not in this context). Finally, we find an emphatic self-reference by Paul in Phlm 19, again intended to add the authority of Paul himself to the pledge that is being made. One should also note the use of emphatic self-reference in Eph 3:1 and Col 1:23. In these passages, Paul (or, more likely, the deutero-Pauline author) is emphasizing Paul's role as apostle and servant. Cf. also Paul's use of αὐτὸς ἐγὼ in 2 Cor 12:13; Rom 9:3, 15:14.

[4] *Ad Her.* 1.5.8. See also Cicero *De Inv.* 1.16.22.

[5] See Martin, *2 Corinthians*, 302; Martin also refers to C. J. Bjerkelund, *Parakalo. Form, Funktion und Sinn der Parakalo-Sätze in der paulinischen Briefen* (Oslo: Universitetsforlaget, 1967), 188. It is significant, then, that the only Pauline letter in which παρακαλῶ does not appear is Galatians, where such tact was not what was called for.

[6] Bruce, *I & II Corinthians*, 229; G. W. Kümmel, Supplemental Notes (pp. 165-214) to H. Lietzmann's *An die Korinther I, II*, Handbuch zum Neuen Testament 9 (Tübingen: Mohr, 1969), 208; A. Plummer, *A Critical and Exegetical*

Such a position, however, is difficult to maintain. These two attributes are not found together in the gospel traditions concerning Jesus.[7] Matthew 11:29 does report Jesus describing himself as πραΰς,[8] but this is hardly sufficient evidence to conclude that here Paul is referring to any sort of traditional material about the earthly ministry of Jesus. The most we can say is that such a description by Paul is certainly in harmony with the traditions about Jesus; otherwise, such a characterization of Jesus would have been nonsense to Paul's hearers.[9]

Both πραΰτης and ἐπιείκεια are common in the wider hellenistic literature as descriptions of virtue. Aristotle defines the virtue of πραΰτης as a slowness to anger.[10] In Jewish literature, such graciousness is often assigned to good rulers,[11] Moses,[12] God,[13] and those who obey God.[14] Likewise, ἐπιείκεια is used to describe the gentleness of rulers,[15]

Commentary on the Second Epistle of St. Paul to the Corinthians, ICC (Edinburgh: T & T Clark, 1915), 273; H. Windisch, *Der zweite Korintherbrief* (Göttingen: Vandenhoeck & Ruprecht, 1924), 292; Witherington, *Conflict & Community*, 437.

[7] ἐπιείκεια is not used at all elsewhere in the New Testament to describe Jesus. Most commonly, these words are used to characterize the life Christians are called to live (πραΰς and related words in Gal 5:23, 6:1; Eph 4:2; Col 3:12; 2 Tim 2:25; Tit 3:2; James 1:21, 3:13; 1 Pet 3:4, 16. Cf. also 1 Clem. 13:4, Barn. 19:4, Did. 15:1, IEph. 10:2. ἐπιείκεια and related words are found in Phil 4:5, 1 Tim 3:3, Tit 3:2 [note that here, both terms appear in the same list], James 3:17. Cf. also IPhil. 1:1-2).

[8] It is interesting to note that here Jesus also uses the word ταπεινός to describe himself, a word which Paul will also use later in v. 1. See also the quotation of Zech 9:9 concerning the coming king in Matt 21:5.

[9] Barrett, *Second Epistle*, 246.

[10] Aristotle *Nich. Eth.* 4.5.1-12.

[11] Cf. Josephus *Ant.* 14.46, 19.330; also LXX Ps 44:5, Zech 9:9.

[12] Num 12:3, Sir 45:4; Philo *Vit. Mos.* 1.26, 2.279.

[13] Philo *Det. Pot. Ins.* 146.

[14] Zeph 2:3, 3:12; Sir 1:27.

[15] LXX Esth 3:13, 8:12; 2 Macc 9:27; 3 Macc 3:15, 7:6; Josephus *Ant.* 10.83; 15.14, 182; Philo *Som.* 2.295 (note also the similar use in Acts 24:4, 1 Pet 2:18).

78 Eloquence and the Proclamation of the Gospel in Corinth

Moses,[16] God,[17] and of the godly.[18] Danker notes that these two terms are also used to describe benefactors.[19]
These two words appear together frequently in hellenistic literature,[20] and should be seen as a hendiadys,[21] together meaning something like a "gentle, humble and modest attitude."[22] Rather than referring to his own virtues and services at this point, a theme that Paul will postpone until the *narratio*, Paul refers to the virtues and services of Christ, which he as Christ's apostle implicitly shares, and which he expects the Corinthians to recognize and value. The πραΰτης καὶ ἐπιείκεια τοῦ Χριστοῦ is not, however, a reflection of Jesus' earthly ministry nor a reflection of his "divine and royal majesty."[23] Leivestad[24] has argued persuasively that in this hendiadys, the less frequent term ἐπιείκεια is clarified by the more common πραΰτης; while in the wider literature πραΰτης does describe the gracious actions of royalty, in the New Testament the word is used to describe a more humble attitude, even submitting to abuse. Thus it is likely that here Paul has in mind Jesus' condescension in the incarnation,[25] in which he became vulnerable to the unrighteous abuse of others, a situation in which Paul also shares.[26]

---

[16]Josephus *Apion* 2.209; Philo *Virt.* 81, 125, 140, 148.
[17]LXX 1 Sam 12:22, Ps 85:5, Wis 12:18, Bar 2:27, Dan 3:42, 4:27; 2 Macc 2:22, 10:4; 2 Esd 9:8; Philo *Spec. Leg.* 1.97. Cf. also IPhil. 1:2.
[18]LXX Wis 2:19 (here of the forbearance of the righteous who suffer at the hands of the ungodly, a theme close to the traditions of Jesus' own suffering, and perhaps in Paul's mind close to his own situation at Corinth).
[19]Danker, *II Corinthians*, 149.
[20]Plutarch *Pericl.* 39.1, *Sert.* 25.4; Lucian *The Dream or Lucian's Career*, 10; Philo *Op. Mund.* 103; cf. also in other early Christian literature Diog. 7:4, 1 Clem. 30:8.
[21]Furnish, *II Corinthians*, 455.
[22]Ragnar Leivestad, "The Meekness and Gentleness of Christ," *NTS* 12 (1966): 159-60.
[23]Herbert Preisker, "ἐπιείκεια," *Theological Dictionary of the New Testament* Vol. 2 (Grand Rapids: Eerdmans, 1964), 589. Cf. Heinz Giesen, "ἐπιείκεια," *Exegetical Dictionary of the New Testament* Vol. 2 (Grand Rapids: Eerdmans, 1991), 26.
[24]Leivestad, "Meekness and Gentleness," 158-60.
[25]Cf. Erhardt Güttgemanns, *Der leidende Apostel und sein Herr* (Göttingen: Vandenhoeck & Ruprecht, 1966), 140; Furnish, *II Corinthians*, 460; Bultmann, *Second Letter*, 182.
[26]Cf. 2 Cor 4:10.

This interpretation is confirmed by Paul's continuation of v. 1, which mentions ταπεινός. While there are a few hellenistic writings in which this word is used in a positive way, meaning "modest" or "obedient,"[27] the overwhelming use of this word in the larger hellenistic world is negative, denoting shameful servility.[28] In Jewish literature ταπεινός has a more positive role as well. To be humbled by force can still be understood as oppression[29] and personal violation,[30] and the term is used to express the smallness and insignificance of something or someone.[31] But this is balanced by a realization that to humble oneself is to properly place oneself in subjection to God's will and judgment,[32] that God in fact humbles the people for the sake of producing repentance and correction,[33] and that God and God's Messiah will save and establish the humbled.[34] While the rest of the Greek world saw in ταπεινός primarily a shameful "lack of freedom and subjection," Israel saw as well one's need to "listen to God and obey him."[35]

It is this term that Paul uses in Philippians 2:8 to describe the humiliation of Christ's incarnation, culminating in his obedient death on the cross.[36] Paul will have more to say to the Corinthians about his own humiliation as an apostle of this same crucified Christ (11:7, 12:21),[37] and

---

[27]Plato *Leg.* 4.716a; Xenophon *Ag.* 11.11, *Resp. Lac.* 8.2; Isoc. *Or.* 3.56; Plutarch *Dion* 33.4.

[28]Demosthenes *Or.* 4.23, 9.21, 57.45; Isocrates *Or.* 3.42, 4.68, 8.116; Plato *Leg.* 6.774c; cf. Walter Grundmann, "ταπεινός," *TNDT* 8:1-5.

[29]Gen 15:13, Ex 1:12.

[30]Deut 21:14, Ezek 22:10.

[31]Sir 29:8, 1 Sam 18:23; cf. also Philo *Leg. All.* 3.19, *Det. Pot. Ins.* 16; Josephus *Bell.* 4.319, 6.395; *Ant.* 5.115, 7.95.

[32]2 Chr 33:12; cf. also Philo *Rer. Div. Her.* 29; Josephus *Ant.* 10.11. See also the conclusion to the parable of the pharisee and the tax collector in Lk 18:14.

[33]Is 1:25, 64:11; LXX Ps 89:15, 146:6.

[34]LXX Ps 17:28; Is 11:4, 53:8.

[35]Grundmann, "ταπεινός," 11.

[36]It should be noted that both πραΰς and ταπεινός are used in the LXX to translate עָנָו (note here how 1 *Clem.* 13:4, quoting Is 66:2, reads πραΰν while the LXX uses ταπεινὸν; cf. also Bultmann, *Second Epistle*, 182). Thus Jesus' statement in Matt 11:29 (drawing on Is 26:6) joins together πραΰς and ταπεινός, while Eph 4:2 and Col 3:12 join together πραΰτης and ταπεινοφροσύνη as characteristics of those who follow Jesus; 1 *Clem.* 30:8 joins all three terms, ἐπιείκεια καὶ ταπεινοφροσύνη καὶ πραΰτης.

[37]Furnish, *II Corinthians*, 460.

10:1 sets the stage for those discussions. However, the word is introduced here no doubt as an echo of charges being made against Paul in Corinth: that when he is present with them, he is ταπεινός.[38] That this was a charge leveled against Paul is confirmed by the criticisms of his speech and action when present (10:10). Thus while Paul's introduction of the terms πραΰτης and ἐπιείκεια in v. 1 may speak of benefits rendered (by Christ), ταπεινός belongs more in the category of discussing one's failings and shortcomings, as the handbooks suggested doing to avoid the appearance of arrogance.

Yet Paul's approach is not quite so simple, because it is not clear that in his view ταπεινός in an apostle is in fact a shortcoming. It may be that "meekness and gentleness may unfortunately be misunderstood" as servility rather than patience.[39] Paul does not share the Corinthian view that ταπεινός is a negative characteristic in an apostle. The word carries a pejorative sense for those in Corinth, but Paul wants to hold out to them "in a double entendre his own self-estimate based on the model of the incarnate Lord."[40] It is not so much that Paul is being ironic here;[41] rather, he responds "by paradoxically making a virtue out of his lowliness, for precisely in his lowliness and weakness (v. 10) does God's power become manifest (12:9, 11:30)."[42]

Paul subtly begins to move the Corinthians to see his point by the way the clause containing ταπεινός is introduced. The relative pronoun ὅς may have two possible antecedents in this sentence. It may refer to αὐτὸς δὲ ἐγὼ Παῦλος, as in fact becomes clear by the end of the verse. But grammatically it may also refer to τοῦ Χριστοῦ, which is in closer proximity to the relative clause itself. As this is being heard by the

---

[38]Barrett, *Second Epistle*, 247; Ernest Best, *Second Corinthians*, Interpretation Commentary (Louisville: John Knox, 1987), 92; Bruce, *I & II Corinthians*, 299; Danker, *II Corinthians*, 150; Furnish, *II Corinthians*, 460; Talbert, *Reading Corinthians*, 111; Witherington, *Conflict & Community*, 437. Bultmann, *Second Letter*, 183 says that to the Corinthians, ταπεινός means Paul is "servile" and "cowardly."

[39]Barrett, *Second Epistle*, 247.

[40]Martin, *2 Corinthians*, 303.

[41]Contra Bultmann, *Second Letter*, 183.

[42]Heinz Giesen, "ταπεινός," *Exegetical Dictionary of the New Testament* Vol. 3 (Grand Rapids: Eerdmans, 1991), 333.

Corinthian congregation, it will not be immediately clear to them which one Paul is describing as ταπεινός: himself, or Christ.[43]

There appears to be a purposeful ambiguity here; though by the end of the verse the antecedent of ὅς is clearly Παῦλος, both possibilities are true. Because Christ is one who came as ταπεινός, so too does his apostle. For Paul, the message he proclaims and his style of proclamation are bound together. To reject him because he is ταπεινός and ἀσθενής (v. 10) is also to turn away from the kerygma given to him by God.[44] By reminding them of Jesus' own meekness and gentleness, and by recalling, even if only briefly and indirectly, Jesus' own character as one who was ταπεινός, Paul shows them that they are making a mistake if they find fault with him because he is ταπεινός.[45] Thus Paul is already preparing his hearers for the central issue of the *probatio.*

The second aspect of Paul's *exordium* that we need to discuss is the tone and impact of the imagery used in vv. 2-6. Most of the attention these verses have received has focused on the background of the imagery used. Malherbe's influential analysis is that Paul is describing his opponents in the terms of Stoicism, with the soul as a kind of fortification, while he describes himself with ironic self-deprecation in Cynic terms as one who wages war by his manner of life.[46] However, other backgrounds for this imagery have been proposed. McCant has suggested that the wisdom tradition of Israel may in fact be the source of Paul's imagery, and points to Prov 21:22, where the "wise one" (σοφός) goes against the strongholds (ὀχύρωμα - cf. 2 Cor 10:4) of the ungodly.[47] In a similar

---

[43]There are other places where Christological statements are introduced with relative clauses in constructions very similar to this one, most notably in Phil 2:6. See also Col 1:15, 1 Tim 3:16. On the present construction as having the form of a Christological confession, see Güttgemanns, *Der leidende Apostel*, 135-41; Martin, *2 Corinthians*, 303; Barrett, *Second Epistle*, 247-48. See also 2 Cor 13:3.

[44]Martin, *2 Corinthians*, 299.

[45]Bultmann, *Second Letter*, 183. See also Leivestad, "Meekness and Gentleness," 164.

[46]Abraham Malherbe, "Antisthenes and Odysseus, and Paul at War," *HTR* 76 (1983): 143-73. For similar language used by Philo in an anti-Sophistic argument, see *De Conf. Ling.* 129. That Paul is here taking the stance of a philosopher, see Windisch, *Der zweite Korintherbrief*, 298; Betz, *Der Apostel*, 68-69; Furnish, *II Corinthians*, 462.

[47]Jerry W. McCant, "Paul's Thorn of Rejected Apostleship," *NTS* 34 (1988): 562. See also Bruce, *I & II Corinthians*, 230, who sees connections both to Prov 21 and to Philo's *De Conf. Ling.* 129: "For any strong building which is erected

way, Witherington suggests that the language here is drawn from the sage of Eccl 9:14-16, as Paul portrays himself as "the poor sage who must deliver his besieged converts from the lofty walls the opponents have built against them, and yet his wisdom is being despised."[48] Witherington's argument, however, is even more difficult to sustain than McCant's since Eccl 9 shares no important vocabulary with 2 Cor 10:2-6, and only loosely shares the imagery of a city under siege. Bultmann[49] points out that the imagery of capture to signify obedience can be found in other parts of the Jewish tradition:

> To restore the souls of those who wish to come to him, and to lead a goodly band of captives back to freedom. I became strong and powerful and led the world captive, and it became to me the glory of the Most High, even of God my Father. (Odes of Solomon 10:3-4)

> And he gave me the rod of his strength, that I might subdue the thoughts of peoples, and lay low the power of mighty men; to make war by his word, and to gain the victory by his might. (Odes of Solomon 29:8-9)[50]

Finally, Martin[51] suggests that the imagery here may derive from the traditions of the Maccabees rather than from any philosophical tradition; Martin points particularly to passages such as 1 Macc 5:65 and 8:10, which also use the word ὀχύρωμα found in v. 4, the latter reference also including αἰχμαλωτίζειν (cf. v. 5). However, rather than looking for one specific tradition from which Paul is drawing here, the best course seems to be the one taken by Danker, who says that such imagery was widespread, and would have been familiar to the Corinthians both from the Jewish scriptural and from the Greco-Roman philosophical traditions.[52]

More important for our purposes than the background of such imagery are the tone and the function of these military themes. Quintilian

---

by means of plausible arguments is not built for the sake of any other object except that of averting and alienating the mind from the honour due to God, than which object what can be more iniquitous?"

[48]Witherington, *Conflict & Community*, 438.

[49]Bultmann, *Second Letter*, 185-86.

[50]Translation from the Odes of Solomon by J. A. Emerton in *The Apocryphal Old Testament*, ed. H. F. D. Sparks (Oxford: Clarendon, 1984), 681-731.

[51]Martin, *2 Corinthians*, 305.

[52]Danker, *II Corinthians*, 151-53. See also Malherbe, "Antisthenes," 143-47.

says that one strategy in the *exordium*, particularly if one thinks the opposition has already swayed the hearers, is to use a hint of threat should the hearers not judge fairly and correctly.[53] Paul's emphatic self-reference in v. 1 may already carry a veiled threat.[54] In the following verses Paul portrays himself as a military commander,[55] one who is ready and able to wage war against all who stand against God and the gospel, and whose weapons, though they may appear weak to the Corinthians, are in fact mighty "in God's cause" (δυνατὰ τῷ θεῷ, v. 4).[56]

There is a significant amount of emotional force in this section. Along with logical argumentation (λόγος), ancient rhetoric recognized the persuasive power of producing an emotional response from the hearers. Quintilian says that there are two basic kinds of emotions upon which a speaker can draw.[57] The milder form is ἦθος, and deals primarily with presenting oneself as a person of moral character and credibility, eliciting affection and appreciation in the hearers. The stronger emotions of anger, dislike, fear, hatred, and pity are termed πάθος. In this section, Paul draws on both. His self-portrayal as a military commander is part of the *ethos* he wishes to present to the Corinthians; to the extent that this serves as a threat which instills fear, Paul draws on *pathos*.

The element of threat from Paul is continued in v. 6, where Paul says directly that he is ready (ἐν ἑτοίμῳ ἔχοντες) to punish. Furnish notes that this phrase also continues the imagery of warfare and conquest.[58] If necessary, Paul will come as God's conquering general. The strong *ethos* which Paul establishes in vv. 1-6 is decisive for all of chapter 10, setting the tone for the opening sections of Paul's argument and establishing what

---

[53]Quintilian 4.1.21.

[54]See Bultmann, *Second Letter*, 182; Martin, *2 Corinthians*, 300.

[55]Windisch suggests a military commander in a messianic war. See *Der zweite Korintherbrief*, 298.

[56]With Furnish, *II Corinthians*, 457, it seems preferable to read this dative as a dative of advantage rather than as a semitic intensive ("divinely powerful"). The threat from Paul comes precisely because he is one engaged in battle for God's cause; so also Bultmann, *Second Letter*, 185.

[57]Quintilian 6.2.8-24.

[58]Furnish, *II Corinthians*, 459. Furnish notes such texts as Polybius *Histories* II 34.2 ("When they had these troops they kept them in readiness [εἶχον ἐν ἑτοίμῳ] and awaited the attack of the enemy") and Philo *Legat. ad Gaium* 259; cf. also 1 Macc 7:29, 12:50.

84 *Eloquence and the Proclamation of the Gospel in Corinth*

Paul sees as a proper relationship between himself and this congregation; they will not have authority over him.

Along with a stress on his own person and an element of threat against the hearers should they not respond with obedience to his words, Paul follows the advice of the rhetorical handbooks in this *exordium* in one more respect. Quintilian advises that the most attractive strategy in the *exordium* is to draw from what the opponent has already said against you.[59] Cicero shares this same view:

> On the other hand, if the speeches of your opponents seem to have won conviction among the audience . . . it behoves you to promise to discuss first the argument which the opponents thought was their strongest and which the audience have especially approved.[60]

We have already noted how Paul begins in v. 1 with what was undoubtedly a charge laid against him at Corinth.

> Vv. 1, 2 are only really intelligible if they cite the actual estimate of Paul in the eyes of his opponents; and we may appeal to v. 10 for confirmation of the view that Paul is quoting their words as "catch phrases" or "slogans" . . . .[61]

The charge, however, appears to be not simply that Paul was ταπεινός, but that he exhibited inconsistency: that he was ταπεινός when it suited him, and that he was bold (θαρρεῖν, v. 1b) when that suited him.[62] It is this perception that led to some thinking (λογίζεσθαι) that Paul lives κατὰ σάρκα (v. 2).[63] The fact that he can write bold letters when absent only makes the situation worse: as was mentioned in

---

[60]Cicero *De Inv.* 1.17.25.

[61]Martin, *2 Corinthians*, 300. Martin also points to remarks by Bultmann, *Second Letter*, 184-185.

[62]See Kennedy, *New Testament Interpretation*, 94.

[63]Malherbe ("Antisthenes," 167-68) points out that a perception of inconsistency regarding Paul's travel plans provokes a similar charge of living κατὰ σάρκα in 2 Cor 1:17.

the previous chapter, hellenistic writers strongly criticized those who pretended to be ταπεινός for the sake of flattery.[64]

Cicero says that in the *exordium* goodwill can be obtained by weakening the effect of the charges made against you by the opponent.[65] We have already seen how Paul leads the Corinthians to re-examine their estimate of him as ταπεινός in their presence in light of the πραΰτης καὶ ἐπιείκεια τοῦ Χριστοῦ, and of Christ's own identity as one who is ταπεινός. In vv. 2-5, Paul picks up the language of the charge laid against him and turns it to his own defense: He does not live κατὰ σάρκα, but it is ἐν σαρκί that he wages his battle; just as some consider (λογίζεσθαι) Paul to live κατὰ σάρκα, Paul for his part is considering (λογίζεσθαι) demonstrating his true confidence when he comes (v. 2).

Verse 6 further weakens the effect of the charges against Paul as he anticipates the punishment that he will administer. This element brings, of course, the aspect of threat that we discussed above. Yet Paul does more than simply threaten in this verse. First of all, he connects his own boldness shown in punishment with the obedience of the Corinthians. If he appears to be slow in coming with a stick of correction (see 1 Cor 4:21, 2 Cor 13:2), it is not because of a failing on his part, but because of the failure of obedience among the Corinthians themselves. Paul has postponed action in the hope that the Corinthians will change their ways, and so avoid Paul's punishment. Thus the Corinthians are already being put on the spot; Paul will further turn the tables on them in chapter 13, so that it will be they and not he who are being examined and judged.

The language of v. 6 about "your obedience" also serves to divide Paul's opposition. Paul's rhetoric implies that it is not the Corinthians themselves who are the opponents, but rather that it is the satanic interlopers whom Paul will punish. The threat to the Corinthians remains, of course, should they fail to act in obedience to Paul. Yet Paul's rhetoric here holds out hope that the Corinthians are still his and will renew their allegiance, and that together they will stand against this threat that has

---

[64]Grundmann, "ταπεινός," 3; Furnish, *II Corinthians*, 456; Forbes, "Comparison," 10-12. Cf. Quintilian 11.1.21-22: "And yet I am not sure that open boasting is not more tolerable, owing to its sheer straightforwardness, than that perverted form of self-praise, which makes the millionaire say that he is not a poor man, the man of mark describe himself as obscure, the powerful pose as weak, and the eloquent as unskilled and even inarticulate. But the most ostentatious kind of boasting takes the form of actual self-derision."

[65]Cicero *De Inv.* 1.16.22.

entered the community from the outside. The anticipated obedience of the Corinthians is distinguished from the hopeless and doomed disobedience of the intruders.[66]

Finally, before we leave the *exordium*, and with the further charge of Paul's poor rhetorical performance looming in v. 10, we should note that v. 6, which closes the *exordium*, is a carefully crafted piece, especially effective when we remember that it was intended to be heard and not simply seen. Martin[67] discusses the artistic use of assonance (καθαιροῦντες and καθαίρεσιν in v. 4 and ἐπαιρόμενον in v. 5; ὑπακοή in vv. 5, 6 and παρακοή in v. 6); he also notes the alliterative use of words beginning with π in vv. 5, 6. But he fails to note that Paul carries this alliteration farther and to greater effect.[68] Verse 6 begins with four words which begin with ε (ἐν ἑτοίμῳ ἔχοντες ἐκδικῆσαι); these are then followed by three words beginning with π (πᾶσαν παρακοήν ὅταν πληρωθῇ), and then two words which begin with ὐ (ὑμῶν ἡ ὑπακοή).[69] If the Corinthians are doubting Paul's power, then he will display it not only when he arrives, but also in what he says now, and even in the way in which he says it.

---

[66]Furnish, *II Corinthians*, 464; Martin, *2 Corinthians*, 306-7; Barrett, "Paul's Opponents," 239; idem, *Second Epistle*, 253-54. It is not clear just how Paul intends to punish these intruders after the obedience of the Corinthians is completed, since presumably the intruders will have been evicted from Corinth by that time; however, such a reading is certainly preferred to the suggestion that Paul intends to punish the Corinthians' past disobedience at that point. The distinction in v. 6 between Corinthians and the intruders is also to be preferred to understanding this as Paul's threat to punish those among the Corinthians who, when the rest of the community begins to return to obedience, remain loyal to the intruders. See Danker, *II Corinthians*, 153; Witherington, *Conflict & Community*, 439.

[67]Martin, *2 Corinthians*, 301.

[68]Cf. Aristotle *Rhetoric* 3.9.9; *Ad Her.* 4.12.18.

[69]The alliteration in the final phrase is heightened by the fact that the intervening word ἡ shares with the surrounding words the rough breathing.

PROPOSITIO: 10:7-11[70]

The function of the *propositio* is to make clear what the speaker wants to be understood as the main point or points under dispute. This may be either a simple, direct statement, or a listing of those points to be covered in the oration:

> In an argument a partition correctly made renders the whole speech clear and perspicuous. It takes two forms, both of which greatly contribute to clarifying the case and determining the nature of the controversy. One form shows in what we agree with our opponents and what is left in dispute; as a result of this some definite problem is set for the auditor on which he ought to have his attention fixed. In the second form the matters which we intend to discuss are briefly set forth in a methodical way. This leads the auditor to hold definite points in his mind, and to understand that when these have been discussed the oration will be over.[71]

We will find that in this section, Paul not only clarifies what is at issue, but also looks ahead to the order in which he will take up the major topics.

The *propositio* was closely related to another section of the oration, the *narratio*. In fact, Quintilian discusses whether at times a clear statement of *narratio* might make a separate *propositio* unnecessary.[72] But that by no means implies that the *propositio* was seen by Quintilian as superfluous. His expectation is that it will normally be an important part of an oration.[73] Although the ancient handbooks agree in discussing the *propositio* following the *narratio*, the two are closely enough related and there is enough flexibility to allow these two elements to be found in the opposite order. Quintilian himself notes that it is "some" who place the *partitio* after the *narratio*,[74] which is the order that he in general expects. But he also notes that Aristotle introduced a "slight novelty" (*aliquatenus novat*) in this regard by placing the *propositio* before the

---

[70]The main discussions of the *propositio* in the ancient handbooks are found in *Ad Her.* 1.10.17 (under the label *divisio*), Cicero *De Inv.* 1.22.31-23.33 (under the label *partitio*) and Quintilian 4.4.1-5.28.

[71]Cicero *De Inv.* 1.22.31; cf. also *Ad Her.* 1.10.17, Quintilian 4.4.5-7.

[72]Quintilian 4.4.1-2.

[73]Ibid. 4.4.3-4.

[74]Ibid. 4.4.1.

narratio.[75] That this order was not in fact unusual can be seen not only from the way in which Quintilian describes it, but also in speeches such as Plato's *Apology*, in which Socrates' opening is followed by a statement of what needs to be dealt with in this speech, i.e., the *propositio* (18b-19a):

> The proper course for me, gentlemen of the jury, is to deal first with the earliest charges that have been falsely brought against me, and with my earliest accusers, and then with the later ones . . . .

This is then followed by the *narratio*, describing how this prejudice against Socrates had arisen:

> Let us go back to the beginning and consider what the charge is that has made me so unpopular, and has encouraged Meletus to draw up this indictment . . . .[76]

Paul begins his *propositio* with what is probably best read as an imperative: τὰ κατὰ πρόσωπον βλέπετε.[77] Paul will begin his

---

[75]Ibid. 3.9.5; cf. Aristotle *Rhetoric* 3.13.

[76]Trans. by Hugh Tredennick, in *Plato. The Collected Dialogues*, ed. Edith Hamilton and Huntington Cairns (Princeton: Princeton University, 1961), 3-26. A similar structure is apparent in Odysseus' speech in *Iliad* 9: After the opening *exordium* "he states his proposition (228-231): the ships will be destroyed unless Achilles returns to help the Greeks. . . . He then moves on to a third part, a narrative of how the situation developed (232-246)" (Kennedy, *Classical Rhetoric*, 12). Similarly, the *De Corona* of Demosthenes, though more complex in structure, shows the same basic shape: The *exordium* in 1-8; in 9-17 Demosthenes protests against irrelevant charges, replies to charges regarding his private life, and introduces discussion of public policy, all of which is best seen as the *propositio*; then, in 18-52, he presents a *narratio* of the events behind these charges.

[77]βλέπετε is read as an imperative by Barrett, *Second Epistle*, 255; Danker, *II Corinthians*, 153; Furnish, *II Corinthians*, 465; Martin, *2 Corinthians*, 307, as well as by the translators of JB, NEB, NRSV. This interpretation is given support by the fact that Paul regularly uses βλέπετε in contexts best read as imperative elsewhere in his letters (1 Cor 8:9, 10:18, 16:10; Gal 5:15; Phil 3:2; see also Eph 5:15; Col 2:8, 4:17. Cf. Barrett, *Second Epistle*, 256 and Furnish, *II Corinthians*, 465, both of whom note some doubt about βλέπετε in 1 Cor 1:26 and prefer to read it there as an indicative). Βλέπετε in the present verse is read as an indicative by John Chrysostom, *The Homilies of Saint John Chrysostom*

propositio by telling the Corinthians what it is that they must examine. τὰ κατὰ πρόσωπον recalls the language of Paul's *exordium* in v. 1, ὃς κατὰ πρόσωπον, and should be interpreted with that previous phrase in mind. At the very least, Paul is telling the Corinthians that they must look at what is right in front of their faces. Since Paul himself is at the moment absent, they must look at the signs of his presence among them still;[78] they are the field assigned to Paul and to which Paul has reached (vv. 13-16); their existence as a community of faith is in fact a letter of reference for Paul (2 Cor 3:1-3), and they know what he did among them (12:12).

It is possible that the verb βλέπετε contains an even more forceful point. Rather than simply reading it as meaning "observe," it may be better to hear in this verb a word of warning to the Corinthians about the present danger they are in,[79] and to understand this verb in the same way it is used in 1 Cor 8:9, Gal 5:15, Phil 3:2:[80] "watch out," "beware." τὰ κατὰ πρόσωπον then, recalling the language of v. 1, would indicate a face-to-face meeting with Paul. Despite how they perceived Paul's presence with them during the painful visit, Paul's opponents should not think that a personal confrontation with him will help their cause (cf. v. 2, 6; 13:1-4).[81]

On either understanding of τὰ κατὰ πρόσωπον, the imperative βλέπετε has the effect of already beginning to turn the tables on the Corinthians; by telling them what they must look to (or look out for), Paul prepares the way for the end of this letter, when he will place *them* under investigation (13:5). Paul's strategy of turning the tables on his accusers also appears in the way that he again appropriates the language apparently

---

Archbishop of Constantinople, on the Epistles of Paul to the Corinthians, The Nicene and Post-Nicene Fathers, no. 12, 22.1 (New York: Christian Literature Company, 1889); by J. A. T. Robinson, *The Body: A Study in Pauline Theology* (Chicago: Henry Regnery, 1952), 26; by the translators of NIV, TEV, NEB mg, JB mg; and as an interrogative by Kennedy, *Second and Third Epistles*, 184; Bultmann, *Second Letter*, 187; and KJV. However, reading it as an indicative (whether in a statement or in a question) seems to require reading τὰ κατὰ πρόσωπον as equivalent to τὰ κατὰ σάρκα, "what can be seen outwardly" (Bultmann, *Second Letter*, 187), "mere externals." As the following discussion will show, such is not the best interpretation.
[78]See Bruce, *I & II Corinthians*, 230-31; Furnish, *II Corinthians*, 465-66.
[79]Furnish, *II Corinthians*, 475.
[80]See also 1 Cor 3:10, 10:12, 16:10; Eph 5:15; Col 2:8, 4:17.
[81]This suggestion is noted in Bultmann, *Second Letter*, 187 n. 6, attributed to a letter from K. Grobel.

used against him. We have already heard how some "considered" (v. 2, λογίζεσθαι) Paul to be lacking; now in v. 7, Paul again picks up that same word and sends it back to his detractors:[82] they (or perhaps it is rather a single "ringleader" in mind,[83] the τις of v. 7 and τοιοῦτος of v. 11) must consider (λογίζεσθαι) something, and consider it carefully.

He is to consider it ἐφ' ἑαυτοῦ, a phrase which can be described as difficult at best. Barrett translates it as "let him have another look at himself."[84] Yet it is more likely that we should understand this in the sense of "by himself;" John Chrysostom understands Paul to be saying that his opponent should not wait to learn from Paul's rebuke when he returns to Corinth.[85]   Such an understanding fits well with the interpretation of τὰ κατὰ πρόσωπον βλέπετε as a warning not to look forward to or depend on a face-to-face confrontation with Paul. Paul's opponent needs to reconsider while he still has a chance.

What this opponent must consider again deals with Paul being Χριστοῦ. There have been several suggestions regarding what this might mean, and what the opponent is apparently denying Paul.[86] It is unlikely that he is denying simply that Paul is a Christian;[87] it seems that this opponent is claiming to belong to Christ in some special way. Nor does it seem likely that what is at stake is a claim to connection with the

---

[82]See Bultmann, *Second Letter*, 188; Furnish, *II Corinthians*, 466; Martin, *2 Corinthians*, 308.

[83]Barrett, *Second Epistle*, 265; Furnish, *II Corinthians*, 466.

[84]Barrett, *Second Epistle*, 256.

[85]Chrysostom, *Homilies* 22.1. ἐπί + genitive is often used to indicate the basis on which something is undertaken or judged (see 2 Cor 13:1; Xenophon *Anab.* 2.4.10, Demosthenes *De Corona* 224). Paul's opponent, then, is urged to undertake this himself, so that it does not need to be forced upon him at Paul's arrival. We should also note that this construction with ἐπί is at home in the courtroom, indicating the one before whom someone appears and pleads a case (see Mt 28:14, Mk 13:9, Acts 2:5:9-10, 1 Cor 6:1, Did. 11:11; see also Demosthenes *De Corona* 224, "ἐκρίνετο ἐφ' ἑαυτοῦ"). If this opponent is playing judge over Paul, Paul warns him that he needs instead to take such action with regard to himself.

[86]For a brief and helpful review, see Barrett, *Second Epistle*, 256-57.

[87]See 1 Cor 3:23, 15:23; Rom 8:9; Gal 3:29. Käsemann argues that the denial that Paul is a Christian at all is involved here: since it is Paul's status as a true apostle that is being placed under doubt, as a false apostle Paul would also be seen as no Christian at all (E. Käsemann, "Die Legitimatät," 11-12). But this can hardly have been the explicit charge made against Paul here.

historical Jesus;[88] Paul claims that in whatever way this opponent is Χριστοῦ, so is he, a claim that he could not make if the issue were having known the historical Jesus. The thrust of the opponent's claims about being Χριστοῦ appears in the next verse (γάρ, v. 8), as Paul begins to talk about the ἐξουσία that has been given to him (see also 11:5, with the implicit charge that Paul is a lesser apostle than these newcomers). To be Χριστοῦ means to carry the ἐξουσία from the Lord himself,[89] a claim which is being denied to Paul, and which Paul here presents as being at the very core of the trouble at Corinth, and the heart of his reply.

In v. 8 Paul moves on to another,[90] though related, topic. Even if Paul goes on to boast about the authority that the Lord has given to him (which Paul will do at some length, though "as a fool," in his *probatio*), he will not be put to shame. The reason that he will not be put to shame is that Paul's authority will have its effect, one way or the other. Paul stresses that the authority was given to him to build up the community at Corinth, not to tear it down. Yet there should be no mistake; if demolition is necessary, Paul is able to do that as well (note that the καθαίρεσιν of v. 8 has been prepared for by καθαίρεσιν and καθαιροῦντες already in v. 4).[91]

---

[88]Bruce, *I & II Corinthians*, 231; but cf. Bultmann, *Second Letter*, 187.

[89]Barrett, *Second Epistle*, 257-58; Betz, *Der Apostel*, 133-34; Best, *Second Corinthians*, 95; Martin, *2 Corinthians*, 308-9.

[90]Barrett, *Second Epistle*, 258 is surely correct in rejecting the translation of περισσότερόν τι as "somewhat excessively" (cf. NRSV, "a little too much;" TEV, "somewhat too much;" NIV, "somewhat freely;" NEB, "somewhat over-boastful;" JB, "rather too much"), and preferring to translate it as a real comparison: "For if I make a further boast . . . about our authority" (cf. Furnish, *II Corinthians*, 466, "somewhat more than I already have in claiming to be Christ's;" Martin, *2 Corinthians*, 308, "Even if I can boast [about being Christ's] and, more than that, about my [our] authority;" KJV, "For though I should boast somewhat more of our authority"). Barrett gives several examples that show Paul customarily uses such forms with a true comparison in mind. The point here is not that Paul may boast a bit too much, but that he can, without shame, go on to boast as much as they about the authority given to him by the Lord.

[91]Contra Barrett, *Second Epistle*, 258: "He [Paul] has no authority to destroy the work of God" (so also Bruce, *I & II Corinthians*, 231). That is, of course, true as long as the community continues to be God's; however, should the Corinthians place themselves on the side of "strongholds" and "arguments" and "every proud obstacle raised against the knowledge of God" (vv. 4-5, NRSV), then Paul is ready and able to tear such things down, and he will warn the Corinthians that they

On this reading of v. 8, the sense of ἵνα at the beginning of v. 9 is clarified.[92] Paul will not be put to shame, because his authority will be exercised, in discipline if necessary. Paul warns them of this, so that (ἵνα) he will not seem to the Corinthians merely to be trying to frighten them into submission with his letters. Such a conclusion could be drawn, and probably is being drawn by some in Corinth, in light of the charge that is being made against Paul there (φησίν, v. 10).[93] The opposition is willing to admit the power of Paul's letters (when he is at a distance); but Paul's personal presence fails to match up to what his letters promise.[94] It is not simply that Paul is being accused of being a poor speaker or leader, though that is likely part of the complaint. The problem here is the same as Paul already mentioned in v. 1: that Paul seems inconsistent. To that concern, Paul answers with v. 11: They will find out his consistency;

---

themselves are in danger of failing to meet the test (13:5). Cf. Danker, *II Corinthians*, 154: "But if occasion calls for it, he may have to do some destroying." See also Martin, *2 Corinthians*, 310.

[92]Other attempted explanations (see Barrett, *Second Epistle*, 258-59) of how to construe the ἵνα clause are forced: to connect it with v. 8a is awkward because of the intervening οὐκ αἰσχυνθήσομαι in 8b; to take it with v. 11 not only turns it into an awkward anticipatory clause, but also requires reading all of v. 10 as parenthetical (John Chrysostom, *Homilies* 12.380; Martin, *2 Corinthians*, 310-11); to treat it as only loosely connected and equivalent to an imperative (Moule, *Idiom Book*, 145) seems a measure of last resort, as does the suggestion that we have an elipsis here that needs to be filled in (BDF #483; Windisch, *Der zweite Korintherbrief*, 305; Barrett, *Second Epistle*, 259: "I will therefore not bring this authority into play, that I may not . . . ." So too, apparently, the understanding of the Vulgate). Bultmann, *Second Letter*, 189, though he would rather read this as a result clause, is on the right track by maintaining the connection between the ἵνα clause and the preceding οὐκ αἰσχυνθήσομαι; Furnish, *II Corinthians*, 467-68 also correctly maintains the connection between vv. 8 & 9.

[93]Kennedy, *New Testament Interpretation*, 93, "The 'indictment' he is answering can be summed up in the quotation at 10:10." This inconsistency, showing up in other issues such as Paul's collection for Jerusalem (as well as his insistence to support himself through manual labor) versus his refusal to accept pay for himself from the Corinthians, but primarily in the discrepancy between his letters and his rhetoric when in person, is at the center of the complaints against Paul. For the repeating of charges in one's *propositio*, cf. Plato *Apology* 19b.

[94]Witherington, *Conflict & Community*, 434 quotes the 4th century B.C. Sophist Alcidamas *On the Sophists* 16a-b, criticizing those rhetors who write well but who, when compelled to speak *extempore* "in every respect . . . make an unfavorable impression and are no different from the voiceless."

when he comes, he will act in accord with his letters (and will no longer be sparing, 12:14, 13:2). Paul draws this *propositio* to a close with language of presence and absence which recalls the way in which the *exordium* began (cf. ἀπόντες in v. 11 and ἀπὼν in v. 1; παρόντες in v. 11 and παρὼν in v. 2), forming an *inclusio* that surrounds these first two opening sections and marks the end of the *propositio*.[95]

In his discussion of the *propositio*, Quintilian spends considerable time discussing *partitio*, "the enumeration in order of our own propositions."[96] If such a strategy is employed, Quintilian insists that the description of what will be discussed should be both clear and brief.[97] But above all, Quintilian warns that "the worst fault of all is to treat your points in an order different from that which was assigned them in your proposition."[98] In his *propositio*, Paul has in fact laid out three main topics which he will discuss in his *probatio*, in the order in which he will address them: Paul too belongs to Christ (10:7, taken up in 11:1-15); Paul is able to boast of his authority without shame (10:8-10, taken up in 11:16-12:13); Paul will act with consistency when he arrives in Corinth (10:11, taken up in 12:14-18). Thus, we see that Paul has prepared for his argument with a *propositio* which has alerted the hearers to the topics which will be discussed in his *probatio*. Before Paul launches into that argument, he gives some further "background" in what should be identified as the *narratio*.

NARRATIO: 10:12-18[99]

The basic description of *narratio* given by the handbooks is simple: "The narrative is an exposition of events that have occurred or are supposed to have occurred."[100] Yet the handbooks are also concerned to point out that the *narratio* is more than just a bare reporting of facts. "For the purpose of the statement of facts is not merely to instruct, but rather to persuade

---

[95]This *inclusio* is also recognized by Martin, *2 Corinthians*, 313.

[96]Quintilian 4.5.1. cf. also *Ad Her.* 1.10.17, Cicero *De Inv.* 1.22.32.

[97]Quintilian 4.5.26-27.

[98]Ibid. 4.5.28.

[99]The major discussions of *narratio* in the ancient handbooks are found in Aristotle *Rhetoric* 3.13.3-5, 16.1-11; *Ad Her.* 1.8.12-9.16; Cicero *De Inv.* 1.19.27-31.30; Quintilian 4.2.1-132.

[100]Cicero *De Inv.* 1.19.27; Quintilian 4.2.31 gives virtually the same definition.

the judge."[101] In fact, Quintilian admits that it is often a good idea to "scatter some hints of our proofs here and there, but in such a way that it is never forgotten that we are making a statement of facts and not a proof."[102] Thus the *narratio* is not intended merely to be informative, but also persuasive; it should be designed to make the *propositio* more credible, and to prepare for the arguments of the *probatio*. As such, the *narratio* may well relate events and details which the judge or hearers already know well, but will do so with a view toward clarifying the nature of the subject which is under consideration.[103] It may not only set forth the facts of the case itself, but also "facts which have a bearing on the case."[104] Aristotle points in particular to the usefulness of highlighting what one wishes the hearers to understand as particularly characteristic about one's self and one's opponents:

> Further, the narrative should draw upon what is emotional by the introduction of such of its accompaniments as are well known, and of what is specially characteristic of either yourself or your adversary.[105]

These guidelines describe what Paul sets out to do in his *narratio*, as he reminds the Corinthians of something that they know well, and that in Paul's view decisively characterizes himself as well as his opponents: Paul reminds the Corinthians that they are his territory, because God first sent *him* to them with the gospel. Before Paul begins his argument in earnest, he wants to be sure this basic perspective is clear.

By the end of his argument, Paul will have turned the tables on his opponents and on the Corinthians themselves. In such a case, Quintilian allows that the *narratio* may be delayed and placed out of what he considers a more typical order of *exordium - narratio - propositio*: "Thus after first rebutting the charge, we make our statement of facts the opening of an incrimination of the other party."[106] This is precisely what Paul has done in 2 Corinthians 10, and by the time he reaches the end of

---

[101]Quintilian 4.2.21.

[102]Ibid. 4.2.54.

[103]Ibid. 4.2.1, 21-23. Cf. Demosthenes *De Corona* 17, "It is necessary, men of Athens, and not improper, to remind you of the position of affairs in those days, so that you may consider each transaction with due regard to its occasion."

[104]Quintilian 4.2.11.

[105]Aristotle *Rhetoric* 3.16.10.

[106]Quintilian 4.2.26.

this *narratio*, he will be in a good position to directly and forcefully challenge his opponents in Corinth.[107]

Quintilian suggests beginning the *narratio* by referring to someone whom you either want to praise or blame.[108] This is what Paul does in v. 12 by referring to those who "commend themselves." Paul's opening is heavy with irony.[109] To be "bold" (τολμᾶν) was a necessary and expected characteristic of an effective orator and leader.

> For if one should take lessons in all the principles of oratory and master
> them with the greatest thoroughness, he might, perhaps, become a more
> pleasing speaker than most, but let him stand up before the crowd and
> lack one thing only, namely assurance [τολμᾶν], and he would not be
> able to utter a word.[110]

τολμᾶν involves a person "pushing himself forward so that he does not hesitate to speak or act on his own behalf,"[111] and was part of the standard debate and counter-claims between philosophy and sophistry.[112] To be bold without the ability to back it up, of course, would be foolish.[113] Yet it would be equally damaging to be perceived as one who lacked τολμᾶν. It may well be that this was part of the complaint against Paul,[114] due to

---

[107]Cicero *De Inv.* 1.19.27 says that there are three types of *narratio*: "one which contains just the case and the whole reason for the dispute; a second in which a digression is made beyond the strict limits of the case for the purpose of attacking somebody, or of making a comparison, or of amusing the audience . . . or for amplification. The third kind is wholly unconnected to public issues, which is recited or written solely for amusement . . . ." 2 Cor 10:12-18 is an example of the second type.

[108]Quintilian 4.2.129.

[109]Irony was a recognized tool of rhetoric; cf. Quintilian 8.6.54-59. Irony was not, of course, the exclusive possession of the Greco-Roman tradition. Paul would have known it also from the Jewish tradition. Cf. Jer 2:28, Ezek 28:3, Amos 4:4-5; John Reumann, "St. Paul's Use of Irony," *LQ* 7 (1955), 140-141.

[110]Isocrates *Antidosis* 192.

[111]Martin, *2 Corinthians*, 319.

[112]Betz, *Der Apostel*, 67-69. For evidence that this was also at home in the discussions of Judaism, cf. Esth 1:18, Job 15:12, 2 Macc 4:2, 3 Macc 3:21, Philo *Som.* 1.54.

[113]Dio Chrysostom *Or.* 13.29, "I did not venture to speak a word of my own [οὐδένα ἐτόλμων διαλέγεσθαι], fearing lest I be laughed at and regarded as a fool." Dio is no doubt engaging in a bit of irony himself here.

[114]Cf. 2 Cor 10:2, 11:21.

his way of answering the community's previous questions, or the way in which he handled discipline problems when he returned to Corinth, or his rhetorical style in dealing with his opponents (or perhaps the combination of all these issues). That we should read Paul's professed lack of τολμᾶν here as ironic[115] is seen in the fact that he has already promised boldness in 10:2, and he will begin to fulfill that promise in 11:21 (τολμῶ κἀγώ).

What Paul says he would not dare to do is to compare (συγκρῖναι) himself with these others. Comparison (σύγκρισις) was a tool widely used in hellenistic culture.[116] It was a common exercise in one's early education.[117] Aristotle recommends comparison as a useful way of developing one's position.

> If he does not furnish you with enough material in himself, you must compare him with others . . . . And you must compare him with illustrious personages, for it affords ground for amplification and is noble, if he can be proved better than men of worth. . . . That is why, if you cannot compare him with illustrious personages, you must compare him with ordinary persons, since superiority is thought to indicate virtue.[118]

There were, of course, recognized dangers to such comparison. Plutarch finds it most unbecoming to compare yourself to the praise and fame of others.[119] Aristotle warns

> And to speak at great length about oneself and to make all kinds of professions, and to take the credit for what another has done; for this is a sign of boastfulness.[120]

Dio Chrysostom was accused of boasting because of his use of σύγκρισις, and he is compelled to downplay his own skill to avoid that charge.

---

[115]Cf. Bultmann, *Second Letter*, 192; Furnish, *II Corinthians*, 480.

[116]One might note, for instance, that it is the basic approach that underlies Plutarch's parallel "Lives."

[117]Witherington, *Conflict & Community*, 376 n. 1.

[118]Aristotle *Rhetoric* 1.9.38-39.

[119]Plutarch *On Praising Oneself Inoffensively* 545 D (cited by Talbert, *Reading Corinthians*, 114).

[120]Aristotle *Rhetoric* 2.6.10. His position sounds remarkably close to Paul's comments in vv. 13-16. Similarly, Epictetus *Disc.* 3.1.21-23, 22.60-61.

> My purpose in mentioning such matters was neither to elate you nor to range myself beside those who habitually sing such strains, whether orators or poets. For they are clever persons, mighty Sophists, wonder-workers, but I am quite ordinary and prosaic in my utterance, though not ordinary in my theme.[121]

Even worse would be to engage in such comparison, and to be found inferior.[122] In one first century letter, a student complains about a bad teacher that he has had to endure, who although he "used to be a mere provincial teacher sees fit to compete (εἰς σύγκρισιν) with the rest."[123]

However, despite these cautions (whose very existence is evidence of how wide-spread the practice was), such comparison was a common part of rhetorical competition.[124] Lucian describes the philosophers he would criticize:

> They accuse everyone else; they amass biting phrases and school themselves in novel terms of abuse, and then they censure and reproach their fellow-men; and whoever of them is the most noisy and impudent and reckless in calling names is held to be the champion.[125]

Furthermore, Lucian puts these instructions into the mouth of a teacher:

> Do not expect to see something that you can compare with So-and-so, or So-and-so; no, you will consider the achievement far too prodigious and amazing even for Tityus or Otus or Ephialtes. Indeed, as far as the others are concerned, you will find out that I drown them out as effectively as trumpets drown flutes.[126]

As for advice given to the student, Lucian's teacher says

---

[121]Dio Chrysostom *Or.* 32.39. Cf. 2 Cor 11:6.
[122]See Bruce J. Malina, *The New Testament World. Insights from Cultural Anthropology* (Louisville: John Knox, 1981), 30-33 for a discussion of honor gained or lost through "contests" within an "agonistic" society.
[123]POxy 2190, lines 28-29 (cited by Furnish, *II Corinthians*, 480); see also Danker, *II Corinthians*, 157.
[124]Betz, "The Problem of Rhetoric," 23. Idem, *Der Apostel Paulus*, 119-20.
[125]Lucian *Icaromenippus* 30.
[126]Lucian *A Professor of Public Speaking* 13.

If anyone accosts you, make marvellous assertions about yourself, be extravagant in your self-praise.[127]

It was this type of comparison and competition that Paul seems to have been facing in Corinth; and it is this kind of comparison that Paul says, with irony, he wouldn't dare undertake. It was not only comparison with one who was superior that would be considered foolish; so too would comparison with someone obviously inferior.[128] In a sense, Paul says that his opponents are correct—he wouldn't dare place himself in the same class as such people. These opponents claim to be in a different league; Paul agrees, and will soon show that they are in league with Satan.[129] That Paul views his refusal of comparison from a point of superiority rather than inferiority is quickly seen in his criticism of the opponents' behavior in v. 12: they are simply self-recommending,[130] making the mistake of self-comparison[131] as the standard for evaluation.

---

[127]Ibid., 21.

[128]See Peter Marshall, "Invective: Paul and His Enemies in Corinth," in *Perspectives on Language and Text*, ed. E. Conrad and E. Newing (Winona Lake, Ind.: Eisenbrauns, 1987), 372; Talbert, *Reading Corinthians*, 114. This may mean that, despite their criticisms to the contrary, the opponents in Corinth did not see Paul as a completely uncultivated speaker, or no comparison with him would have been undertaken. For numerous examples from Philo of the concept that where there is no similarity there can be no comparison, see Forbes, "Comparison," 25-26 n. 20.

[129]See Garland, "Paul's Apostolic Authority," 374.

[130]Paul's comments about self-recommendation and his lack of letters of reference in 3:1 and 5:12 may indicate that Paul himself was being criticized as someone who had come to Corinth only on his own self-recommendation. If that is the case, then here he turns that charge back on his opponents. So Furnish, *II Corinthians*, 480.

[131]The omission of "οὐ συνιᾶσιν. ἡμεῖς δὲ" by D, F, G and some of the Latin texts in vv. 12b-13a, which would imply that the αὐτοὶ in v. 12 refers to Paul himself, and that he does engage in self-comparison, is surely to be rejected (contra Windisch, *Der zweite Korintherbrief*, 309; Lietzmann, *An Die Korinther*, 143; Käsemann, "Die Legitimität," 56-57; Bultmann, *Second Letter*, 192-93; BDF #416.2). Despite arguments that Paul was claiming such self-comparison as the legitimate practice of a spiritual person (cf. 1 Cor 2:15-16), it is difficult to see how v. 12 relates to v. 13 other than as a contrast; the opponents measure themselves by themselves (i.e., without a divinely authorized standard), while Paul will use only the measure given to him by God; so Martin, *2 Corinthians*, 315; see also Furnish, *II Corinthians*, 470-71; Talbert, *Reading Corinthians*, 114. Barrett (*Second Epistle*, 164) prefers the longer reading, but his explanation for the

Paul's style and grammar in vv. 12-13 have at times been viewed as convoluted at best. Windisch described this section as "notably clumsy," with "oddly confused expressions" and "intolerable constructions."[132] Lietzmann described these phrases as "gehackten, grimmig hingeworfenen Satzbrocken."[133] Barrett says Paul "ties himself in grammatical knots."[134] Martin is willing to attribute the obscurity of this section to Paul's "emotional involvement," which produces a situation where "his dictation runs ahead of his mind."[135]

However, although these sentences are not among the most easily comprehended in the Pauline letters, it is not so clear that they are careless or without a good deal of skill and intention. The repetition of forms of "measure" (μετροῦντες, ἄμετρα, μέτρον, ἐμέρισεν, μέτρου) sounds a cadence that emphasizes Paul's point: this is about boundaries, and Paul has not overstepped his.[136] In addition, a four-fold repetition of verbs prefixed by σύν in v. 12 (συγκρῖναι, συνιστανόντων, συγκρίνοντες, συνιᾶσιν) serves to highlight "the boastful conspiracy on the part of Paul's opponents."[137] Far from being haphazard, the central section of v. 12 exhibits a tight chiastic structure:

$$\begin{array}{c} \text{ἑαυτοῖς} \\ \text{ἑαυτοὺς} \\ \text{μετροῦντες} \\ \text{καὶ} \\ \text{συγκρίνοντες} \\ \text{ἑαυτοὺς} \\ \text{ἑαυτοῖς} \end{array}$$

Thus, rather than seeing here a confusion in Paul's expression, we can recognize further irony in that Paul outwardly declines to compare himself

---

omission, based on a misunderstanding in the Latin tradition, is unnecessarily involved. More likely, the omission resulted from simple haplography (ου . . . ουκ; so Martin, *2 Corinthians*, 315; Metzger, *Textual Commentary*, 583).

[132] Windisch, *Der zweite Korintherbrief*, 313 (noted by Martin, *2 Corinthians*, 317).

[133] Lietzmann, *An Die Korinther*, 143.

[134] Barrett, *Second Epistle*, 261.

[135] Martin, *2 Corinthians*, 317.

[136] Cf. Martin, *2 Corinthians*, 320.

[137] Danker, *II Corinthians*, 158.

with these others, while at the same time producing a remarkably balanced and powerful sentence.

> Paul stated in v. 11 that he would demonstrate that his actions were equal to his words. In this and succeeding statements the apostle shows how skillful he can be with his words. Thus he leaves to the imagination the comparable weight of action promised in v. 11.[138]

In v. 13, Paul begins to clarify what kind of measure he will use: it will be the κανών which God has given. And that κανών is then defined in terms of the geographic reach of Paul's mission: ἐφικέσθαι ἄχρι καὶ ὑμῶν.[139] Barrett points out how both κανών and μετρεῖν are used by Aristophanes to describe measuring a geographic area.[140] κανών does appear in an imperial edict from the time of Tiberius with the meaning of "a measured area or a limited domain of service."[141] Paul's only measure for boasting, then, will be what God has done through him in bringing the gospel into new territory,[142] and in this case specifically to Corinth.

Though Furnish[143] rightly points out that κανών does not appear in Paul's description of the mission agreement in Galatians 2:1-10 (and so concludes that there is no necessary reason to connect the present verses with a misunderstanding [or violation] of that agreement), it is

---

[138]Ibid.

[139]Cf. Bultmann, *Second Letter*, 194. Such a geographic understanding of Paul's idea of κανών here is denied by Käsemann, "Die Legitimatät," 43-51; Georgi, *Opponents of Paul*, 287-88 n. 47; Hermann Beyer, "κανών," *TDNT* 3:599-600. But Barrett, "Christianity at Corinth," in *Essays on Paul* (Philadelphia: Westminster, 1982), 18 rightly points out that the ἐφικέσθαι ἄχρι καὶ ὑμῶν confirms that Paul is thinking in terms of territory to which he has come as pioneer. See also Martin, *2 Corinthians*, 320.

[140]Barrett, *Second Epistle*, 265 (Aristophanes *Birds* 992-1021).

[141]Witherington, *Conflict & Community*, 440 n. 46. The evidence is found in *New Documents Illustrating Early Christianity Vol. 1*, ed. G. H. R. Horsley (North Ryde: Macquarrie University, 1981), 36-45, cited by Witherington. That κανών can also mean "jurisdiction" or "area of responsibility" in general, see 1 Clem. 1:3, 14:1, 41:1.

[142]Note Romans 15:17-20, where Paul's boast (καύχησιν) is that he does not dare (οὐ τολμήσω) to speak of anything except the way in which Christ has proclaimed the gospel through him "from Jerusalem to Illyricum," and will continue this mission into unevangelized territory.

[143]Furnish, *II Corinthians*, 472.

nonetheless tempting to wonder with Barrett[144] whether that agreement may not have included an unfortunate ambiguity about whether or not such a "division of labor" was intended to be geographic. Certainly Paul understood Corinth to be his territory; even though the community contained some Jews, it was a Gentile city, and Paul, following his call from God to be the apostle to the Gentiles, had first brought the gospel there. He was, then, the planter (1 Cor 3:6), the master architect (1 Cor 3:10), and in fact their father in Christ as no one else could ever be (1 Cor 4:15);[145] their very faith is bound up with Paul's apostleship (1 Cor 9:1-3). "Corinth rightly belonged to his 'sphere of service' *qua* apostle to the Gentiles."[146]

Thus, when Paul says in v. 15 that he will not boast εἰς τὰ ἄμετρα, he is not simply saying that he will refuse to boast "excessively" (NRSV: "beyond limits"), but that he will not boast beyond the specific mission area (NEB: "beyond our proper sphere"),[147] "in the labors of others." Whether or not a charge was being made against Paul that he had "overextended himself" (ὑπερεκτείνειν, v. 14) by coming to Corinth,[148] it is clearly Paul's view that these interlopers have gone beyond not simply reasonable or polite limits, but the limits which God has set by bringing Paul to Corinth first with the gospel.

This is the basic foundation of the *narratio* of which Paul wants to remind the Corinthians; he was the first to bring the gospel to them, and that he did so is evidence that Corinth is within the κανών which God has

---

[144]Barrett, *Second Epistle*, 265. Less convincing is Barrett's suggestion ("Cephas and Corinth," in *Essays on Paul* [Philadelphia: Westminster, 1982], 35-36) that it was Peter himself who had headed this mission to Corinth. That appeals to Peter's authority were part of the problem is possible; that Peter himself was in Corinth "preaching another Jesus" (11:4) hardly seems likely. Cf. Martin, *2 Corinthians*, 323.

[145]The image of the founder of a group or community as their "father" was common in hellenistic culture; see T. R. Stevenson, "The Ideal Benefactor and the Father Analogy in Greek and Roman Thought," *Classical Quarterly* 42 (1992): 425. Philosophers also exhorted their listeners with paternal language; see Epictetus *Disc.* 3.22.82, Quintilian 2.2.4-5; Abraham J. Malherbe, "Exhortation in First Thessalonians," *NovT* 25 (1983): 244. Such paternal language also was used by patrons to their clients; see Witherington, *Conflict & Community*, 467 n. 6.

[146]Martin, *2 Corinthians*, 322.

[147]Furnish, *II Corinthians*, 471.

[148]Suggested by Martin, *2 Corinthians*, 316, 321.

appointed to him as apostle. These newcomers can make no such claim. Paul has thus characterized for the Corinthians both himself and his opponents, and has staked out his ground for the direct attack on them that will begin in chapter 11.

Paul has also prepared for his *probatio* by indicating that he by no means is done with Corinth. The present tense of ἐφικνούμενοι in v. 14 may well serve to remind the Corinthians that not only did Paul reach them, but that Paul continues his reach to them with ongoing pastoral care and responsibility.[149] It is, in fact, that continuing identity of Corinth as Paul's field of labor that is the reason that he will be able to be powerful not only in his letters, but in his actions when he comes (v. 11).[150]

Paul also has hope for a healthy future with Corinth. The increase in πίστις to which Paul looks forward in v. 15 is not trust in the gospel, but a growth in their faithfulness to Paul's ministry (note the hope, already expressed in v. 6, that the Corinthians will complete their obedience).[151] That Paul has such continued (or renewed) allegiance in view here is confirmed by Paul's conviction that this will result in Paul being praised (μεγαλυνθῆναι) among the Corinthians (ἐν ὑμῖν), and that this would happen according to the κανών given to Paul, i.e., according to his sphere of ministry, and would in turn propel Paul's ministry into new areas beyond Corinth.

Paul further prepares for his *probatio* by a subtle but important shift in terminology in v. 13, from describing the activity into which he finds himself forced as σύγκρισις, a more accepted rhetorical term, to calling it "boasting" (καύχησις), a more offensive label and one which raises an important issue for Paul: On what does one place trust and confidence?[152] For Paul, that is the issue at the heart of this activity. καυχᾶσθαι does not mean "bragging" so much as it is a question of trust: "For Paul then, as for the OT and Philo, the element of trust contained in καυχᾶσθαι is primary."[153]

Paul sums up his point in the *narratio* with a reference in v. 17 to Jeremiah 9:23-24 (LXX 9:22-23). Paul has already used this same

---

[149] Furnish, *II Corinthians*, 472.

[150] Bultmann, *Second Letter*, 193-94.

[151] See Martin, *2 Corinthians*, 323-24; Furnish, *II Corinthians*, 481-82.

[152] Witherington, *Conflict & Community*, 441.

[153] Bultmann, "καυχάομαι", in *TDNT* 3:645-654, here 649. Note Phil 3:3, where καυχάομαι is set in a parallel construction with πεποιθέναι. Note also that 2 Cor 10:7-8 has likewise set these two verbs in parallel.

reference to counter the Corinthians' tendency to engage in competition against each other (1 Cor 1:31). While Jeremiah calls the people to "boast" in knowing the Lord, Paul's abbreviated reference commands that one's boast be ἐν κυρίῳ; and here, the κύριος is Jesus Christ (cf. Gal 6:14; Phil 3:3).[154] It is only the Lord Jesus who will be Paul's boast, Paul's source of confidence, and only the Lord who can be the criterion for measurement. Here Paul has reached a turning point in his argument, since the main concern of the *probatio* will deal with the question of the proper criterion for apostolic ministry.

Certainly "boasting in the Lord" includes, in Paul's argument, "to boast of what Christ had wrought through him in his allotted field of service."[155] That has been Paul's point throughout this *narratio*. But "to boast in the Lord" does not stop there; Paul will go on in his *probatio* to explore just what it means to "boast in the Lord." Since this is a Lord at whose meekness and even humiliation Paul has already hinted in v. 1, "Christ, not Demosthenes or Isocrates or Cicero, is Paul's model for wise and persuasive behavior. Though a sage, he will follow Jeremiah's warning and will therefore boast in his foolishness, weakness and poverty."[156]

Paul wraps up his *narratio* with v. 18, marking this section with an *inclusio* with συνιστάνειν in vv. 12 and 18.[157] Quintilian says that the *narratio* should bring one to the point where the issue to be determined begins.[158] Paul has laid out the groundwork for true καυχᾶσθαι, and so is ready to undertake the "foolish boasting" of his *probatio*. There are important issues Paul must clarify for the Corinthians. Just what does it mean to boast ἐν κυρίῳ? How is it that one can know whom the Lord

---

[154]Furnish, *II Corinthians*, 482.

[155]Bruce, *I & II Corinthians*, 234; Scott Hafemann, "Self-Commendation and Apostolic Legitimacy in 2 Corinthians," *NTS* 36 (1990): 82.

[156]Witherington, *Conflict & Community*, 441; cf. also Best, *Second Corinthians*, 98, "There is indeed only one standard by which measurement should be made—Christ. Paul seeks to imitate Christ (1 Cor 11:1) and to manifest the life of Jesus in his life (2 Cor 4:10). This is the standard by which the Corinthians ought to be assessing both him and his rivals and by which we ought to assess ourselves."

[157]Noted by Talbert, *Reading Corinthians*, 113-14; Danker, *II Corinthians*, 159; Martin, *2 Corinthians*, 324.

[158]Quintilian 4.2.132.

commends,[159] or if one is δόκιμος? That will be the crux of Paul's *probatio*, and after that he will return to this theme of δόκιμος in his *peroratio* in 13:5, by which time he will be able to turn the tables on the Corinthians, and address the issue to them, just as they are now asking whether Paul truly is δόκιμος.[160]

PROBATIO: 11:1-12:18[161]

Cicero defines the *confirmatio* (equivalent to Quintilian's term *probatio*) thus:

> Confirmation or proof is the part of the oration which by marshalling arguments lends credit, authority, and support to our case.[162]

Paul now begins his *probatio*, seeking to confirm his ἐξουσία among the Corinthians which he introduced in the *propositio* (10:8), and to show that he is indeed δόκιμος.

The *probatio* was more than just logical argumentation, though of course that was necessary. Quintilian recognizes the need to consider the emotional impact of what one says.

> We on the other hand have to compose our speeches for others to judge, and have frequently to speak before an audience of men who, if not thoroughly ill-educated, are certainly ignorant of such arts as dialectic: and unless we attract them by the charm of our discourse or drag them by its force, and occasionally throw them off their balance by an appeal to their emotions, we shall be unable to vindicate the claims of truth and justice.[163]

---

[159]Barrett, *Second Epistle*, 269.

[160]Cf. Bultmann, *Second Letter*, 197.

[161]The *probatio* (Quintilian's term) receives more attention in the handbooks than any other aspect of arrangement. The major discussions are found in Aristotle *Rhetoric*, the majority of books 1 & 2, 3.17.1-18.7 (using the term πίστεις to identify these arguments); *Ad Her.* 1.10.18-2.29.46 (under the label *confirmatio*); Cicero *De Inv.* 1.24.34-51.97 (also under *confirmatio*); Quintilian, book 5.

[162]Cicero *De Inv.* 1.24.34. Cf. *Ad Her.* 1.10.18.

[163]Quintilian 5.14.29.

Paul will draw on both *ethos* and *pathos* to supplement his logical argumentation. Quintilian advises that the speaker must not bore his hearers with bare syllogistic reasoning, but "vary and diversify it with a thousand figures."[164] As Paul indicated in the *propositio*, his arguments will be organized around three major issues.

Argument 1: Who belongs to Christ? (11:1-15)

Paul begins his *probatio* with a plea that his hearers be willing to put up with what he has to say, a common rhetorical theme.[165] Since the following verses more logically give reasons why the Corinthians should listen to Paul than why they are in fact listening to him, it makes better sense to read ἀνέχεσθε in 11:1 as an imperative[166] than as an indicative.[167]

Paul asks the Corinthians to put up with a bit of foolishness (ἀφροσύνη) from him. But this talk of foolishness then disappears from the discussion until Paul prepares to present his "Foolish Boast" in 11:16-12:13.[168] The intervening verses have seemed to some to be an intrusion, an unnecessary sidetrack; "Paul's uneasiness about the whole business of boasting (v. 17) leads him into a nervous prolixity."[169] Yet it would seem better to describe the rest of this section (vv. 2-15) as a "digression,"[170] one that is intended to give the reason that Paul, despite what was said in 10:12-18, will in fact engage in some boasting: it is

---

[164]Ibid. 5.14.32.

[165]Danker, *II Corinthians*, 161 notes Demosthenes *De Corona* 160 ("For many reasons you may fairly be asked to listen to my account of that policy, but chiefly because it would be discreditable, men of Athens, that you should be impatient of the mere recital of those arduous labours on your behalf which I had the patience to endure"). Perhaps a closer parallel to our verse is found at the beginning of the *probatio* in Isocrates *Antidosis* 13, "I beg you now to listen to my defense."

[166]So Barrett, *Second Epistle*, 271; Furnish, *II Corinthians*, 485; Martin, *2 Corinthians*, 327-28; BDF #448.6; KJV, TEV, NEB, NRSV, JB mg.

[167]So John Chrysostom, *Homilies*, 23.1; Bultmann, *Second Letter*, 199-200; Lietzmann, *An Die Korinther*, 144; JB, NIV.

[168]Note that ἀνέχεσθαι and ἀφροσύνη appear together in 11:1 and then again in 11:19, with 11:16 having already repeated the general thrust of v. 1 (ὡς ἄφρονα δέξασθέ με).

[169]Furnish, *II Corinthians*, 498.

[170]Bruce, *I & II Corinthians*, 239; Talbert, *Reading Corinthians*, 119.

because of the opponents in Corinth, and the effect they are having there. By making the initial move in v. 1 toward that foolish boast, Paul in effect places all of the argumentation (not just the Foolish Boast in 11:16-12:13) under the heading of "foolishness."[171] By delaying that boasting and dealing first with the issues of 11:2-15, Paul makes clear that he is being forced into this foolish game (cf. 12:11).

11:2 gives the first reason that Paul offers as to why the Corinthians should tolerate this from him. Paul draws on the familiar biblical image of God as the groom, and God's people as the bride.[172] Paul places himself in the role of the bride's father,[173] who promised the church at Corinth in marriage when he evangelized them.[174] The wedding awaits in the future, at the Lord's Parousia.[175] Now Paul is afraid that he may not be able to fulfill his obligation as the bride's father, and present the church as a "pure virgin" to that one promised groom, τῷ Χριστῷ. Surely the emphasis is just as much on ἑνὶ ἀνδρὶ as it is on παρθένον ἁγνὴν.[176] Defection from Paul, in Paul's view, cannot be separated from defection from the one true gospel, and so defection from Paul means to go after another husband, ἄλλον Ἰησοῦν (v. 4).[177]

Paul's reference in v. 3 to Eve's deception by the serpent[178] foreshadows his invective in 11:15, when the opponents are called

[171]Barrett, *Second Epistle*, 271.
[172]Cf. Is 50:1-2, 54:1-8, 62:5; Jer 31:32; Ezek 16; Hos 1-3.
[173]So Bultmann, *Second Letter*, 200; Barrett, *Second Epistle*, 272; Danker, *II Corinthians*, 162; Furnish, *II Corinthians*, 499; Best, *Second Corinthians*, 101; Talbert, *Reading Corinthians*, 119. In light of Paul's statements about his role as the Corinthians' father in the faith (cf. 12:14, 1 Cor 4:15), this position seems preferrable to understanding Paul's role here as the groom's friend (cf. John 3:29, ὁ φίλος τοῦ νυμφίου), as suggested by Martin, *2 Corinthians*, 332; Witherington, *Conflict & Community*, 445.
[174]Cf. Bruce, *I & II Corinthians*, 234; Best, *Second Corinthians*, 101-102.
[175]Barrett, *Second Epistle*, 272; Best, *Second Corinthians*, 101-102; Bruce, *I & II Corinthians*, 234; Bultmann, *Second Letter*, 201; Danker, *II Corinthians*, 162; Furnish, *II Corinthians*, 486, 499; Martin, *2 Corinthians*, 333.
[176]Martin, *2 Corinthians*, 332-333.
[177]Cf. Bultmann, *Second Letter*, 200.
[178]The tradition of Eve's deception had become quite developed in the inter-testamental period. Cf. 4 Macc 18:8, 1 Enoch 69:6, Apoc. Abraham 23, Apoc. Moses 17, Life of Adam and Eve 44:2-5, Jub. 3:17-35. However, there is nothing in Paul's remarks here that indicates any specific source other than the account of Gen 3.

servants of Satan.[179] It is they who present the danger of drawing away the νοήματα of the Corinthians, which are supposed to be εἰς τὸν Χριστόν, and which Paul seeks to capture εἰς τὴν ὑπακοὴν τοῦ Χριστοῦ (10:5). By implication, they do this by sharing in the serpent's πανουργία.[180]

The second reason that Paul gives the Corinthians for putting up with him is given in v. 4: since they put up with others well enough (others who come with a different Jesus, a different spirit, a different gospel), they should be able to show a bit of tolerance to him as well.[181] This is the first time we hear directly that there have been other preachers coming to Corinth,[182] though Paul's discussion of μέτρον and κανών in 10:12-18 was certainly directed at this situation. ὁ ἐρχόμενος, in the light of the singular forms in 10:7, 10-11, probably indicates the ringleader of the opposition at Corinth.[183] If Paul knows who this is, he refrains from identifying or naming him; such was a common rhetorical tactic, either because the opponent's name carried respect among the audience, or

---

[179.]The identification of the serpent of Gen 3 with Satan or the devil is at least as old as Wis 2:24. Cf. Furnish, *II Corinthians*, 486; Martin, *2 Corinthians*, 334.

[180.]Betz (*Der Apostel*, 104-105) suggests that Paul uses πανουργία here because it was a standard part of a philosopher's anti-Sophistic stance. Such a suggestion is made more attractive by the indication in 12:16 that Paul was being charged as a πανοῦργος. Paul's use of this word in 11:3 may well have been motivated by a charge being made against him, but it does not mean Paul was intentionally drawing on philosophical traditions here. Martin (*2 Corinthians*, 334) points out that while the LXX Gen 3:1 describes the serpent as φρονιμώτατος, other traditions (Aquila, Symmachus) read πανοῦργος; cf. Otto Bauernfeind, "πανουργία, πανοῦργος," *TDNT* 5:725 n. 17.

[181.]Though v. 4 may also give the reason why Paul is concerned about being able to bring the Corinthian church to its wedding day as a pure bride (vv. 2-3), it seems best to take the γάρ in v. 4 as referring primarily to the opening statement of v. 1. Cf. Barrett, *Second Epistle*, 274; Furnish, *II Corinthians*, 488.

[182.]The imperfect ἀνείχεσθε in P34, ℵ, D², F, G, and several other uncial and minuscule manuscripts is to be regarded as an alteration of the text, perhaps to make this condition more hypothetical, thus saving the church from the shame of actually having welcomed such preaching. But the present tense indicative, making this a "real condition," fits the context better; clearly, they have tolerated such preachers. See Bultmann, *Second Letter*, 202; Furnish, *II Corinthians*, 489; Martin, *2 Corinthians*, 328.

[183.]So Barrett, *Second Epistle*, 275; Martin, *2 Corinthians*, 335. For ὁ ἐρχόμενος as a generic reference, see Bultmann, *Second Letter*, 202; Furnish, *II Corinthians*, 488.

because to leave him unnamed had the effect of robbing him of some significance.[184] Yet there is nothing insignificant about the trouble at Corinth. The fact that Paul can say the rival preaching contained a different spirit and a different gospel derives from the prior conviction that it involves another Jesus. It does not seem that any overt Christological doctrines are at issue; Paul addresses no response to such.[185] Yet in Paul's eyes, the difference between himself and his opponents is grounded in Christology. "It is the character of Jesus as setting the norm for Christian existence that is at stake."[186]

The third supporting reason for the appeal of v. 1 is given in v. 5. Paul here understates the case; he will soon make clear that it is not simply that he is equal to these "superior apostles,"[187] but that they are not apostles at all.[188] Again, his irony is apparent; picking up the terminology

---

[184]See Peter Marshall, "Invective," 366; Martin, *2 Corinthians*, 353.

[185]Cf. Bultmann, *Second Letter*, 203.

[186]Martin, *2 Corinthians*, 336.

[187]Whether or not this term was being applied immoderately by these preachers to themselves (Witherington, *Conflict & Community*, 446 n. 26), it certainly reflects the Corinthians' appraisal of them.

[188]There is no indication that Paul is switching attention from one group, viewed more positively (the "superior apostles") and often identified with the leadership of the Jerusalem church, to a different group that is rejected as satanic and often identified with the opposition in Corinth. Furthermore, compared to the "superior apostles" Paul appears to be ἰδιώτης τῷ λόγῳ (v. 6), something unlikely if Paul were being placed against the Palestinian leadership of the church. Those who do see two different groups in chapter 11 include Käsemann, "Die Legitimität," 41-48; Martin, *2 Corinthians*, 336-42; C. K. Barrett, "Paul's Opponents;" idem, "Ψευδαπόστολοι," in *Essays on Paul* (Philadelphia: Westminster, 1982), 87-107. Even less likely is Margaret Thrall's suggestion ("Super-Apostles, Servants of Christ, Servants of Satan," *JSNT* 6 (1980): 42-57) that Paul's variation in tone regarding the other apostles is because he is not fully informed about what is actually happening in Corinth, and that behind his remarks concerning the servants of Satan in 11:14-15 lies the tradition of Jesus' rebuke of Peter (Mt 16:23, Mk 8:33). That there is only one group of apostles in view (and though they claimed Jewish heritage, there is no indication that they were authorized or claimed authorization from the Jerusalem leadership) is apparent when one remembers the ironic tone of this section. For those who see only one group of apostles in chapter 11, see Bultmann, *Second Letter*, 203; Furnish, *II Corinthians*, 48-54, 502-505; Danker, *II Corinthians*, 164; Best, *Second Corinthians*, 103-104; Witherington, *Conflict & Community*, 446-47.

of λογίζεσθαι from 10:2, 7, 11, Paul "considers himself" not less than these others who have gained a hearing among the Corinthians.

Vv. 5-11 discuss 2 issues in which it seems Paul was being criticized as inferior: his eloquence as a speaker (vv. 5-6), and his refusal of financial support from Corinth (vv. 7-11). To be ἰδιώτης τῷ λόγῳ did not necessarily mean that one was unskilled or untrained,[189] although there were criticisms about the sophistication of Paul's rhetoric at Corinth (10:10). Isocrates discusses those who are ἰδιώτης not in terms of those who are untrained or unskilled, but as those who, though trained, nevertheless choose not to become competitors or teachers, but return from the school to private life.[190] Dio Chrysostom, though certainly not unskilled, can call himself ἰδιώτης; he is no professional teacher or philosopher.[191] Thus, though Paul's rhetorical skill was also being criticized at Corinth, the main thrust of the charge behind 11:6 is that Paul is an amateur.[192]

It is this realization that makes the transition from v. 6 to vv. 7-11 sensible. Paul refused to accept the kind of salary from the Corinthians that any decent teacher would expect; this made it look to his opponents in Corinth as though Paul did not deserve to be paid, and thus Paul seems to be an ἰδιώτης, in contrast to these newcomers who did accept (if not demand) payment. Though Paul has discussed his refusal of Corinthian support before (1 Cor 9:1-18), he needs to address it again in the light of recent developments in Corinth.

Theissen[193] may be correct in suggesting that in not accepting support from the community in which he was living and serving, Paul opened

---

[189]Cf. NRSV, "untrained in speech;" NIV, "I may not be a trained speaker."

[190]Isocrates *Antidosis* 201-204. Cf. also Philo *Agr.* 143, 159-60, who contrasts ἰδιώτης with the Sophists who are always engaging in contests; also Plato *Ion* 532 D, where Socrates contrasts professional rhapsodes and actors with "ordinary people."

[191]Of course, there may well be, both in Dio and in Paul, a bit of ironic false humility. See Dio Chrysostom *Or.* 12.15-16, 42.3; cf. 32.39; Danker, *II Corinthians*, 165.

[192]E. A. Judge, "Cultural Conformity and Innovation in Paul: Some Clues from Contemporary Documents," *TynB* 35 (1984): 12-14, 35; Witherington, *Conflict & Community*, 447 n. 29. See also Betz, *Der Apostel*, 59-60; Kennedy, *New Testament Interpretation*, 95; Pogoloff, *Logos and Sophia*, 43. Cf. TEV, "Perhaps I am an amateur in speaking."

[193]Theissen, "Legitimation and Subsistence," 40-46.

himself to the charge of not following a command of the Lord (1 Cor 9:14, Lk 10:7-8), and thus became vulnerable to the accusation that his refusal of such support amounted to ἁμαρτία (11:7) and ἀδικία (12:13).[194] However, the concern addressed by Paul here is not, as in 1 Corinthians 9, over this practice as a "right" (ἐξουσία) which Paul voluntarily relinquishes; rather, the issue at hand in 2 Corinthians appears in 11:11. Paul was compared to these newcomers who were willing to accept the Corinthians' money and so be bound to them in a relationship that included obligations; Paul's refusal of such a relationship was being taken as a sign of his lack of love for them.[195]

Paul portrayed himself in 10:3-6 as a military commander waging war on the side of God. In 11:8 Paul reinforces that *ethos* by again using military terms, saying that he "plundered" (ἐσύλησα) other churches,[196] taking their resources as "wages" to further his campaign in Corinth.[197] Even now Paul will not take the Corinthians' money. If his usual practice was, as it seems to have been, to accept support money once he had established a church and moved on from there,[198] he would not follow that practice with Corinth; he will continue to refuse their money (ἐτήρησα καὶ τηρήσω, v. 9b). Paul then uses an oath (ὁ θεὸς οἶδεν, v. 11) to

---

[194]As Furnish, *II Corinthians*, 491 notes, the expression ἁμαρτίαν ποιεῖν in 11:7 is unique in the Pauline corpus. ἁμαρτία elsewhere in Paul's writings is understood to be an enslaving power; only here and in Romans 4:8 (quoting LXX Ps 31:2) does ἁμαρτία indicate a specific wrong action. Likewise, 2 Cor 12:13 appears to be the only time in the Pauline writings where ἀδικία describes a specific action rather than an abstract concept. This adds weight to the suggestion that the charge of ἁμαρτία was one which came from Paul's opponents in Corinth.

[195] Thus whether the ἁμαρτία is seen as primarily against a command of the Lord or against the Corinthians, Witherington's suggestion (*Conflict & Community*, 448) that ἁμαρτία here means "mistake" rather than "sin" fails to grasp the seriousness of the charge against Paul.

[196]Thus Paul is not the client of these other churches either. Perhaps Paul intends this to cut off any further charge of inconsistency in allowing financial relationships with other churches which he did not allow with Corinth. See Furnish, *II Corinthians*, 508.

[197]Furnish, *II Corinthians*, 492; Martin, *2 Corinthians*, 346; Danker, *II Corinthians*, 168; Barrett, *Second Epistle*, 282.

[198]See Furnish, *II Corinthians*, 507; Witherington, *Conflict & Community*, 208.

confirm that the reason for this action is NOT a lack of love for the Corinthians.

The reason for Paul's resolution not to accept the Corinthians' money is given in v. 12. It is because there are those who want to boast that they are as Paul: true apostles who deserve the support of the church. It is to cut off this opportunity (ἀφορμὴν) that Paul will refuse the Corinthians' money;[199] then all will see that Paul and these other so-called apostles are not the same. Now it becomes clear why Paul brought up the issue of financial support in this discussion. His opponents were claiming that they worked on the same level as Paul; now he has laid bare their lie.[200]

Having shown how he and these others do not, in fact, work on the same principles, Paul will expose them for what they are. Paul returns to the discussion of the "super apostles" that had been suspended after v. 5, but now Paul speaks without irony and declares that they are only false apostles, in fact in league with Satan.[201] Just as this section began with words about Satan's activity in the guise of the serpent, so at the end of the section Paul discusses Satan's activity in the guise of these false apostles.[202] Likewise, just as Paul's opening section of this discussion looked to the End and the Church's marriage to Christ (11:2), so too he closes this section with a forward look to God's final judgment on such ministers of Satan (11:15).[203] This *inclusio* frames the first argument of the *probatio*.[204]

---

[199]It is surely better to read the second ἵνα with the second ἀφορμὴν than with ἐκκόψω. Paul is not hoping that by his actions he and the others will be seen to be the same, as vv. 13-15 make clear. Rather, those who have come to Corinth are boasting that they are as much apostles as Paul, and so should receive support from the Corinthians. See Furnish, *II Corinthians*, 494.

[200]See Best, *Second Corinthians*, 107.

[201]Cf. Dio Chrysostom *Or.* 45.1, "bearing up under the hatred, not of this or that one among my equals, or peers as they are sometimes called, but rather of the most powerful, most stern man, who was called by all Greeks and barbarians both master and god, but who was in reality an evil demon" (δαίμονα πονηρόν).

[202]For an example of the tradition of Satan changing himself into an "angel of light," cf. Life of Adam and Eve 9:1.

[203]See Martin, *2 Corinthians*, 353. For τέλος as the eschatological judgment of God, cf. Rom 6:21-22, Phil 3:19.

[204]So also Talbert, *Reading Corinthians*, 119.

Argument 2: Paul's Foolish Boast (11:16-12:13)[205]

Having discussed the true nature of his rivals, Paul is now ready to take up the theme that was mentioned in 10:8-10 as the second topic to be expected in the *probatio*: Paul's boasting. That theme had been introduced in 11:1, to which πάλιν λέγω in v. 16 points. 11:1 had asked them to put up with some foolishness (ἀφροσύνης) from him; now that he is picking up that topic,[206] he wants to make sure that they do not

---

[205]The majority of rhetorical analysis done on 2 Corinthians 10-13 has focused on this section. Betz (*Der Apostel* and *Paul's Apology: II Cor. 10-13 and the Socratic Tradition*, Center For Hermeneutical Studies Colloquy No. 2 [Berkeley, 1970]) spends much of his work discussing this section of boasting as part of Paul's socratic defense against charges of being a false philosopher. One criticism of Betz's analysis is that it doesn't take enough account of how Paul seems to be answering his opponents "in kind;" he boasts, because they are already boasting. S. H. Travis (*Paul's Boasting in 2 Corinthians 10-12*, Studia Evangelica, No. VI [Berlin: Akademic Verlag, 1973]) sees this as a parody of boasting, but from Hebrew rather than Greek models. While his study broadens our understanding of the context of "boasting," it is not clear that his study clarifies Paul's rhetorical strategy in these verses. J. Zmijewski (*Der Stil der paulinischen "Narrenrede"* [Cologne: Peter Hanstein, 1978]) has explored the literary form of this section, but has used modern literary theory rather than ancient models. J. Paul Sampley, "Paul, His Opponents in 2 Corinthians 10-13, and the Rhetorical Handbooks," has provided a helpful study of the extent to which Paul follows the guidelines laid out in the handbooks for obtaining good-will from one's audience. Judge ("Paul's Boasting") discusses these verses as a parody of the rhetorical practice of self-advertisement; Forbes ("Comparison"), much in agreement with Judge, also sees this section as a parody of hellenistic practices, with the addition that Paul has been charged as a "flatterer," and responds that his opponents were pretentious imposters. The studies by Judge and Forbes are particularly helpful, though we will disagree with them as to where parody is to be found, and where Paul is being more straightforward.

[206]Though Paul has indicated in the *propositio* that the topic of who truly belongs to Christ would be part of his argument, 11:2-15 does have the appearance of being a digression, since 11:16 resumes a subject introduced in 11:1. Cf. Quintilian 4.2.104: "And if we do introduce a digression, it must always be short and of such a nature that we give the impression of having been forced from our proper course by some uncontrollable emotion." Such a description would seem appropriate for 11:2-15.

misinterpret what he is about to do: he is not a fool, he only plays one.[207] Martin[208] points out that the ἄφρων is not one who is "dimwitted," but is one who has lost the correct μέτρον of self and world. In the eyes of Paul's opponents, he lacked what it took to be an apostle, and so in his ministry he acted beyond his proper μέτρον, he acted the part of ἄφρων. Paul, for now, is willing to concede that point, and he will play out that role by boasting.

Paul's boasting in this section has been compared to the guidelines for "proper" boasting in Plutarch's *On Praising Oneself Inoffensively*.[209] To boast about oneself is "offensive" (539 B), "held in the greatest contempt" (540 A), and "most unstatesmanlike" (545 D).[210] Yet Plutarch recognizes that there are times when self-praise is necessary and justified, and so may be done without blame, especially if "mistaken praise injures and corrupts by arousing emulation of evil and inducing the adoption of an unsound policy where important issues are at stake" (545 D). Such would seem to match Paul's situation in 2 Corinthians 10-13, and so justify his self-praise according to hellenistic standards. The parallels between Plutarch's guidelines and Paul's strategy in 2 Corinthians 10-13 are impressive.[211] While such correspondence does not indicate a direct

---

[207]Bultmann, *Second Letter*, 210, where he also points out how the ἀνέχεσθέ μου in v. 1 is echoed by δέξασθέ με in v. 16. Note also that ἀνέχεσθε is used twice in this section, in vv. 19 and 20, making an additional connection back to v. 1.

[208]Martin, *2 Corinthians*, 362.

[209]In *Plutarch's Moralia* 7:110-167. Trans. Phillip H. De Lacy and Benedict Einarson (Cambridge: Harvard University, 1959). For discussions of this text in relation to Paul's boasting, see especially Betz, "Paul's Apology," 17; Forbes, "Comparison," 8-9; Talbert, *Reading Corinthians*, 118.

[210]Quintilian 11.1.15 also recognizes the problem: "In the first place, then, all kinds of boasting are a mistake, above all, it is an error for an orator to praise his own eloquence, and further, not merely wearies, but in the majority of cases disgusts the audience." For similar advice for the philosopher, see Epictetus *Disc.* 3.24.118.

[211]For example, Plutarch advises that "self-praise goes unresented if you are defending your good name or answering a charge" (540 C. Cf. 2 Cor 10:1-2, 10; 11:11; 12:13, 16); "a man reproached for his very triumphs is entirely pardonable and escapes all censure if he extols what he has done" (541 E. Cf. 2 Cor 11:7-11); one may praise another "whose general character is similar" (542 C. Cf. 2 Cor 12:2-5); one should redirect some of the credit to God (542 E. Cf. 2 Cor 12:9-10); one should include "certain minor shortcomings, failures, or faults" (543 F. Cf.

borrowing by Paul of this rhetorical tradition,[212] it seems clear that Paul would have been excused in this case for his boasting, and commended for the way in which he proceeds. Nevertheless, Paul is not in complete agreement with the tradition embodied in Plutarch.[213] Even though by hellenistic standards Paul's boasting is justified, it remains for him "foolishness" (Cf. 11:1, 16-17, 21, 23; 12:11).[214]

The boasting itself doesn't begin until v. 22; vv. 16-21 are "introduction" to the boast, so that the Corinthians will not miss the point. He wants them to receive him, even if it is as a fool, in order that he may boast a bit.[215] The implication is that boasting is done by fools, including his rivals in Corinth; but unlike them, Paul recognizes the foolishness. The τῶν ἀφρόνων in v. 19 are certainly Paul's rivals at Corinth,[216] and the Corinthians themselves may not escape being fools, as is indicated by the irony in vv. 19-21. The Corinthians are so "wise" that they can put up with abuse.[217] That irony is intensified by the proximity of ἀφρόνων and φρόνιμοι in v. 19.[218]

---

2 Cor 11:32-33, 12:7-8); one should show that one's position has come "with much hardship and peril" (544 D. Cf. 2 Cor 11:23-29).

[212]See Travis, *Paul's Boasting*; cf. also John Chrysostom, *Homilies* 24.3, who finds Paul's reasons for boasting vital; since Paul boasts for the benefit of his hearers, his actions are commendable. Chrysostom supports this practice not from hellenistic writers, but from the Old Testament: Samuel (1 Sam 12:3) and David (1 Sam 17:34-36) boast for the sake of others or of the truth. "For he that looks to the advantage of his hearers even though he should praise himself, not only deserves not to be found fault with, but even to be crowned."

[213]Cf. the critique by John Dillon in Betz's "Paul's Apology;" McCant, "Paul's Thorn of Rejected Apostleship," 559.

[214]Judge, "Paul's Boasting," 37-50; Travis, *Paul's Boasting*, 527-32; Forbes, "Comparison," 20; Talbert, *Reading Corinthians*, 118-119.

[215]μικρόν τι is no doubt a purposeful understatement, meant to ridicule the excessive claims being made by his rivals. Cf. Martin, *2 Corinthians*, 362.

[216]See Bultmann, *Second Letter*, 211. Referring to them in v. 20 with the indefinite pronoun may be an example of the rhetorical strategy of "non-naming" one's opponents in order to rob them of status. See Furnish, *II Corinthians*, 511.

[217]The litany of their abuse is given added weight by the careful construction of v. 20b: by the five-fold repetition of εἰ τις + verb (anaphora), and by the assonance of the end of each phrase (οι, ει, ει, αι, ει). Cf. Martin, *2 Corinthians*, 364. Note the advice in *Ad Her.* 1.4.8: "We shall make our adversaries unpopular by setting forth their violent behavior, their dominance . . . ."

[218]Furnish, *II Corinthians*, 497.

In v. 21, Paul (again ironically) apologizes for being too weak to abuse them the way they want. This theme of "weakness" will become vital in Paul's strategy for leading the Corinthians to a more adequate vision of apostolic authority, but for now that theme is suspended. The boasting that Paul will do first will be κατὰ σάρκα (v. 18), which is always ἐν ἀφροσύνῃ (v. 17). This boasting, at least at first, will not be κατὰ κύριον, not the boasting ἐν κυρίῳ of 10:17. Paul will, eventually, come to that; but not yet. For now, Paul will demonstrate that he too can be bold (τολμῶ κἀγώ, v. 21), if that is what they want. He threatened to do this when he comes to Corinth (10:2), and now he will demonstrate that he is able to follow through.[219]

There has been a difference of opinion among scholars over how the boast of 11:22-29 should be understood. Some have understood this to be a parody of the claims of Paul's opponents; while they no doubt boasted in successes and victories, Paul boasts in his sufferings.[220] Others have read this boasting in difficulties as a standard method in gaining goodwill from an audience, a tactic probably used by Paul's rivals as well.[221]

While it is true that the context of this list is highly ironic, it does not follow that this list should be read as a parody of the opponents' grand claims.[222] Paul's letters contain several other lists of hardships, without

---

[219]Martin, *2 Corinthians*, 369.

[220]Bultmann, *Second Letter*, 215; Plummer, *Second Epistle*, 322; Furnish, *II Corinthians*, 532-33, 535-36; E. A. Judge, "St. Paul and Classical Society," *Jahrbuch für Antike und Christentum* 15 (1972): 35; idem, "St. Paul and Socrates," 114; Georgi, *Opponents of Paul*, 279-80; Forbes, "Comparison," 18-19; Garland, "Paul's Apostolic Authority," 378-79; Witherington, *Conflict & Community*, 452 (here, not a direct parody of the opponents' claims, but of Augustus' *res gestae*).

[221]John T. Fitzgerald, *Cracks in an Earthen Vessel: An Examination of the Catalogues of Hardships in the Corinthian Correspondence*, SBLDS 99 (Atlanta: Scholars, 1988), 24-25,; Sampley, "Paul, His Opponents," 168; Talbert, *Reading Corinthians*, 122; Danker, *II Corinthians*, 180-81 (understood as Paul assuming the role of the "endangered benefactor"); Witherington, *Conflict & Community*, 450; Glenn Holland, "Speaking Like a Fool: Irony in 2 Corinthians 10-13," in *Rhetoric and the New Testament: Essays From the 1992 Heidelberg Conference*, JSNT Sup. 90 (Sheffield: JSOT, 1993), 259.

[222]Contra Garland, "Paul's Apostolic Authority," 379.

any apparent parody being intended.[223] Indeed, such listings of hardships are recommended in the rhetorical handbooks:

> We shall win good-will . . . if we dilate on the misfortunes which have befallen us or the difficulties which still beset us;[224]

> From the discussion of our own person we shall secure goodwill by praising our services without arrogance and revealing also our past conduct toward the republic, or toward our parents, friends, or the audience . . . ; likewise by setting forth our disabilities, need, loneliness and misfortune.[225]

Furthermore, Plutarch advises:

> For it is with reputation and character as with a house or an estate: the multitude envy those thought to have acquired them at no cost or trouble; they do not envy those who have purchased them with much hardship and peril.[226]

This is the kind of boasting that Paul undertakes in 11:23-29. Vv. 23-27 speak of what Paul has endured in the past; vv. 28-29, as *Ad Her.* advised, move on to present distress.[227]

It was common for philosophers to list the difficulties they had endured and overcome. The tradition can be seen as early as Plato:

> What they will say is this, that such being his disposition the just man will have to endure the lash, the rack, chains, the branding iron in his eyes, and finally, after every extremity of suffering, he will be crucified, and so will learn his lesson that not to be but to seem just is what we ought to desire.[228]

Perhaps closer to Paul's list are those from the Stoic tradition:

> The sage of the Stoics is not impeded when confined and under no compulsion when flung down a precipice and not in torture when on the

---

[223]Rom 8:35-39; 1 Cor 4:9-13; 2 Cor 4:8-9, 6:4-10, 12:10a.
[224]Cicero *De Inv.* 1.16.22.
[225]*Ad Her.* 1.5.8.
[226]Plutarch *On Praising Oneself Inoffensively* 544 D.
[227]Cf. Sampley, "Paul, His Opponents," 168.
[228]Plato *Republic* II.361 E.

rack and not injured when mutilated and is invincible when thrown in wrestling and is not blockaded by circumvallation and is uncaptured while his enemies are selling him into slavery.[229]

Or again:

> Do you not know that in the long course of time many different things must needs happen; fever must overcome one man, a brigand another, a tyrant a third? Because such is the character of the air about us, such that of our associates; cold and heat and unsuitable food, and journeys by land and by sea, and winds and all manner of perils; this man they destroy, that man they drive into exile, another they send on an embassy, and yet another on a campaign.[230]

Paul's list of hardships in 2 Corinthians 11:23-29 certainly stands out from these other examples by the length and the degree to which Paul develops this theme; perhaps even more importantly, Paul's list is unrelieved by any mention of what Paul accomplished despite such hardships, and there is no thought of boasting in Stoic "indifference" (ἀταραξία).[231] These hardships are not so much overcome as they are endured in faith and obedience as Paul lives out his call to be an apostle. Despite those differences, the form that Paul is using would have been recognizable to the Corinthians.[232]

---

[229]Plutarch *Conspectus of the Essay, "The Stoics Talk More Paradoxically than the Poets"* 1057 E, cited by Furnish, *II Corinthians*, 281. Furnish also notes Epictetus *Disc.* 3.29.24, Dio Chrysostom *Or.* 8.16, Seneca *Moral Epistles* 30.3 as providing parallels to Paul's list of hardships. See also Epictetus *Disc.* 1.1.22-25, 4.24, 11.33, 18.22-23; 2.19.24; Horace *Satires* 2.7.83-87; Seneca *De Providentia* 6.1-9, *Ep.* 82.14; Robert Hodgson, "Paul the Apostle and First Century Tribulation Lists," *ZNW* 74 (1983): 67, 77-80; Witherington, *Conflict & Community*, 388.

[230]Epictetus *Disc.* 3.24.28, cited by Danker, *II Corinthians*, 185. Danker notes that such lists are part and parcel of the figure of benefactor, and are used by philosophers in the role of the "ultimate benefactors of humanity."

[231]See Hodgson, "Tribulation Lists," 68; Witherington, *Conflict & Community*, 388.

[232]Wolfgang Schrage, "Leid, Kreuz und Eschaton: Die Peristasenkataloge als Merkmale paulinischer theologia crucis und Eschatologie," *EvT* 34 (1974): 141-75 argues that these lists find their roots for Paul not in Greco-Roman philosophy, but in Jewish apocalyptic traditions. Schrage's primary mistake is to assume that Paul could not draw upon and combine these traditions. See Fitzgerald, *Cracks*, 28-30; Garrett, "God of This World," 99; Hodgson, "First Century Lists," 60; Steven J.

Thus it is certainly possible, if not likely, that Paul's rivals had been engaging in this kind of boast. The comparative mode of Paul's boast (note especially v. 23b) makes it likely that Paul's rivals were similarly boasting of what they had suffered; Paul is answering them in kind, and showing that he can outdo them.[233] This list should not be read as a parody; Paul is here boasting κατὰ σάρκα (11:18), as the world boasts. Though his unrelieved listing of such suffering and even social degradation may have made his readers uncomfortable by the end of the list, this should not first and foremost be read (yet) as "boasting in weakness" (v. 30). Paul is here listing what he has endured in his faithful obedience as an apostle,[234] a listing which is intended not to parody but to match and overwhelm the claims of his opponents, to add to Paul's own *ethos* in the eyes of the Corinthians, as well as to create *pathos* in his hearers.[235]

The boast is carefully constructed to have its rhetorical effect and to show the Corinthians that Paul can engage in this kind of contest, foolish though it is. The boast is introduced by the assonance of v. 21b: λέγω τολμῶ κἀγώ.[236] The four rhetorical questions that follow, together with their answers, show an ascending pattern both in number of syllables (7-9-9-12)[237] and in number of words (3-3-4-5).[238] The crescendo created rhythmically is reinforced in the fourth element by the change in the answer from κἀγώ to ὑπὲρ ἐγώ; Paul is not simply claiming equality, but superiority, a move for which Paul has already prepared the readers by the scathing attack of 11:13-15. The climax of these questions is further indicated by the parenthetical παραφρονῶν λαλῶ in v. 23. To be

---

Kraftchick, "Death in Us, Life in You: The Apostolic Medium," in *Pauline Theology Vol. II: 1 & 2 Corinthians* (Minneapolis: Fortress, 1993), 171-72.

[233]So also Holland, "Speaking Like a Fool," 259.

[234]Cf. Käsemann, "Die Legitimatät," 54-55; Michael L. Barré, "Paul As Eschatological Person," *CBQ* 37 (1975): 501.

[235]If Paul's purpose for the hardship list here is to create a certain *ethos* to counteract his opponents' claims, then it is significant that in the Pauline letters it is only those hardship lists in 2 Cor 10-13 (11:23b-29, 12:10a) which are grammatically singular; all the others (Rom 8:35-39; 1 Cor 4:9-13; 2 Cor 4:8-9, 6:4-10) are plural.

[236]See Martin, *2 Corinthians*, 372.

[237]The parenthetical παραφρονῶν λαλῶ in v. 23 is not included in these counts; but it too, as we will see, serves to create a crescendo in v. 23a.

[238]See Barré, "Paul as Eschatological Person," 525 n. 11.

διάκονος Χριστοῦ is obviously for Paul the highest claim in this list. If the opponents have claimed this designation for themselves, Paul is willing to reflect their claim in his boast. Yet he is clearly not comfortable with it: he points out not only the insanity of such boasting, but also the insanity of attributing this status to his rivals at Corinth.[239]

The remainder of v. 23 is made up of four phrases, each introduced by ἐν. Here too a progression can be observed as the difficulties mentioned become more severe: κόποις, φυλακαῖς, πληγαῖς, θανάτοις.[240] Vv. 24-25 then serve to make more explicit the kinds of θανάτοις in which Paul has found himself.[241] The numbers included in vv. 24-25 will serve to increase the *pathos* of this recounting.[242]

Just as ἐν θανάτοις πολλάκις in v. 23 served as a heading for vv. 24-25, so too ὁδοιπορίαις πολλάκις at the beginning of v. 26 serves as a heading for the things listed in the remainder of that verse: these are all examples of the dangers Paul has faced while "on the road."[243] This list too is highly structured. The first four phrases each end in a genitive indicating source (the second two including the preposition ἐκ/ἐξ), followed by four phrases introduced with ἐν. The repetition of κινδύνοις at the beginning of each phrase further heightens the effect of this listing.[244] The difficulties mentioned here also seem to come to a

---

[239]Ibid., 506 n. 17; Plummer, *Second Epistle*, 321. Thus Barrett, *Second Epistle*, 294 is not correct in claiming that Paul's use of this title here indicates that he has turned his attention from the rivals in Corinth to the leaders in Jerusalem; see Martin, *2 Corinthians*, 373.

[240]Such a progression in severity is noted by Martin, *2 Corinthians*, 369, 376. Such listings were used to give "pathetic amplification" (Kennedy, *New Testament Interpretation*, 90-91) to one's speech. Kennedy directs attention to the discussion of *frequentatio* in *Ad Her.* 4.40.52, and of συναθροισμός *(congerie,* or "accumulation") in Quintilian 8.4.27. Here, however, Quintilian's discussion of another form of amplification (*incrementum*) seems more appropriate: "It is also possible to heighten our style less obviously, but perhaps yet more effectively, by introducing a continuous and unbroken series in which each word is stronger than the last" (Quintilian 8.4.8).

[241]So also Barré, "Paul as Eschatological Person," 505.

[242]One should note also the pattern in v. 25: three times - one time - three times - one time (clearly implied, though not stated explicitly with ἅπαξ). For the use of numbers in hellenistic lists of exploits, see Furnish, *II Corinthians*, 515.

[243]So also Martin, *2 Corinthians*, 378; cf. Windisch, *Der zweite Korintherbrief,* 357; Barré, "Paul as Eschatological Person," 504.

[244]A good example of the rhetorical figure of "anaphora." Cf. Quintilian

climax at the end, with κινδύνοις ἐν ψευδαδέλφοις. It is difficult not to connect this word with the ψευδαπόστολοι in 11:13; both words may well have been coined by Paul. The climax then is reached when Paul points out how these same people whom the Corinthians have welcomed into their community have caused him such trouble.[245] Thus the *pathos* of this list is increased.

At the beginning of v. 27, we should read κόπῳ καὶ μόχθῳ as the third heading in this list,[246] and understand the rest of v. 27 as examples of what Paul has had to endure because of his "toil and labor."[247] This verse undoubtedly addresses an issue the Corinthians found disturbing: that Paul chose to work with his own hands to support himself financially. The same phrase is used in this sense in 1 Thess 2:9, and the related verb κοπιῶμεν in 1 Cor 4:12 is described as ἐργαζόμενοι ταῖς ἰδίαις χερσίν. Paul's way of not allowing himself to become anyone's "client" has not been easy:[248] it has meant that he has endured "many a sleepless night, hungry and thirsty, often without food, cold and naked."[249]

Just as we noted a progression toward a climax in the rhetorical questions of vv. 22-23a, and in the lists of v. 23b and v. 26, so too the list in v. 27 may be intended to climax with the mention of "nakedness." Paul probably intends, of course, not actually being without clothing, but being

---

9.3.30. See Danker, *II Corinthians*, 183: "The effect is one of an avalanche of suffering that climaxes in the rhetorical questions in v. 29."

[245] So also Zmijewski, *Der Stil*, 259; Martin, *2 Corinthians*, 379. This is more likely than the more general references to false brethren understood here by Bultmann, *Second Letter*, 217 and Barrett, *Second Epistle*, 299-300.

[246] So also Martin, *2 Corinthians*, 380. Cf. Furnish, *II Corinthians*, 537.

[247] Undoubtedly to be read together as one thought, a figure called συνωνυμία in Quintilian 9.3.45; cf. Danker, *II Corinthians*, 183. The rhyme of the pair increases its effect.

[248] Contra Judge, "Early Christians," 126-27, it is not the case that "Paul provided himself with a secure social position, consciously or unconsciously, by adopting the conventions of the sophistic profession." Paul's insistence upon self-support meant that he did not travel among the elite, and it did not give him a financially comfortable life. See 1 Cor 9:19, 2 Cor 11:7; Hock, *Social Context*, 37.

[249] We should note again the careful way in which Paul has constructed this portion of his list. It begins with a pair of words (κόπῳ καὶ μόχθῳ), followed by a single word modified by πολλάκις; then another pair (λιμῷ καὶ δίψει), followed again by a single word modified by πολλάκις; the list then ends with a final pair of words (ψύχει καὶ γυμνότητι).

ill-clothed as a result of his decision to support himself with what his hands can earn.[250] Yet it is also a word that carries with it, from the Hebrew tradition, a particular burden of shame.[251] It is characteristic of those defeated, taken prisoner, and led off in shame (Is 20:2-4; 2 Macc 11:12); by extension, it becomes a description of those who are defeated by God and come under condemnation (Ezek 23:29, Hos 2:3, Amos 2:16, Mic 1:8; cf. also Heb 4:13; Rev 3:17, 16:15, 17:16). Thus v. 27 reaches its climax with a term that emphasizes the loss of dignity and status that Paul willingly accepted for the sake of his apostolic ministry.

Paul's list ends in v. 28 by his mentioning, besides all the things he could have said but has passed over,[252] something that again (as with ψευδαδέλφοις in v. 26) points directly to the Corinthian situation: Paul has to worry about his churches (and apparently had to worry about the Corinthians more than about the rest!).[253] Paul ends the list on a note that will increase the *pathos* of this listing by letting the Corinthians know that they have laid yet another burden on the back of their apostle.[254]

Paul's hardship list is followed in v. 29 by two rhetorical questions which highlight again the suffering that comes as a part of his apostolic ministry. Barré's attempts to argue that both these questions deal with Paul's (and his opponents') claims to be involved in the great eschatological struggle are finally not convincing.[255] His argument relies too much on dubious chiastic connections between v. 29 and vv. 20-21; to read ἀσθενεῖ / ἀσθενῶ and σκανδαλίζεται as boasts about being engaged in eschatological struggle relies on the doubtful suggestion that

---

[250]So Hock, *Social Context*, 84 n. 94; Furnish, *II Corinthians*, 519. The description of the true philosopher as one who was ill-clothed is common in hellenistic writings; Furnish notes Epictetus *Disc.* 3.22.45-47; Lucian *The Cock* 9 and *The Downward Journey* 20. Note also 1 Cor 4:11, where "nakedness" is found in another hardship list, accompanied as in our passage by hunger and thirst, and by the strain of manual labor.

[251]Cf. Martin, *II Corinthians*, 380.

[252]The most probable meaning of χωρὶς τῶν παρεκτός; see the discussion in Martin, *2 Corinthians*, 381.

[253]So also Martin, *2 Corinthians*, 391.

[254]The degree to which Paul wants to emphasize this final point can be seen in the way in which he stretches out the expression, giving it additional weight: article-noun (ἡ ἐπίστασίς μοι), article-adjectival phrase (ἡ καθ᾽ ἡμέραν), article-noun (ἡ μέριμνα).

[255]Barré is followed by Forbes, "Comparison," 20. See the criticism in Furnish, *II Corinthians*, 520.

the interrogative pronouns in v. 29 must be read as a reference to the same people indicated by the indefinite pronouns in vv. 20-21; finally, to argue that πυροῦμαι in v. 29 must have an eschatological reference fails to account for the wider use of this verb in other hellenistic writings where it does have a "psychological" meaning,[256] which fits this context better.

Paul has been accused of being weak (10:10). He is willing to accept that charge, in the sense that he willingly joins himself to those who are weak.[257] When members of his churches are made to stumble, as is happening with the Corinthians, Paul burns with anger against those who would destroy his work.[258]

Paul has finished his boasting κατὰ σάρκα, and in v. 30 signals a shift in his approach.[259] Paul had been charged with being weak (10:10); he sarcastically told the Corinthians, at the beginning of this "fool's boast," that he was too weak to abuse them (11:21); he closed the hardship list with the claim of joining his children in their weakness. Paul is now ready to pick up that theme in earnest. He is weak; he will not

---

[256]For example, in 2 Macc 4:38, 10:35, 14:45; Philo *Vit. Mos.* 2.280, it is used to describe anger; in 3 Macc 4:2, it is used to describe grief; in Philo *Leg. All.* 1.84, it is used to describe thanksgiving.

[257]Forbes, "Comparison," 19, is certainly correct in noting that "weakness" should not be understood only in psychological terms. "Weak" and "strong" carry connections to the social structure; the "weak" are those who are seen as lacking status; the "strong" are those who enjoy status. Thus, Paul's "weakness" is not his own awareness of inadequacy, but his acceptance of humiliation in the eyes of others.

[258]Cf. Martin, *2 Corinthians*, 382-83. So also Bruce, *I & II Corinthians*, 244; Barrett, *Second Epistle*, 302; Furnish, *II Corinthians*, 520.

[259]This reading understands 11:30 as looking ahead to the boast that Paul is about to make, and not a comment on the preceding section; this is in agreement with Philip E. Hughes, *Paul's Second Epistle to the Corinthians* (Grand Rapids: Eerdmans, 1962), 418; Bruce, *I & II Corinthians*, 244; Talbert, *Reading Corinthians*, 122; Danker, *II Corinthians*, 185; Witherington, *Conflict & Community*, 458; Best, *Second Corinthians*, 115; Holland, "Speaking Like a Fool," 260; contra Windisch, *Der zweite Korintherbrief*, 362; Bultmann, *Second Letter*, 217-18; Furnish, *II Corinthians*, 539; Martin, *2 Corinthians*, 383; Barrett, *Second Epistle*, 302; Forbes, "Comparison," 20; Hafemann, "Self-Commendation," 86-87. Bultmann's comment (*Second Letter*, 218), though written concerning 12:1, actually fits the transition at 11:30 better: "Paul now drops the motif of comparison, and the καυχᾶσθαι ἐν ταῖς ἀσθενείαις motif becomes the theme. With this feature the ἀφροσύνη is actually abandoned, since the καυχᾶσθαι is no longer κατὰ σάρκα (v. 18)."

shrink from that charge, but will in fact make that his boast; he will show that this is in fact "boasting in the Lord" (10:17), since Paul is the apostle of the Christ who was crucified in weakness (13:4). That this startling approach is in fact the one to which Paul commits himself is confirmed by a solemn oath (11:31).[260]

Though the short narrative in 11:32-33 has been seen by some as being out of place, either an afterthought (another adversity to add to the list)[261] or even an interpolation,[262] it makes perfect sense as the beginning of Paul's boasting according to "weakness," as vv. 30-31 indicated he would do.[263] While the boasts in 11:22-29 were not meant to parody directly the claims of Paul's opponents, here the boast does become such a parody.[264]

The suggestion that 11:32-33 is a conscious reversal of the Roman military award for the first soldier to scale the enemy's walls (the *corona muralis*) is compelling.[265] Residents of an important Roman colony and political center such as Corinth would have been familiar with the award; there is a statue from Corinth dated from the late first to early second century wearing such a crown.[266] While awards were given to the first one up the wall, Paul tells how he came down the wall—and that in a

---

[260]It is not clear whether one should read the oath primarily with v. 30 (Barrett, *Second Epistle*, 302; Furnish, *II Corinthians*, 540; Martin, *Second Corinthians*, 384) or with vv. 32-33 (Bruce, *I & II Corinthians*, 244; Witherington, *Conflict & Community*, 458). The previous use of an oath to guarantee the nature of Paul's boasting (11:10) seems to weigh in favor of the former interpretation (so Martin). An oath is often prompted by the crucial point in the issue under consideration or the point where the vulnerability in one's argument is sensed; see J. Paul Sampley, "'Before God I Do Not Lie' (Gal. 1:20): Paul's Self-Defense in the Light of Roman Legal Praxis," *NTS* 23 (1977): 481-82.

[261]Hans Lietzmann, *An die Korinther*, 151. Cf. Bultmann, *Second Letter*, 218: "Is it then a simple addition to verses 23-29? We see no reason for it."

[262]Windisch, *Der zweite Korintherbrief*, 363-64.

[263]Cf. Furnish, *II Corinthians*, 541. Thus vv. 32-33 are not a "climax" or "continuation" of the list in 11:22-29 (Martin, *2 Corinthians*, 383), nor a movement from the general description of 11:22-29 to a specific example (Forbes, "Comparison," 20; Sampley, "Paul's Opponents," 168).

[264]Betz, *Der Apostel*, 70-100.

[265]See Judge, "Paul's Boasting," 47; Furnish, *II Corinthians*, 542; Travis, *Paul's Boasting*, 530; Martin, *2 Corinthians*, 372; Forbes, "Comparison," 20-21; Talbert, *Reading Corinthians*, 123.

[266]Furnish, *II Corinthians*, 542.

basket!²⁶⁷ Paul has already used military imagery in this letter (10:4-5) as part of the *ethos* he presents to the Corinthians. 11:32-33 should be read with those earlier images still in mind.²⁶⁸   It signals a surprising modification of that earlier *ethos*;²⁶⁹ Paul is now boasting in weakness.

The strategy of parody continues with the narrative of Paul's visit to Paradise in 12:1-4.²⁷⁰ It is an event which Paul does not precipitate,²⁷¹ and in which he has no active role: he is "caught up" (passive in both vv. 2 & 4).²⁷² He doesn't even know his own condition during the event.²⁷³ Although it is introduced as an example of "visions and revelations" (v. 1), Paul sees nothing to report, and hears only what cannot be reported (v. 4). Though the mystery religions certainly valued secret revelations,²⁷⁴ it is not likely that the Corinthians would here admire Paul's piety in not revealing this mystery.²⁷⁵ Even the secrets of the mystery religions were

---

²⁶⁷Danker's suggestion (*II Corinthians*, 185-86) that this episode shows how much Paul endures, rather than showing his humiliation, confuses the tactic in 11:23-29 with the section that begins at 11:30.

²⁶⁸See Martin, *2 Corinthians*, 384-85, 387; Witherington, *Conflict & Community*, 459 n. 79.

²⁶⁹Furnish, *II Corinthians*, 542.

²⁷⁰Danker (*II Corinthians*, 189-90) notes that the theme of *apotheosis* was a common one in the Greco-Roman world. Quintilian 6.2.29-30 notes the emotional impact of relating visions in one's speech.

²⁷¹Whether Paul's use of the third person in this description is explained from rabbinic practice (Talbert, *Reading Corinthians*, 123) or from hellenistic rhetorical tradition (as a way of boasting about someone else with whom the speaker could be compared rather than praising oneself directly; cf. Plutarch, *On Praising Oneself Inoffensively*, 542 C-D; Furnish, *II Corinthians*, 544; Danker, *II Corinthians*, 188 points to Demosthenes *De Corona*, 321), it is surely Paul himself that has experienced this (cf. 12:7).

²⁷²Cf. Bultmann, *Second Letter*, 222: "It is a mere happening toward which Paul need take no position, from which no consequences follow for his activity . . . . Precisely because the experience is a mere happening for which Paul is not responsible, he may boast of it." See also Talbert, *Reading Corinthians*, 123; Best, *Second Corinthians*, 118.

²⁷³The repetition about not knowing whether he was in or out of the body probably should be read as "contribut[ing] to the satirical tone by adding a note of feigned suspense at the threshold of the ultimate disclosure." (Danker, *II Corinthians*, 190).

²⁷⁴Cf. Apuleius *Metamorphoses* 11.23; Barrett, *Second Epistle*, 311; Furnish, *II Corinthians*, 527; Martin, *2 Corinthians*, 405.

²⁷⁵Suggested by Danker, *II Corinthians*, 191.

shared with the fellow members of the cult.[276] The "sealed revelations" of the Jewish tradition are reported only as those revelations themselves are (finally) disclosed.[277] Paul reports a revelation that reveals nothing; such things are not where Paul finds the basis for his ministry, and he doesn't want the Corinthians' attention focused on such things either.

Yet Paul, no doubt ironically, goes on to worry that perhaps because of this "revelation," people will think too highly of him for the wrong reasons. Paul has not, in fact, refrained from boasting (v. 6), and "abundance of revelations" (v. 7a) is hardly how the Corinthians would describe an event which happened fourteen years earlier, and which had no point that could be told.[278] However, Paul's concern through this irony is genuine: what the Corinthians see and hear from Paul in his apostolic ministry is what they need to consider (λογίσηται, v. 6).[279]

The third parody is the story of Paul's non-healing, 12:7-9.[280] Paul presents the Corinthians with the paradox of an apostle who cannot heal himself of whatever the "thorn in the flesh" was. The σκόλοψ τῇ σαρκί has been interpreted as: 1) Some kind of spiritual or psychological distress. Thus the Vulgate translation as *stimulus carnis*, and Luther's suggestion (*Table Talk* 24.7) that Paul was referring to temptations of despair and doubt.[281] However, there is nothing in the context, or in the Pauline corpus, to suggest that such struggles weighed on Paul. 2) Physical illness or disability.[282] This had been suggested as early as Tertullian (*On Modesty* 13) and Irenaeus (*Against Heresies* 5.3.1). Modern scholars who support this understanding include Barrett,[283]

---

[276]Furnish, *II Corinthians*, 545; Lincoln, "Paul the Visionary," 216.

[277]Dan 12:4, 9; note also Is 8:16 (where the revelation is shared with the group) and Rev 10:2-4 (where the mention that some has been "sealed" is placed in the context of much that is reported).

[278]Holland, "Speaking Like a Fool," 262.

[279]Note the use of λογίζεσθαι, apparently a prominent word in the evaluations going on in Corinth; cf. 10:7, where it is also found with βλέπειν.

[280]Betz, *Der Apostel*, 92-93; Witherington, *Conflict & Community*, 461.

[281]These are cited by Talbert, *Reading Corinthians*, 124.

[282]Cf. Philo *Praem.* 119: those who follow virtue will be free from all disease, and any infirmity which they suffer is not for punishment, but "to remind the mortal that he is mortal, to humble his over-weening spirit and to improve his moral condition."

[283]Barrett, *Second Epistle*, 314-15.

Bruce,[284] Furnish,[285] Danker,[286] and Witherington.[287] Galatians 4:13-14 is often used to show that Paul suffered from a particular physical illness.[288] However, there the illness strikes one as something unexpected by Paul, not the kind of chronic problem that is indicated by 2 Cor 12:7 (note the present tense of κολαφίζη). 3) Paul's adversaries, who work to destroy his apostolic ministry. This interpretation was suggested by John Chrysostom.[289] It is followed by Munck,[290] Barré,[291] Loubser,[292] Forbes,[293] Murphy-O'Connor,[294] and Young & Ford.[295]

Though the Corinthians were probably more sure than we can be about what this σκόλοψ was,[296] this last suggestion seems to fit the best. The only other place where Paul uses κολαφίζειν is 1 Cor 4:11, where it clearly refers to hostility from those who oppose him (see 1 Cor 4:12-13).[297] Such persecution would not be something shared by the whole church, as suggested by Furnish[298] as a reason to reject this theory. Nor is it convincing to argue that Paul would not pray to have persecution removed, "since persecution was the fuel on which Paul seemed to thrive."[299] This was opposition which was endangering his own community, and Paul hardly sought out persecution! Nor is the aorist tense of παρεκάλεσα a reason that the σκόλοψ cannot be opponents, arguing that Paul is still wrestling with that problem in Corinth.[300] Paul

---

[284]Bruce, *I & II Corinthians*, 248.

[285]Furnish, *II Corinthians*, 549-50.

[286]Danker, *II Corinthians*, 193.

[287]Witherington, *Conflict & Community*, 462.

[288]For the range of specific ailments suggested by modern scholars, see Furnish, *II Corinthians*, 548-49; Martin, *2 Corinthians*, 413-16.

[289]*Homilies on 2 Corinthians*, 26.2, 29.2.

[290]Munck, *Paul and the Salvation of Mankind*, 186 n. 1.

[291]Michael L. Barré, "Qumran and the Weakness of Paul," *CBQ* 42 (1980): 216-27.

[292]Loubser, "A New Look," 515.

[293]Forbes, "Comparison," 21.

[294]Murphy-O'Connor, *Theology*, 119.

[295]Young and Ford, *Meaning and Truth*, 76.

[296]Martin, *Second Corinthians*, 416: "We will probably never know the truth or, at least, never know for sure we have the truth."

[297]So also Barré, "Qumran," 226.

[298]Furnish, *II Corinthians*, 549-50.

[299]Martin, *2 Corinthians*, 415.

[300]As argued by Witherington, *Conflict & Community*, 462 n. 97.

has had opposition follow him before, and the aorist tense may refer to his arrival at the realization that such opposition will not be removed. σκόλοψ in the LXX is used to describe personal enemies (see Num 33:55, Ezek 28:24). ἄγγελος σατανᾶ easily recalls from 11:13-15 the διάκονοι αὐτοῦ (i.e., σατανᾶς, who transforms himself into ἄγγελος φωτός, just as his ministers transform themselves). The short hardship list in 12:10 further clarifies Paul's weakness in this context with words that indicate the idea of hostility and opposition: ὕβρεσιν (and the opponents were certainly people of ὕβρις), ἀνάγκαις (and Paul is about to say, in v. 11, how the Corinthians have forced him [ἠναγκάσατε] to boast in this situation), διωγμοῖς καὶ στενοχωρίαις(with the first—and more specific—term giving further clarity to the meaning of the second).[301] If the reference here is to Paul's rivals (and at the moment, particularly his rivals in Corinth) being the σκόλοψ, the section further adds to the *pathos* in Paul's argument, just as ψευδαδέλφοις (11:26) and ἡ μέριμνα πασῶν τῶν ἐκκλησιῶν (11:28) have done.[302]

It is now, in this healing story without healing, that we finally get the oracle from the Lord that might have been expected in 12:1-4;[303] and it is a word affirming Paul's weakness![304] The weakness for which Paul was criticized (10:10) is not only Paul's boast (11:30); it is also the vehicle for God's own power, and the criterion of apostolic ministry.[305] This is what "boasting in the Lord" (10:17) is finally seen to be, because

---

[301]See also Barré, "Qumran," 225.

[302]David M. Park's suggestion ("Paul's ΣΚΟΛΟΨ ΤΗ ΣΑΡΚΙ: Thorn or Stake?," *NovT* 22 [1980]: 179-83) that σκόλοψ here should be understood as a military image (death by impaling) is provocative. It would match the military language Paul has used already in the letter. However, as painful as this σκόλοψ was for Paul, the image of Paul impaled by it seems more severe than this context can support (see Furnish, *II Corinthians*, 528-29; Martin, *2 Corinthians*, 412).

[303]The statement in 12:9 has a form similar to both Jewish and Greek oracles. See David E. Aune, *Prophecy in Early Christianity and the Ancient Mediterranean World* (Grand Rapids: Eerdmans, 1983), 249-50.

[304]See Lincoln, "Paul the Visionary," 218-19; Witherington, *Conflict & Community*, 463 n. 99. Philo *Vit. Mos.* 1.69 contains a similar declaration, "Your weakness is your strength." In Philo, however, the point seems to be that God makes up for the weakness of the people, and will rescue them. For Paul, the point is that God has chosen weakness as a vehicle for divine power.

[305]Cf. Käsemann, "Die Legitimatät," 60-64. Moule, *Idiom Book*, 15 notes that the perfect tense in 12:9 is a true perfect, and indicates that this is a statement which Paul considers to have continuing authority in his ongoing ministry.

Paul's weakness is nothing less than the place where the power of the crucified Lord is revealed (12:9; cf. 13:3-4).

12:11-13 forms a concluding section for Paul's foolish boasting. The two asyndetic clauses at the beginning of v. 11 come with the force of someone suddenly waking from a dream. Paul awakens from his foolishness, and is ready to call a halt to it. Here the role of the fool is dropped. There are several elements in 12:11-13 which recall the opening of the foolish boast, thus forming an *inclusio*[306] and marking this as the closure to that boast: ἄφρων in 12:11 recalls the ἀφροσύνη with which the boast began in 11:1; the claim not to be inferior (οὐδὲν γὰρ ὑστέρησα τῶν ὑπερλίαν ἀποστόλων)[307] in 12:11 recalls a similar claim (μηδὲν ὑστερηκέναι τῶν ὑπερλίαν ἀποστόλων) in 11:5; the ironic description of Paul's refusal to be a financial burden for the Corinthians as ἀδικίαν in 12:13 recalls 11:7, where Paul's practice was ironically labelled ἁμαρτίαν.

V. 12 gives the reason that Paul should have been commended by the Corinthians themselves (and the reason that he is certainly not inferior to these others): τὰ σημεῖα τοῦ ἀποστόλου were performed (by God, through Paul) among them. There is an important question, however, and considerable disagreement, over what Paul is referring to as "signs of an apostle," and over what the relationship is between these and the three dative nouns which close the verse: σημείοις τε καὶ τέρασιν καὶ δυνάμεσιν. Most scholars and translations have taken these as functioning to express means: "The apostolic signs were performed among you . . . , by signs and wonders and deeds of power."[308]

However, this interpretation is not entirely satisfactory. Though Paul clearly performed such deeds (see Rom 15:19, Gal 3:5), these are hardly the sort of criteria for which he has been arguing throughout this letter. More helpful is the suggestion that the three datives at the end of v. 12 should be understood as expressing accompaniment: "The marks of a true apostle were there, in the work I did among you, which called for such

---

[306]Cf. Talbert, *Reading Corinthians*, 115.

[307]Danker, *II Corinthians*, 197-98 notes the wordplay in the repeated οὐδέν of 12:11, and identifies it as an example of humor: In his nothingness he is still superior to these arrogant rivals. Cf. also Forbes, "Comparison," 22.

[308]Trans. from Furnish, *II Corinthians*, 552. See Windisch, *Der zweite Korintherbrief*, 553; Bultmann, *Second Letter*, 231; among translations, see KJV, TEV, JB, NRSV.

constant fortitude, and was attended by signs, marvels, and miracles."[309] Paul, then, is not saying that these are adequate signs of apostolic ministry, but that the signs of an apostle (preaching that planted the church, ministry carried out in the weakness of the Crucified) had been there along with the things others were claiming (or demanding)[310] as authorization. Yet the direction of interpretation indicated, for instance, by TEV seems strangely out of place here: "The many miracles and wonders that prove that I am an apostle were performed among you. . . ." Paul's entire argument to this point has been

> to build a case that there are more important criteria to determine whether or not a person is a true apostle . . . . Paul is pleading with the Corinthians to dispense with the secondary criteria (signs, wonders, mighty works) and judge would-be apostles by the yardstick of the primary criterion, namely, the *signa apostolica* of the crucified Jesus (13:1-4).[311]

That Paul is pointing beyond such miraculous signs as the (true) "signs of an apostle" is indicated by the phrase ἐν πάσῃ ὑπομονῇ. This points us back to the kind of ministry characterized by the experiences listed in 11:23-29.[312] A similar phrase stands at the head of a hardship list in 2 Cor 6:4-5. Thus, Paul's discussion of the "signs of an apostle" in 12:12 must be understood

> in einem bestimmten Horizont, nämlich in den des Abschnittes 11:23ff, mit seiner Aufzählung der geduldig ertragenen Christusleiden.[313]

At the close of this section, Paul touches on another of the criteria for apostolic ministry which the Corinthians were using and which had apparently become a particularly difficult issue between the Corinthians and Paul: the Corinthians' expectation that a true apostle would accept (and perhaps demand) monetary support from the church (v. 13). The

---

[309]Trans. from NEB. See Barrett, *Second Epistle*, 321; Martin, *2 Corinthians*, 436-37.

[310]It seems likely that it is the Corinthians who are looking for such "signs of an apostle" (cf. 13:3). While Paul's rivals were apparently willing to accept and fulfill such criteria, Paul himself was not. See Barrett, *Second Epistle*, 321.

[311]Martin, *2 Corinthians*, 428, 438.

[312]Furnish, *II Corinthians*, 555.

[313]Käsemann, "Die Legitimität," 63.

issue has come up in this letter before (11:7-12, 20), but the treatment has not been entirely adequate. V. 13 serves as a transition both to a more adequate treatment of this issue of financial support, and to the third and final section of the *probatio*.

Argument 3: Paul's Upcoming Visit (12:14-18)

Though there is an obvious connection between 12:13 and 12:14 (note the use of καταναρκάω in both verses), it is best to see v. 14 as the beginning of a new section.[314] The ἰδού[315] in v. 14 highlights Paul's return to something that had been a concern at the beginning of the letter: his return to Corinth (cf. 10:2, 11). In the light of this return, he picks up the topic re-introduced in v. 13: the issue of apostolic support. When Paul first dealt with this issue (11:7-12), his stated motivation for his continuing refusal of support from the Corinthians was so that his rivals (who demanded such support) could not claim to be just like him (11:12). Since then, through his foolish boast, Paul has shown that indeed there is no true comparison between himself and his rivals.

With that point secured, Paul returns to the discussion of support, but now he gives a different (and perhaps in his mind more adequate) motivation for his practice, which will remain consistent when he returns to Corinth: He is their father in Christ, a theme that has surfaced in this letter before (11:2). Paul states a generally accepted expectation that parents will support their children, and not the other way around.[316] Paul is willing to completely spend himself on their behalf.[317] As a parent, and not merely a client, Paul in fact wants more from the Corinthians than his rivals want: he seeks not their possessions, but their very selves. His

---

[314]Scholars who have treated v. 14 as the beginning of a new section include Bruce, Furnish, Danker, Talbert, Best; others have treated 11-18 as a single unit: Plummer, Barrett, Bultmann, Martin.

[315]Martin (*2 Corinthians*, 439) sees ἰδού as a sign of a new section; this contra Bultmann, *Second Letter*, 233.

[316]See Philo *Vit. Mos.* 2.245.

[317]The use of a simple verb form followed by an intensified form (here, δαπανήσω καὶ ἐκδαπανηθήσομαι) would be rhetorically effective, and is used elsewhere by Paul (1:13, ἢ ἃ ἀναγινώσκετε ἢ καὶ ἐπιγινώσκετε; 4:8, ἀπορούμενοι ἀλλ᾿ οὐκ ἐξαπορούμενοι. These cited by Furnish, *II Corinthians*, 558).

rhetorical question[318] at the end of v. 15 adds *pathos* to this section. Can the Corinthians be so unfeeling as to answer more love with less?[319]

ἔστω δέ at the beginning of v. 16 indicates something that can be agreed upon. Here, it looks ahead to the next phrase:[320] at least all can agree that Paul has not financially burdened them. In fact, it is not clear that the Corinthians would have formulated the statement in this way. It was obvious that Paul had not accepted their money, but they probably saw this as an insult. Paul's statement attempts to make common ground out of his interpretation of the situation: he has not burdened them.

In answer to the charge[321] that Paul has used the collection for Jerusalem as a covert means of getting the Corinthians' money,[322] Paul brings in Titus[323] as a witness. Presumably, the Corinthians hold Titus as

---

[318]Most have understood v. 15b as a question (Barrett, Bultmann, Danker, Furnish, TEV, NEB, JB, NIV, NRSV). The suggestion that it be read as a statement (KJV; E. B. Allo, *Saint Paul: seconde épître aux Corinthiens* [Paris: Gabalda, 1956]) is not as satisfactory, and fails to capture the irony and *pathos* here.

[319]It seems unlikely, though possible, that περισσοτέρως in v. 15 is meant to indicate that Paul loved the Corinthians more than his rivals did (though no doubt Paul would see it so); we might then expect an emphatic ἐγώ (see Bultmann, *Second Letter*, 234). Even less likely would be that Paul meant he loved the Corinthians more than he loved other churches; Paul is already fighting the appearance of such favoritism (11:7-11). Rather, the thought seems to be that the more Paul invests in his relationship with the Corinthians, the more hostility he receives. Now on the verge of visiting them again, he wonders what response his love will provoke.

[320]This is against A. T. Robertson, *A Grammar of the Greek New Testament in the Light of Historical Research* (Nashville: Broadman, 1923), 392; Witherington, *Conflict & Community*, 467; NIV. But the context here (esp. vv. 17-18) argues for reading οὐ κατεβάρησα ὑμᾶς as the position Paul suggests all can agree upon (Martin, *2 Corinthians*, 444).

[321]The way in which Paul reports this charge recalls language used earlier by Paul to describe his opponents (ἔλαβον recalls λαμβάνει in 11:20; πανοῦργος recalls πανουργία in 11:3; and δόλῳ recalls ἐργάται δόλιοι in 11:13). Perhaps this is Paul's final "sideways glance" at his rivals in Corinth. He is not the "crafty one" who "takes" them "by deceit." He has already shown that these are the traits of his opponents.

[322]For an example of such a scam, see Josephus *Ant*. 18.81-84; see also Lucian *The Runaways* 14, 20.

[323]For Titus' role in organizing the collection, see 2 Cor 8:6.

above reproach.[324] But Paul is the one who sent and encouraged Titus; they walk the same path. Paul then closes his *probatio* in vv. 17-18 with four rhetorical questions (the first two expecting a negative answer, the second two expecting a positive answer). This is all Paul can do. At this point, he leaves the issues of his opponents and of the suspicions about support and the collection behind. Paul is now ready to wind up his arguments with an impassioned *peroratio*.

PERORATIO: 12:19-13:10[325]

Quintilian (6.1.1) says that there are two forms of *peroratio*: that which summarizes the proofs already presented, and that which appeals to the emotions of the hearers.[326] Both appeals, of course, can and usually are combined in the *peroratio*. We will see such a combination in 2 Cor 12:19-13:10.

Though the theme of Paul's return to Corinth that appeared in 12:14 also shows up in 12:20-13:4, 10, a significant shift occurs at 12:19. First

---

[324]Correctly, Danker, *II Corinthians*, 203; Witherington, *Conflict & Community*, 468. The claim that Paul's associates were also coming under suspicion (Barrett, *Second Epistle*, 325; Martin, *2 Corinthians*, 446 [but cf. also p. 448!]) is not supported by anything in this context, and would in fact be contrary to Paul's strategy here: he appeals to Titus' irreproachable character.

[325]The discussions of the *peroratio* (ἐπίλογος) in the ancient handbooks are found in Aristotle *Rhetoric* 3.19; *Ad Her.* 2.30.47-31.50; Cicero *De Inv.* 1.52.98-56.109; Quintilian 6.1.1-55. Puskas identifies the *peroratio* as 12:14-13:10, which fails to recognize that the argument of 12:14-18 is a final and new contribution to the *probatio*; Witherington identifies the *peroratio* (of 2 Corinthians as a single unit) as 13:5-10, which ignores, as we shall see, the signs that the *peroratio* has begun with 12:19. Other scholars, though not identifying the unit as the *peroratio*, have seen the final major unit of this letter as 12:19-13:10 (Bruce, Bultmann, Martin).

We understand 13:11-13 as an epistolary postscript, and so outside this rhetorical analysis.

[326]Cicero *De Inv.* 1.52.98 lists three parts of the *peroratio*: 1) the *enumeratio* or *recapitulatio*, which is the summing up of the proofs; 2) the *indignatio*, or exciting ill-will against one's opponents; 3) the *conquestio*, or arousing sympathy or pity for oneself. The second and third of these appear to be treated by Quintilian as one topic. Paul, however, leaves behind any further attempt at this point to excite anger against his rivals; perhaps he thought that had been done sufficiently already (cf. 11:2-4, 12-15, 19-21).

of all, when the upcoming visit to Corinth is discussed in this section, it does not serve, as it did in 12:14, as part of the defense of Paul's actions, but rather as admonition and appeal to the Corinthians regarding what will happen when Paul comes.[327] Furthermore, in 12:19 Paul stops to look back over what he has said, and to make sure that the Corinthians do not misunderstand what this has been. A similar move at the beginning of the *peroratio* can be seen in Plato *Apology* 34 B:

> There, gentlemen, that, and perhaps a little more to the same effect, is the substance of what I can say in my defense. It may be that some one of you, remembering his own case, will be annoyed that whereas he, in standing his trial upon a less serious charge than this, made pitiful appeals to the jury with floods of tears, and had his infant children produced in court to excite the maximum of sympathy, . . . I on the contrary intend to do nothing of the sort . . . . Why do I not intend to do anything of this kind? . . . The point is that for my own credit and yours and for the credit of the state as a whole, I do not think that it is right for me to use any of these methods at my age and with my reputation . . . . I leave it to you and to God to judge me as it shall be best for me and for yourselves.[328]

Paul certainly has been forced into a position of defending his apostolic authority in Corinth. With that defense now finished, in 12:19 Paul begins to shift the rules of this confrontation, and to prevent any false conclusions being drawn by the Corinthians.[329]

12:19b explains why both parts of the Corinthians' possible misinterpretation, ὑμῖν ἀπολογούμεθα, are incorrect.[330] First, it is not to the Corinthians (ὑμῖν) that Paul is answerable, but to God (κατέναντι

---

[327]See Martin, *2 Corinthians*, 487.

[328]Trans. Hugh Tredennick, in *Plato. The Collected Dialogues*, ed. Edith Hamilton and Huntington Cairns (Princeton: Princeton University, 1961). See also Isocrates *Antidosis* 321-22.

[329]It is unclear whether 12:19 should be read as a question (with Calvin, KJV, NIV, NRSV) or as a statement (with Nestle/Aland, Luther, JB, NEB, TEV). Furnish, *2 Corinthians*, 560 may well be right in suggesting that 12:19 should be read as a statement, since to read it as a question would blunt the effect of the preceding questions, with which 12:19 does not belong. It makes little difference, however, which is chosen; in either case, Paul treats the interpretation of his words as a defense presented to the Corinthians as a possible misinterpretation, and one that he will now deny.

[330]See Bultmann, *Second Letter*, 237.

θεοῦ ἐν Χριστῷ λαλοῦμεν).[331] Paul will not recognize them as a judicial body, since they have no authority over him or his apostolic ministry; such a position belongs only to the Lord. Despite the foolishness into which he has been forced, "he does not have to answer to the Corinthians,"[332] and to present a defense to them would be to give too much credit where none is due.[333]

Secondly, Paul denies that he is, in reality, making an apology. To do so would be to play into the hands of his opponents, since then he would be acting out of self-interest.[334] Rather, all that he has done (primarily in this writing, but also in all of his actions with the Corinthians, despite their criticism of him) has been for the purpose of building them (ὑπὲρ τῆς ὑμῶν οἰκοδομῆς). In the opening section of the *peroratio* (12:19-21), Paul appeals primarily to the Corinthians' emotions: he seeks to arouse *pathos* in the form of both pity and fear. We should note that it is in 12:19 that Paul for the first and only time in this letter refers to his readers as ἀγαπητοί,[335] a word full of emotion and surely intended to draw an emotional response in return. Secondly, the list in 12:20 which describes the situation Paul fears he will find when he arrives seems intended to bring before the Corinthians the charges that

---

[331]Furnish, *II Corinthians*, 179 rightly says that this is not simply an oath formula intended to underscore the truth of Paul's words, as in Rom 9:1 or 2 Cor 11:10. Rather, this is an expression that all of Paul's apostolic ministry is placed before God (and God alone) for evaluation. Thus, this marks a return to the position Paul established in 1 Cor 4:1-5: Paul will not be judged by the Corinthians, or even by himself, but by God alone. Thus, this is more than the common appeal to the gods and heroes to witness to the truth of the speaker (see Isocrates *Or.* 2.46; Demosthenes *De Corona* 141, *Ep.* 2.16).

[332]Witherington, *Conflict & Community*, 468.

[333]See Furnish, *II Corinthians*, 566-67.

[334]Furnish, *II Corinthians*, 566-67; Martin, *2 Corinthians*, 458-59.

[335]The same address appears in 2 Cor 7:1, which according to our interpretation was originally a separate letter, and in every other Pauline letter except Galatians.

Paul himself may have to bring against them when he comes,[336] and is the beginning of the threat that Paul will clarify in the next section.

In 12:21, Paul describes the feared outcome of his next visit as his being humiliated again,[337] and his needing to mourn over his congregation.[338] They will be the cause of pain for their apostle. These words will evoke pity and sympathy from his congregation, unless they have lost all feeling for him.[339]

Yet Paul is not only trying to win their sympathy here; there is also a subtle threat to the Corinthians, but one that they could scarcely miss.[340] This time, if Paul is humbled, he will not be humbled as he was the previous time. This time, he will be humbled not by the Corinthians, but by God. What would this mean? It is unlikely that Paul is expressing simply his desire not to repeat his experience of failing to convince and

---

[336]As has been recognized by many, the list in v. 20 includes those things in particular that were likely to result from the situation Paul understood to be going on in Corinth with the coming of the rival apostles: the resulting divisive attitudes and actions, and the breakdown of trust within the community (see Barrett, *Second Epistle*, 329-30; Bultmann, *Second Letter*, 237; Furnish, *II Corinthians*, 567-68; Martin, *2 Corinthians*, 462; Danker, *II Corinthians*, 206).

The impact of the mutual dissatisfaction which will result if Paul finds such things in Corinth is intensified by the chiastic structure of 12:20a: A) οὐκ θέλω; B) εὑρῶ; B') εὑρεθῶ; A') οὐ θέλετε. Cf. Plummer, *Second Epistle*, 368; Furnish, *II Corinthians*, 561; Martin, *2 Corinthians*, 453.

[337]It is not entirely clear whether πάλιν should be connected with ἐλθόντος or with ταπεινώσῃ. However, it is probably better to take it with ταπεινώσῃ, since in the previous verse Paul has already mentioned that he is coming, and to say immediately he is coming "again" seems unnecessary (see Martin, *2 Corinthians*, 464-65; Furnish, *II Corinthians*, 562).

[338]The list of v. 21 which concentrates on sexual sins is probably not intended to indicate that Paul had another specific group in mind at Corinth (as suggested by Barrett, *Second Epistle*, 332), but that these sins were typical of pagan culture (and from 1 Corinthians, all too typical of the Corinthian congregation as well), and Paul is stressing that he will have to deal with any disruptions in the church that he finds (see Martin, *2 Corinthians*, 462).

[339]Quintilian 6.1.23 says that the appeal to emotions that will carry the most weight is the appeal to pity. Paul was charged with being "humiliated" (ταπεινός) among the Corinthians (10:1); now the prospect of that being repeated becomes part of Paul's appeal to the Corinthians. Once again, Paul has taken a criticism against himself and turned it into part of his argument.

[340]For a helpful treatment of how Paul's discussion of his upcoming visit functions as a threat, see Olson, "Confidence Expressions," 223-24.

be supported by his own congregation.[341] We should remember that v. 21a is parallel to v. 20a,[342] and so Paul's humiliation and mourning is parallel to the Corinthians finding Paul not as they want. Paul's words in v. 19b about the purpose behind his authority being for building up would surely recall his earlier words (10:8), which also included mention of using his authority for tearing down. From what Paul will say in 13:2, it is clear that Paul has no intention of "sparing" the Corinthians and leaving as he did the previous time. The "humiliation" that Paul fears now is that he will find the Corinthian church in such a state that he will have to exercise his authority in severe discipline against them; to have to resort to this action will mean that this letter, and in some sense his work and mission among them, have failed.[343] Paul's rivals considered it a mark of honor to be able to treat the community with harshness (11:20); if Paul must exercise his authority with harsh discipline, it will be humiliation for him.

   In the second section of the *peroratio* (13:1-4), Paul begins to move beyond emotional appeal (though there is still plenty of *pathos*, primarily in the form of fear, that may come from his words here) to a summary of Paul's main point in this argument.[344] Paul begins by reminding the Corinthians that he is about to make his third visit. 13:1 reflects the language already used at the end of the *probatio* in 12:14; but now, Paul's point is not that he will maintain the same financial policies, but that the time to bring this situation to resolution has arrived.[345] They have sought

----

[341]So Barrett, *Second Epistle*, 330; Bruce, *I & II Corinthians*, 252.

[342]Bultmann, *Second Letter*, 238-39. Bultmann is correct in connecting Paul's humiliation by God with his needing to be severe with his congregation; however, his suggestion that οὐ has dropped out of the text (thus Paul fears that God will not humble him again and thus not keep Paul's anger in check) is unnecessary and unwarranted.

[343]See Furnish, *II Corinthians*, 567; Martin, *2 Corinthians*, 465-66.

[344]Betz, *Galatians*, 313 notes that the *peroratio* is particularly important for interpretation. Since it is there that a writer will review the most important point or points that he/she wants noticed and remembered, the *peroratio* becomes key to understanding the major concern(s) of the letter. Cf. *Ad Her.* 2.30.47.

[345]It isn't entirely clear what Paul sees as the "two or three witnesses" which establish his case and his right to bring discipline (apparently referring to Deut 19:15, though not introduced with a formal citation formula. The same instruction appears, with perhaps even more similarity to 2 Cor 13:1, in Matt 18:16). Since 13:1 has specifically mentioned this as the third trip to Corinth, it seems best to understand each of the three visits (the founding visit, the "painful" visit, and the

proof that Christ speaks through Paul; though the boasting was foolish, he has provided such proof for them in this letter; he will provide further proof when he arrives by "not sparing" them (13:2b-3a). They may get "proof," but not the proof they want: not signs and wonders and performances for them to judge, but Paul's apostolic discipline.[346] He will not again leave Corinth, outshouted by his opponents and looking for another chance for reconciliation. This will be the decisive confrontation.

V. 4 brings Paul's review to what must be considered the principal thrust of his argument in this letter: his own weakness is connected with the weakness of the crucified Christ; and in that weakness God's power is active (12:9; note also 10:1). "With Christ himself ἀσθένεια and δύναμις are joined,"[347] because Christ willingly took upon himself the role of weakness (Phil 2:6-8), and by his resurrection was vindicated in power by God (Phil 2:9-11; Rom 1:4). Paul wants the Corinthians to see him in a similar way;[348] he has, up to this point, been "weak" with them (cf. 10:10); but whatever the Corinthians do, Paul will be vindicated by God (cf. 10:18). ζήσομεν in 13:4 certainly does not have an eschatological reference; the fact that it will be εἰς ὑμᾶς indicates that Paul is thinking of his upcoming visit to Corinth.[349]

---

upcoming visit) as three witnesses (Plummer, *Second Epistle*, 372; Windisch, *Der zweite Korintherbrief*, 413; Bruce, *I & II Corinthians*, 253). Martin (*2 Corinthians*, 469) doubts that the founding visit can be thought of as a "warning;" however, there is no reason that this could not be, since Paul certainly let them know from the beginning the need for discipline and the consequences of continuing sin and rebellion. Bultmann (*Second Letter*, 243) suggests that the three witnesses are the previous visit, this letter itself, (see also Martin, "Apostasy," 460 for the possibility of a letter counting as a "witness"), plus the upcoming visit. More important than identifying what Paul sees as these witnesses is to hear his point: "You have had due warning, as prescribed; I am now about to take action" (Barrett, *Second Epistle*, 333).

[346]See Martin, *2 Corinthians*, 455. Cf. also Bultmann, *Second Letter*, 242: "The word of Christ who speaks in him is thus not characterized by its demonstrative form, but by its material content. It is not a performance to astound but an accosting word."

[347]Bultmann, *Second Letter*, 243.

[348]See Martin, *2 Corinthians*, 476.

[349]Thus most commentators: Plummer, *Second Epistle*, 375; Bultmann, *Second Letter*, 244; Furnish, *II Corinthians*, 571; Martin, *2 Corinthians*, 477. Barrett (*Second Epistle*, 337) sees here primarily an eschatological reference, though he too recognizes that Paul sees this eschatological life anticipated in

In the final section of the *peroratio* (13:5-10), Paul returns to an argument that aims not so much at summary as at an emotional appeal to the Corinthians. He does this by reversing the roles in this situation: it is not Paul who has to make a defense (12:19) and offer proof that he is "approved" (10:18); it is in fact the Corinthians themselves who must be examined.   Yet Paul also makes clear that he and they are bound together;[350] he is not out simply to win an argument, and he has no absolute need to punish them. How he comes to Corinth will depend upon their response to this letter.

Regarding the *peroratio*, Quintilian says "Nor must we restrict ourselves to recapitulating the points of our own speech, but must call upon our opponent to reply to certain questions."[351] That is precisely what Paul begins to do in 13:5. They must examine themselves, and see if they are ἐν τῇ πίστει. "Faith" here must have the same meaning as in 10:15 —the obedience of life placed under the gospel.[352] Despite their rebellion against Paul and his fears regarding what he will find when he arrives (12:20-21), Paul is willing to assume that they will pass such a test: Christ is indeed in them (οὐκ in v. 5 anticipating a positive answer; v. 5b should be read as slightly ironic; though there is, of course, the chance that the Corinthians will fail the test and be ἀδόκιμοι, Paul is not arguing that is the case—at least not yet).[353] But if the Corinthians pass the test, then they need to recognize that Paul cannot be ἀδόκιμος either (13:6), since he is the one who brought them the gospel in the first place. If the Corinthians find themselves δόκιμος, then they must recognize that Paul has been vindicated.[354]

13:7-9 returns to the point made in 12:19: Paul does not care whether or not he appears vindicated in the eyes of the Corinthians. His

---

relation to the Corinthians.

[350]Note the remarkable string of emphatic pronouns in these verses: ἑαυτοὺς (3x) in v. 5; ἡμεῖς in v. 6; ἡμεῖς and ὑμεῖς in parallel constructions in both vv. 7 & 9. See Furnish, *II Corinthians*, 571-73.

[351]Quintilian 6.1.5.

[352]Cf. Bultmann, *Second Letter*, 144-45; Furnish, *II Corinthians*, 577.

[353]Aristotle *Rhetoric* 3.7.7 discusses the common (κατακόρως, "*ad nauseam*") use of such questions as we find in 13:5b: "the hearer agrees, because he is ashamed not to share what is a matter of common knowledge."

[354]Barrett, *Second Epistle*, 338; Furnish, *II Corinthians*, 578; Danker, *II Corinthians*, 212; Martin, *2 Corinthians*, 457; Witherington, *Conflict & Community*, 466.

concern is that they do κακὸς μηδέν, but that they practice τὸ καλόν. Of course, in this instance that also means that they will come back to obedience to their apostle.[355] Paul has no need to come and display his power in punishment. He is willing to appear weak among them again, and so, at least in the eyes of some, to fail to provide proof that he is δόκιμος. If the Corinthians respond favorably to this letter, he will not need to exercise his authority in punishment, and so will be without proof that he can be "outwardly strong."[356] Yet this would mean the Corinthians' "completion" (κατάρτισις, v. 9), and for their sake he is willing to appear "as though" (ὡς, v. 7) ἀδόκιμος. Faced with the threat of Paul's apostolic discipline, "weakness" is no longer a charge which the Corinthians can hold in contempt against Paul (10:10); it is, as Paul has shown, the true criterion of apostolic ministry and the object of his boast (11:30, 12:9-10).[357] It is also now something the Corinthians had better hope and pray for, and change their ways.

Paul's closing words (13:10) reiterate what he said at the very beginning of this letter (10:1-2): he will not be bold unless he is forced to do so.[358] His closing words nearly repeat his statement in 10:8 regarding his authority; that theme was also hinted at in 12:19,[359] but there the possibility of καθαίρεσις was not explicitly mentioned. It is mentioned here; in fact it is the final word before the epistolary closing. Despite Paul's desire to come for the Corinthians' upbuilding, he will exercise his apostolic authority in humbling discipline if necessary.

---

[355]Barrett, *Second Epistle*, 339, sees the possibility that the Corinthians may do τὸ καλόν and yet still reject Paul as their apostle. However, in Paul's view, if they reject him and his cross-determined ministry, they also reject the One who sent him. Remember, the rivals are nothing less than "servants of Satan" (11:14-15), who come offering another Jesus, another spirit, and another gospel (11:4). See Martin, *2 Corinthians*, 484; David M. Hay, "The Shaping of Theology in 2 Corinthians: Convictions, Doubts, and Warrants," in *Pauline Theology Volume II: 1 & 2 Corinthians* (Minneapolis: Fortress, 1993), 141.

[356]Martin, *2 Corinthians*, 482. See also Danker, *II Corinthians*, 472; Witherington, *Conflict & Community*, 472.

[357]See Furnish, *II Corinthians*, 579.

[358]Martin, *2 Corinthians*, 486. Note also that the same language about being absent now (ἀπών) but soon present (παρών) appears in 13:10 and 10:1-2.

[359]The *inclusio* formed by οἰκοδομῆς / οἰκοδομήν in 12:19 and 13:10 helps mark the boundaries of the *peroratio*.

CHAPTER FOUR

SPECIES AND STASIS

RHETORICAL SPECIES

We are now in a position to make some observations about the rhetorical species of 2 Corinthians 10-13. Though, as we noted in chapter 1, rhetorical theory and epistolary theory were not completely brought together (and thus the rhetorical categories may not fit all letters), the high degree of rhetorical structure and design shown in these chapters makes the consideration of rhetorical species appropriate and necessary.

Betz identifies the species of these chapters as judicial rhetoric.[1] Vital to his interpretation is 12:19, where Paul's denial that he is making an apology is in fact taken as the key to identifying it as such: Paul makes his defense in the philosophical line of Socrates, a defense that claims not to be a defense at all. Betz is joined in this identification by George Kennedy, Young and Ford, and Puskas.[2]

There is much to commend this identification. Certainly 12:19 recognizes that the Corinthians will likely read what has preceded as a defense, a piece of judicial rhetoric. In addition, judicial rhetoric deals primarily with what has happened in the past; much of Paul's concern in this letter deals with his past experiences with Corinth: his founding of the community (10:13-16), his practice regarding money and support (11:7-9, 12:16-18), the experiences of Paul's ministry (11:23b-12:10). In addition, we should notice the accumulation of forensic terms and concepts in the *peroratio*:[3] ἀπολογούμεθα (12:19), κατέναντι θεοῦ . . . λαλοῦμεν (as the true judge, 12:19), μαρτύρων (13:1), δοκιμήν (13:3).

However, not everyone has been convinced that these chapters are best identified as judicial rhetoric. Furnish rightly points out that this letter begins (10:1-2, 11, 17) and ends (13:5, 11-12) with entreaty and admonition, and that one should not, therefore, miss the "overall hortatory

---

[1]Betz, *Der Apostel*, 40.

[2]Kennedy, *New Testament Interpretation*, 93; Young and Ford, *Meaning and Truth*, 39-40; Puskas, *The Letters of Paul*, 65.

[3]See Witherington, *Conflict & Community*, 465.

character" of this letter.[4] Talbert likewise, referring to 13:10, says "in this statement, one finds the hortatory purpose of the whole of 2 Cor 10-13."[5] John T. Fitzgerald, examining 2 Cor 10-13 in terms of letter types rather than according to the species of rhetoric, agrees with these recognitions of the basic hortatory (deliberative) purpose of 2 Cor 10-13.[6] However, he notices the forensic elements combined with this,[7] so that he finally concludes that "2 Corinthians 10-13 is an excellent example of a mixed letter type. The outward structure is that of an appeal, but a strong use is made of elements from a legal setting."[8]

Despite the lack of vocabulary concerned with "advantage" which is typical of deliberative rhetoric,[9] the identification of 2 Cor 10-13 as deliberative is supported by the obvious concern with the future action of the Corinthians that occupies the opening and closing sections of the letter (10:1-6, 12:20-21, 13:5-10), and by Paul's explicit statements concerning what he is doing: he is not (despite the way it seems) presenting a defense (12:19); his concern is that the Corinthians do what is right (13:7).

Witherington, like Fitzgerald, also notes the "mixed" nature of the rhetoric in this letter, but places the emphasis upon the forensic elements: "I would say that the appeal is made in a largely forensic piece, though there is some mixing of forensic and deliberative rhetoric in the letter."[10]

---

[4]Furnish, *II Corinthians*, 48.

[5]Talbert, *Reading Corinthians*, 129. It should be noted, however, that Talbert specifically identifies the rhetorical species of 2 Cor 10-13 as epideictic (p. xiv). There is certainly a great deal in these chapters about praise and blame, honor and shame. But epideictic and deliberative rhetoric are not so easily separated. Aristotle (*Rhetoric* 1.9.35) notes that the two species are closely related, since what one would praise in one setting is the same thing that one would advise in another. Since the appeal to the Corinthians is explicit in this letter, it probably would be better to identify it as deliberative than as epideictic.

[6]Fitzgerald, "Paul, The Ancient Epistolary Theorists," 193-94.

[7]Fitzgerald notes that with 12:19 and 13:1 in particular forensic elements are combined with this hortatory document, and in tension with his earlier observation says "2 Corinthians 10-13 is an apology" (p. 196).

[8]Ibid., 200. A similar conclusion is reached by Stanley Stowers, *Letter Writing*, 109.

[9]Mitchell, *Paul and the Rhetoric of Reconciliation*, 33-39; Witherington, *Conflict & Community*, 333 n. 23.

[10]Witherington, *Conflict & Community*, 339 n. 33.

For Witherington, the deliberative elements serve the more central purpose of Paul's defense.[11]

Witherington's approach, however, fails to give sufficient weight to the attention Paul pays to what the Corinthians will do, to the nature of his future visit with them, and to what Paul himself says he is doing. Witherington also notes, in agreement with Mitchell, that the time frame of the beginning and ending of a work are particularly important for determining the species of rhetoric.[12] However, since Witherington treats all of 2 Corinthians as a single letter (and so points to the past time references in chapters 1 and 2) and because he notes the reference to Paul's past warnings in 13:2 (but fails to take adequate measure of the pervasive view in 13:1-10 toward Paul's upcoming visit, his actions then, and the Corinthians' response to this letter), he identifies these past time signals as indications of judicial rhetoric. However, we should note that both the beginning (10:1-6) and ending (12:19-13:10) of the proposed "four chapter letter" are concerned primarily with what will happen in the future as a result of decisions that the Corinthians must now make. Thus Witherington's assertion that the deliberative elements here only serve the more important judicial rhetoric cannot be sustained.

It is clear that 2 Cor 10-13 cannot simply and exclusively be identified with any one species of rhetoric.[13] The situation that Paul must address is too complex to fit neatly into one single category. Neither is it sufficient to say that it is primarily one type, with elements of another included to serve that primary purpose. In these chapters, deliberative and judicial rhetoric are bound together. Paul's ultimate purpose concerns decisions made by the Corinthians, and so is deliberative in focus. However, those decisions are tied to their judgment concerning Paul, and so Paul necessarily is involved in judicial rhetoric as well. In fact, we can say that the species of rhetoric changes as Paul moves through his argument and new possibilities are opened to him.[14] He is able to make his (deliberative) goals clear at the beginning of this letter. However, he

---

[11]Ibid., 465 n. 1. For such combining of judicial rhetoric with other types, cf. Kennedy, *Art of Rhetoric*, 311.

[12]Mitchell, *Paul and the Rhetoric of Reconciliation*, 24-25; Witherington, *Conflict & Community*, 333.

[13]Wire, *Corinthian Women Prophets*, 4 states "Modern rhetoric has given up the prescriptive side of classical rhetoric with its canon of the single-function speech . . . ."

[14]See the treatment of rhetorical species in Richard N. Longenecker, *Galatians*, Word Biblical Commentary (Dallas, TX: Word, 1990), esp. 184-86.

must engage in what can only be identified as judicial rhetoric, a defense of his apostolic practice, before he can properly place the issue before the Corinthians at the end of the letter. We will note a similar alternation in the *stasis* of Paul's argument as it progresses. An examination of the issue of *stasis* in this letter will now be taken up.

STASIS

As we discussed in chapter one, the *stasis* of an argument arises at that point in the matter where the dispute centers, where objections are raised, and where questions are brought forward.

> The issue is determined by the joining of the primary plea of the defense with the charge of the plaintiff.[15]

> Issues, whether principal or secondary, thus come into being as a result of conflict arising in the course of debate or discussion.[16]

> In rhetoric, a stasis refers to the pause following an affirmation or accusation (κατάφασις) and preceding a response or answer (ἀπόφασις) . . . . Only when the response takes some issue with the κατάφασις does a stasis arise . . . . The stasis of the disagreement is determined by joining the accusing statement made by the first party with the defensive response of the second party.[17]

As is indicated by the quote from Hermogenes above, any particular speech or argument may contain more than one *stasis*, and within the primary *stases* may be subordinate *stases*.[18] The principle *stases* involved in 2 Cor 10-13 will be identified by careful attention to three passages which our rhetorical analysis has already highlighted as key for Paul's argumentation: 10:1-6 (further clarified by 10:10), 10:17-18 (further clarified by 11:30 and 12:9), and 12:19. We will note the ways in which Paul appears to be answering charges or accusations from rivals or detractors in Corinth, or is himself making accusations and anticipating

---

[15]*Ad Her.* 1.11.18. See also Quintilian 7.1.6.
[16]Hermogenes *On Stases*, 369.
[17]Troy Martin, "Apostasy," 438.
[18]See also Hermogenes *On Stases*, pp. 382-83, 408; Seneca the Elder *Controversiae*, Loeb Classical Library, trans. Michael Winterbottom (Cambridge: Harvard University, 1974) 1.1.13, 2.5.10, 7.1.16-17, 7.3.6, 7.7.10, 9.6.10; Kennedy, *Art of Rhetoric*, 325-26; Martin, "Apostasy," 438.

their probable response. As we examine the *stases* involved in this argument, we will also see how they shed light on the coherence of Paul's argument in this letter, as well as the coherence of his position with that taken in 1 Corinthians 1-4. We turn first to a brief examination of the *stasis* in 1 Corinthians 1-4.

1 Corinthians 1-4

The issue on which Paul focuses attention in the first four chapters of 1 Corinthians is laid out in 1:10-17. Paul has heard reports (v. 11) that the Corinthian congregation is splitting into factions, with the distinction being made over allegiance to various apostles.[19] Paul objects to any such parties, including a party that would identify itself with him (1:14-17). There is no evidence of a direct attack against Paul in 1 Corinthians,[20] and here Paul is arguing at least as much against those who would claim his side as against those who would prefer another.[21] As Paul's argument progresses, there are indications that he felt a particular negative judgment on himself and his ministry from some of the people at Corinth, perhaps from those who claim allegiance to other leaders rather than to Paul. However, in Paul's view all the parties have misunderstood the nature of apostolic ministry and preaching. Paul points to himself as an illustration of God's ways. Following a discussion of how God has used what is foolish and weak to confound the wisdom of the world (1:18-31), Paul explains why in his own ministry he has not used "superiority of word or wisdom" (ὑπεροχὴν λόγου ἢ σοφίας— 2:1), and why he came to them "in fear and great trembling" (ἐν φόβῳ καὶ τρόμῳ πολλῷ—2:3). Since the power of God has been revealed through the cross of Christ, Paul's message is and will remain a word of the cross in form as well as in content.

---

[19]The party claiming to "belong to Christ" may well be people who rejected the notion of "belonging" to any apostle at all, though scholarly opinions also include this phrase as possibly Paul's own corrective comment on the situation in Corinth, or even as a pious interpolation. See C. K. Barrett, *A Commentary on the First Epistle to the Corinthians* (New York: Harper Row, 1968; reprint Peabody, Mass.: Hendrickson, 1987), 44-46; Mitchell, *Paul and the Rhetoric of Reconciliation*, 82 n. 101.

[20]Pogoloff, *Logos and Sophia*, 152; Martin, *Corinthian Body*, 52-55.

[21]See Pogoloff, *Logos and Sophia*, 195.

The apparent lack of ὑπεροχὴν λόγου καὶ σοφίας seems to have been a criticism being lodged against Paul by some in Corinth.[22] In 2:6 Paul must claim that he does indeed impart God's wisdom, but only to those who are mature, who are spiritual; the Corinthians' internal bickering proves that they are not such people (3:1-4). In chapter 3, Paul places all apostles in proper perspective: they are servants of God, and of the church. In fact, it is not the Corinthians who belong to the various apostles, but the apostles who belong to the Corinthians as the field and building of God in which apostles labor (3:21-23).

In 4:1-5 Paul summarizes his arguments around this issue, and there we can most clearly see his response to the Corinthians and thus the *stasis* of this argument:

> Think of us in this way, as servants of Christ and stewards of God's mysteries. Moreover, it is required of stewards that they be found trustworthy. But with me it is a very small thing that I should be judged by you or by any human court. I do not even judge myself. I am not aware of anything against myself, but I am not thereby acquitted. It is the Lord who judges me. Therefore do not pronounce judgment before the time, before the Lord comes, who will bring to light the things now hidden in darkness and will disclose the purposes of the heart. Then each will receive commendation from God.

In this passage, Paul denies the Corinthians the right to judge him or his apostolic ministry. He belongs to them as a servant of God, but he remains *God's* servant, and will be judged only by God. By judging (whether in rejection or approval) Paul's apostolic ministry, the Corinthians have claimed a right that belongs only to God, and a judgment that awaits the final day. Here Paul removes all such judgment from the Corinthians and their criteria and places it in an eschatological context.[23]

---

[22]Thiselton, "Realized Eschatology in Corinth," 513 rightly notes "The main issue in 1 Cor 1-4 turns not in the first instance on questions about wisdom as such, but upon the Corinthians' attitudes toward ministry." See also Witherington, *Conflict & Community*, 124.

[23]See Thiselton, "Realized Eschatology in Corinth," 514; Wayne A. Meeks, "Social Functions of Apocalyptic Language in Pauline Christianity," in *Apocalypticism in the Mediterranean World*, ed. D. Hellholm (Tübingen: Mohr, 1983), 699. One of the common functions of future eschatological language in Paul is to point out the tentative, provisional nature of this world's arrangements (and the believer's position as provisional to the extent that he or she shares existence on this side of the eschaton). See John G. Gager, "Functional Diversity

The ground of that eschatological context is the event of the cross, by which God has overthrown the scribe, the debater, and the wise of this age (1:18-25). The wisdom Paul brings doesn't belong to this age or its doomed rulers (2:6-8), and "to decide to preach only Christ crucified meant also a decision to cast aside eloquence (λόγος) and wisdom (σοφία) as instruments of proclamation,"[24] for such things belong to this age. God's action through the cross is the crisis for the world which demolishes all other criteria. The Corinthians' bickering and competition over apostles is pointless, since it embodies the unspiritual values of this age that is passing away (3:1-4),[25] and it is God alone who will judge the apostles (3:12-15).[26] Thus, in these opening chapters of 1 Corinthians, Paul argues against the Corinthians' judgments of himself and his apostolic ministry on the *stasis* of jurisdiction (*translatio* or μετάληψις).

Primary and Secondary Stases in 2 Corinthians 10-13

As we have noted in this study, few scholars have paid sufficient attention to the issue of rhetorical *stasis*. The only systematic discussion of *stasis* in these chapters comes from J. Paul Sampley. Without using the term *stasis,* Sampley discusses how Paul treats various topics in 2 Corinthians 10-13 in different ways.[27] Thus, for example, according to Sampley Paul treats the charge of fraud (12:16) from the *stasis* of denial (*coniecturalis,* στοχασμός; 12:17-18). The charges that Paul is unskilled (11:6) and weak (10:10) are dealt with on the *stasis* of quality (*qualitas, generalis,* ποιότης); lack of eloquence should not be confused with lack of

---

in Paul's Use of End-Time Language," *JBL* 89 (1970): 325-37.

The list of scholars who have claimed that most or all of the trouble dealt with in 1 Cor was caused by an over-realized eschatology is long; see Barrett, *First Epistle*, 109; Bruce, *1 & 2 Corinthians*, 49-50; Ernst Käsemann, "On the Subject of Primitive Christian Apocalyptic," in *New Testament Questions of Today* (Philadelphia: Fortress, 1969), 125-26; E. Earle Ellis, "Christ Crucified," in *Reconciliation and Hope. New Testament Essays in Atonement and Eschatology Presented to L. L. Morris* (Exeter: Paternoster, 1974), 73-77; Thiselton, "Realized Eschatology," 510-26.

[24]Black, *Paul, Apostle of Weakness*, 103.

[25]See Ernst Käsemann, "For and Against a Theology of Resurrection," in *Jesus Means Freedom* (Philadelphia: Fortress, 1969), 61.

[26]This is not the only time Paul denies the value of rhetorical eloquence by drawing upon eschatological themes. See Rom 16:18-20, 2 Cor 2:15-17.

[27]Sampley, "Paul, His Opponents," 165-67.

knowledge, and Paul's weakness is shown to be a vehicle for God's power. Sampley reads 11:8 as the Corinthians' interpretation of Paul's monetary support from other churches: they see it as robbery.[28] Sampley then sees Paul's response in 11:9 ("my needs were supplied by the friends who came from Macedonia") as an argument on the *stasis* of definition (*definitiva, proprietas,* ὅρος).

Sampley is basically correct in identifying these *stases*, yet even his analysis is insufficient. He fails to distinguish between primary and secondary *stases*, and most of his examples must be classified as secondary.[29] Furthermore, though he notes the possibility of the *stasis* of jurisdiction,[30] he apparently finds no example of it in these chapters. By contrast, the analysis below will show that this *stasis* is key not only to Paul's position in 1 Corinthians 1-4, but also key to his strategy in 2 Corinthians 10-13.

2 Corinthians 10:1-18

We begin to hear the accusations from some against Paul at the opening of this section: he is bold when at a distance, but humbled when with them (v. 1). The same idea is expressed again in v. 10: his letters thunder, but he doesn't follow through with an impressive performance in person. Finally, in v. 12, we find an indication that the Corinthians want Paul to engage in a display and comparison of his eloquence, but he

---

[28]Sampley's interpretation of this verse differs from the one offered in this study, in which Paul is understood to be the one who says he "plundered" these other churches as part of his *ethos* as a military figure in God's battle, and in order to show that he is not the client of any of his churches. See discussion above in chap. 3.

[29]In addition to the discussion of primary *stases* below, we would make a few alterations in Sampley's identification of these secondary *stases*. The *stasis* in 11:7-11 is, as Sampley identifies it (167), one of definition; however, the term which Paul wants to avoid is not "robbery," but "sin" (v. 7). Paul wants to show that what he has done in accepting money from Macedonia was not an offense against Corinth, but for their good. In 11:12-15 Paul is not simply denying the fact of his vacillation (165), but is making a further argument about his refusal of Corinthian support, this time on the *stasis* of quality, and specifically on the ground of a countercharge which shifts the blame to another (μετάστασις); it is because of the designs of those "ministers of Satan" that Paul must continue to refuse financial support from Corinth.

[30]Ibid., 176 n. 9.

has failed to join the game; some suspect it is because he doesn't dare, since he knows he is outclassed by his rivals.

Throughout this opening section, Paul stakes out ground for himself which does not allow the Corinthians to pass judgment on him or his ministry; that is, Paul continues to argue from the same *stasis* which he adopted in 1 Corinthians 1-4 in response to the Corinthians' desire to judge him: that of jurisdiction. In the opening words, Paul's emphatic reference to himself reminds the Corinthians who it is they are presuming to judge. Paul continues in vv. 3-6 by adopting the *ethos* of the military figure who threatens, if necessary, to take action against his opponents in Corinth. Paul does not look for the Corinthians' approval, but for their obedience (v. 6). That *ethos* sets the tone for all of chapter 10.

Paul continues his refusal to submit himself or his ministry to the evaluation of the Corinthians in vv. 7-11. It is they who must watch out (βλέπετε, v. 7).[31] Paul is the one who has been given authority by the Lord himself. That authority is not intended to be used in tearing down (v. 8), but there is an element of threat here as well. Paul will return to this theme at the end of his letter (13:10), and the hint of warning seems clear: if necessary, Paul will do some demolition. Such a position hardly allows for the Corinthians to pass judgment on him.

The *stasis* of jurisdiction continues in vv. 12-18. Paul refuses to engage in any kind of comparison or competition with his rivals in Corinth, reminding the people that he has a unique role in their community as the founding apostle. The standards by which they would measure him are judged by him to be τὰ ἄμετρα (v. 13, 15).

Paul reaches a pivotal point in his argument at 10:17-18, where he puts all boasting, approval, and commendation into proper perspective. Using the same verse from Jeremiah that he had used in 1 Cor 1:31, Paul again places the judgments and the criteria of the Corinthians into eschatological crisis. The boasting and commendations which are going on in Corinth, and which they want Paul to join, mean nothing. The true basis of testing is not the social values which have been adopted by the Corinthians, but the judgment of God. Such judgment is an eschatological event, so that Paul looks forward in hope "that on the day

---

[31]See above in chap. 3, where the interpretation of this phrase as a warning is defended.

of the Lord Jesus" he and the Corinthians can boast in one another (2 Cor 1:14; see also 1 Cor 4:5).[32]

In 1 Cor 1:31, Paul draws on Jer 9:24 to sum up the argument of 1:26-30 that God's ways of working are the opposite of the standards enshrined by the world: God works through the foolish, weak, and low (1:27-28), just as God worked supremely through the weakness of the cross and the foolishness of the proclamation of Christ crucified (1:18-25). The function of the same verse from Jeremiah in 2 Cor 10:17 is similar: boasting and commendation are taken out of the hands and the values of the Corinthians. 10:18 clarifies Paul's point in v. 17 regarding boasting: such judgment belongs to God alone. Thus, the *stasis* on which Paul is arguing in this section is the same as that adopted in 1 Cor 1-4 where Paul argues against a different round of apostolic "evaluation" by the Corinthians; in both cases he argues on the *stasis* of jurisdiction.

It appears that this is how Paul would prefer to deal with such issues. However, there is an inherent problem with attempting to argue from the *stasis* of jurisdiction. To convince the judges that your case is better than your opponents' may be difficult; but to convince those who have set themselves up as judges that they themselves are wrong to have done so is even more difficult. It threatens the judges' own position, status, and honor. If one refuses to "play the game," insisting instead that the game itself is illegitimate, and then fails to convince the judges, the case is lost by forfeit. That is why, when the *stasis* of jurisdiction was used in an argument, it was often only a part of the argument, joined with other *stases* in case the argument on jurisdiction failed to convince.[33]

There is a further reason why an argument based on the *stasis* of jurisdiction might have been ineffective in Paul's situation. By the time of Paul, the practice of "declamation" had become fashionable in intellectual and literary circles, and among those aspiring to social values of eloquence and rhetorical power.[34] Declamation provided an opportunity to practice one's rhetorical skill and display one's eloquence by arguing with others over a particular case, whether real or fictional.

---

[32]Furnish, *II Corinthians*, 483; Dewey, "A Matter of Honor," 216; Beverly Gaventa, "Apostle and Church in 2 Corinthians: A Response to David M. Hay and Steven J. Kraftchick," in *Pauline Theology Vol. II: 1 & 2 Corinthians*, ed. David M. Hay (Minneapolis: Fortress, 1993), 197.

[33]Hermogenes *On Stases*, 408.

[34]For a review of the practice of declamation, see Kennedy, *Art of Rhetoric*, 312-322.

As for declamations of the kind delivered in the schools of the rhetoricians, so long as they are in keeping with actual life and resemble speeches, they are most profitable to the student, not merely while he is still immature, for the reason that they simultaneously exercise the powers both of invention and arrangement, but even when he has finished his education and acquired a reputation in the courts. For they provide a richer diet from which eloquence derives nourishment and brilliance of complexion, and at the same time afford a refreshing variety after the continuous fatigues of forensic disputes.[35]

The popularity of such displays extended beyond Rome and reached "some of the more Romanized towns of Spain and Gaul and in the East."[36] It appears that the Corinthians shared this outlook "which appreciated style, technique, and artistic effects as virtues in themselves."[37]

However, in such disputes the *stasis* of jurisdiction did not serve a useful function; it failed to join the debate seriously. Hermagoras lists it as the last of the *stases* and does not give it great respect, probably because it was not useful for the kinds of rhetorical exercises that interested him.[38] Hermagoras is not the only ancient rhetorician to downplay the usefulness of jurisdiction. Quintilian[39] lists jurisdiction as the *stasis* with the least strength: it is a "last hope." The first three *stases*, omitting jurisdiction, are at times listed by the rhetorical handbooks as sufficient.[40]

It would not be surprising, then, when Paul is being compared with other speakers, if his arguments based on jurisdiction were not well received. Even if 1 Cor 1-4 settled the immediate problem, it did not end the Corinthians' desire to judge apostles.[41] Paul apparently sensed the need to move beyond this *stasis*, because he adopts a different *stasis* in the following section.

---

[35]Quintilian 10.5.14.

[36]Kennedy, *Art of Rhetoric*, 335.

[37]Ibid., 316. For evidence that the Second Sophistic movement was underway in Corinth during Paul's time, see Witherington, *Conflict & Community*, 443 n. 11.

[38]Kennedy, *Art of Persuasion in Greece*, 308; see also Braet, "Status," 83-84.

[39]Quintilian 3.6.83.

[40]Quintilian 7.4; *Ad Her.* 1.11.18; Cicero *De Or.* 2.26.

[41]Mitchell, *Paul and the Rhetoric of Reconciliation*, 303 concludes "Paul's rhetoric of reconciliation in 1 Corinthians was a failure."

2 Corinthians 11:1-12:18

We hear charges against Paul again in 11:5-6:   Paul is an amateur (ἰδιώτης), and is inferior to the other apostles. Though Paul will stress his role as the congregation's founder (11:2-4) and his motives for their good (11:7-11) in contrast to the evil of his rivals (11:12-15), he will no longer deny their right to make a decision regarding Paul's ministry. In fact, such a decision now becomes required, because the choice between Paul and these rivals must be made; the two bring mutually exclusive ministries. Paul will, for the moment, treat the Corinthians as a jury.

The major *stasis* on which the *probatio* is argued has already been prepared for by 10:17-18. There, Paul has shown that self-commendation is pointless, since it is only the one whom the Lord commends who is δόκιμος. Paul will do some boasting, even though it can only be foolishness (11:1, 16-17). However, another important issue has been raised by 10:18. Whom does the Lord commend? Granted that this commendation is an eschatological event, the church must still recognize the Lord's anticipated commendation in the present age. What will be the criteria?

Paul's response to this question shows up most clearly in two verses that we have already identified as central to his argument in this section. True boasting will be in weakness (11:30), because it is in the weakness of the apostle that God's power is brought to fullness (12:9); indeed, in some sense the very existence of Christ's power in Paul depends on Paul's weakness.[42]   In 12:9, Paul says it is the power of Christ (ἡ δύναμις τοῦ Χριστοῦ) that will dwell in him in this way.   The Corinthians are looking for evidence of Christ speaking in Paul (13:3); the problem is that they are looking for the wrong things.   They have forgotten that Christ may be described with "meekness and gentleness" (10:1, already laying the groundwork for this rhetorical move).[43]   They have failed to realize that the cross sets the paradigm for apostolic ministry.

---

[42]T. B. Savage, "Power Through Weakness: An Historical and Exegetical Examination of Paul's Understanding of the Ministry in 2 Corinthians (Ph.D. diss., Cambridge University, 1986), 204.

[43]The κύριος of 10:17-18 should be understood as Jesus. See 1 Cor 1:30-31, 15:31; Gal 6:14; Phil 1:26, 3:3; Rom 15:17. It is this Christ, crucified in weakness (13:4), in whom Paul will boast and who will commend the δόκιμος.

In his "fool's boast" Paul does not deny the accusations against him; he is weak, he is nothing (11:29, 12:11). However, he argues that this is in fact the only legitimate way to live out the apostolic ministry of a crucified Lord. Thus Paul here argues on the *stasis* of quality, and specifically on the basis of justification (ἀντίληψις):[44] The actions are admitted, but no wrongdoing is confessed since the actions are claimed to be honorable on other grounds.

> His irony comes through as he does not directly negate what the opponents say about him; rather he accepts it in an *ad hominem* way, and turns their negative and prejudicial assessment of him into an affirmation of positive and personal credit.[45]

That other ground which makes Paul's weakness not only honorable but necessary is the cross of Christ. Paul's claim to proper apostolic conduct is based on the conformity of his life to the weakness and suffering of Jesus on the cross.[46] Weakness is not a hindrance to apostolic ministry, but in fact it is the necessary mark of an apostle, since an apostle must embody what he proclaims, and that is above all the cross. "Il ressemble à celui qu'il annonce, le Christ crucifié."[47]

From Paul's point of view, the conflict between himself and his opponents is over whether or not the cross will be the only criterion for proper apostolic ministry. By this argument based on quality, focused on the paradigmatic nature of the cross, Paul provides the standard by which the Corinthians must discriminate between competing apostles and their differing models of the life of faith.[48] "The cross becomes a watershed

---

[44]In contrast to the weakness of the *stasis* of jurisdiction in the eyes of ancient rhetoricians, the *stasis* of quality / justification was felt to be the strongest possible position (unless the charges could be denied altogether). See Quintilian 7.4.4. The *stasis* of quality could also be seen as the best opportunity to display one's skill: "The question of quality therefore makes the highest demands on the resources of oratory, since it affords the utmost scope for a display of talent on either side, while there is no topic in which emotional appeal is so effective" (Quintilian 7.4.23).

[45]Martin, *2 Corinthians*, 301.

[46]Best, *Second Corinthians*, 134.

[47]Eric Fuchs, "La Faiblese, glorie de l'apostolat selon Paul: Étude sur 2 Corinthiens 10-13," *ETR* 55 (1980): 241.

[48]Calvin Roetzel, "As Dying, and Behold We Live: Death and Resurrection in Paul's Theology," *Int* 46 (1992): 18.

between Paul and the opponents."[49] It is not a Christological doctrine as such which has become the focus of debate, but whether or not the cross is so central to human understanding and experience of God that it must continue to be the determining paradigm for the proclamation of the gospel. Paul's answer is clear and startling:

> The power of the preaching of the gospel resides paradoxically in the fact that the act of preaching is itself weak and vulnerable, in conformity with the cross of Christ.[50]

By insisting on the cross as the canon by which all apostolic proclamation and ministry must be judged, Paul not only gives reason for the Corinthians' continued loyalty to himself, but also calls into question all the ways in which they joined hellenistic society in idealizing the value of power, eloquence and beauty:[51]

> To revel in an exalted Christ, now powerfully present in the community and endowing the members with an abundance of spiritual gifts, without discerning that he bears the marks of one crucified, results in a skewed Christianity.   Such a Christianity will naturally find afflictions, hardships, and other expressions of "weakness" to be either an embarrassment or evidence of inauthenticity.[52]

Thus Paul not only challenges the judgments that the Corinthians have been making, but also their basic assumptions and criteria. These criteria have been eliminated by God's eschatological act at the cross. The eschatological tone of these chapters should not be missed. Witherington, as we have noted, finds the principal species of these chapters to be judicial, and he credits that as the reason for what he perceives as a lack of eschatological emphasis:

---

[49]Charles B. Cousar, *A Theology of the Cross: The Death of Jesus in the Pauline Letters* (Minneapolis: Fortress, 1990), 140.

[50]John William Beaudean, Jr., *Paul's Theology of Preaching* (Macon, Ga.: Mercer University, 1988), 202-03.

[51]Judge, "Cultural Conformity," 14; Roetzel, "As Dying," 10.

[52]Cousar, *Theology of the Cross*, 166. See also Murphy-O'Connor, *Theology*, 150.

> This forensic concentration on the past may help explain why 2
> Corinthians focuses so much on the past saving acts of God in Christ
> and so little on what may be called future eschatology.[53]

Such a statement fails to recognize the strong eschatological themes that
run through this section. However, the focus of these themes is not the
same as we saw in 1 Cor 4 or even in 2 Cor 10:17-18. In much of 2 Cor
10-13, and in the *probatio* in particular, we see a shift concerning Paul's
role in the eschatological images he uses.[54]

In 1 Cor 4:1-5, Paul stands with the Corinthians as those who must
await the eschatological judgment of God. In contrast, in the
eschatological themes in 2 Cor 10-13 Paul has a distinctive role over
against the Corinthians. Paul opens the *probatio* by casting himself in the
role of the one who has promised the Corinthian church as a bride for
Christ, and looks ahead to the eschatological day when that marriage will
be completed. This image draws on the Old Testament language of the
people Israel as the bride of the Lord (cf. Is 54:5-6, 62:5; Ezek 16:8).
That biblical image was not only a declaration of what God had already
done, but was also an expression of eschatological hope:

> On that day, says the Lord, you will call me, "My husband," and no
> longer will you call me, "My Baal." . . . And I will take you for my wife
> forever; I will take you for my wife in righteousness and in justice, in
> steadfast love, and in mercy. I will take you for my wife in faithfulness;
> and you shall know the Lord (Hos 2:16-20).

Secondly, Paul's tirade against the ψευδαπόστολοι in   11:13
presents the conflict at Corinth as an eschatological one: this trouble is
nothing less than the deceit of Satan at work in his servants. In the
present time Paul is the one who denies Satan and his minions the
opportunities they seek, but he also looks ahead to the ultimate end of
such schemes in the judgment of God (v. 15b).

---

[53]Witherington, *Conflict & Community*, 334.

[54]Gager, "Functional Diversity," 337 notes the way that Paul is willing to vary
his expression of eschatological themes in order to meet the needs of the situation:
"We have seen that he argues differently in different situations, adapting his
language to meet specific occasions."

> Paul viewed the false apostles . . . as an eschatological phenomenon. It
> would be difficult to account otherwise for the passionate feelings that
> evidently were evoked on each side.[55]

Thirdly, Paul's journey to the "third Heaven" (12:2-4) is not simply a mystical event; it is an eschatological one. Paul may not know how it happened, nor have anything he can report from it; but he is caught up out of the present age for a moment. The verb which Paul uses to describe what happens to him during this event (ἁρπάζειν) is the same verb he uses in 1 Thess 4:17 to describe what will happen to all believers at the Lord's coming. In a sense, Paul becomes an eschatological figure who experiences an anticipation of the final transference of believers to the presence of Christ.[56]

Finally, we may reflect again on the role of Jeremiah in these four chapters. Not only is Jeremiah quoted in 10:17, but the language of "building" and "tearing down" which frames this letter (10:8, 13:10) also comes from Jeremiah, specifically from the account of Jeremiah's call (Jer 1:9-10).[57] Though there is not an exact verbal correspondence between Paul's expression and the wording of Jeremiah 1:10 (in Jer, ἀνοικομεῖν and καταφυτεύειν; in 2 Cor, οἰκοδομή and καθαίρεσις), the reference to Jeremiah seems clear, especially in light of the other parallels between Jeremiah and Paul.[58] Paul's reflection on his call as one that is grounded in God's decision before Paul was even born (Gal 1:15) recalls a similar declaration to Jeremiah (Jer 1:5); the ministries of both men could be described as marked by suffering and opposition from their own communities; both are called to a ministry that includes the Gentiles (Jer 1:5, Gal 1:16). Drawing on the model of Jeremiah, Paul claims the authority to build up the community (and hopefully to avoid the need to tear it down, though that too is within his role as apostle, clearly

---

[55]Barrett, *Second Epistle*, 286.

[56]Ibid., 309. See also Furnish, *II Corinthians*, 544-45; Martin, *2 Corinthians*, 405; James D. Tabor, *Things Unutterable: Paul's Ascent to Paradise in Its Greco-Roman, Judaic, and Early Christian Contexts*, Studies in Judaism (Lanham, Md.: University Press of America, 1986), 81-95, 123-24.

[57]See also Jer 24:6, 31:28.

[58]Derk William Oostendorp, *Another Jesus: A Gospel of Jewish-Christian Superiority in 2 Corinthians* (Kampen: J. H. Kok, 1967), 21; Karl H. Rengstorf, "ἀπόστολος ," *TDNT* 1:440; William L. Lane, "Covenant: Key to Paul's Conflict with Corinth," *TynB* 33 (1982): 9-10; Young and Ford, *Meaning and Truth*, 69-74.

threatened in 13:10)[59] because he has been entrusted with the eschatological ministry of serving the community of the church.

In all of these eschatological themes, Paul is more than just one of the crowd; he has assumed a decisive role. If the Corinthians refuse to leave all judgment for the Lord's Day, then Paul will show how that eschatological event is already impinging on the Corinthians' experience through his own ministry as their apostle. This shift in the way Paul portrays his role will continue in the concluding section of the letter, where it will reinforce a final shift in *stasis*.

2 Corinthians 12:19-13:10

12:19 begins with a statement of what Paul anticipates the Corinthians may conclude: that he is offering his defense to them. Paul's response to this, which establishes the *stasis* from which Paul will argue in the *peroratio*, follows immediately: Paul is not defending himself to the Corinthians, but is speaking κατέναντι θεοῦ ἐν Χριστῷ.[60] God, not the Corinthians, is the judge before whom Paul speaks.[61]

> Paul is not a minister who was intended to pass any sort of qualifying examination which would turn him into a candidate approved by the Corinthians.[62]

Thus Paul re-establishes the *stasis* of jurisdiction with which he began in chapter 10.[63] However, now his position has been fortified with an explanation of the nature of apostolic ministry as necessarily cruciform,

---

[59]Witherington, *Conflict & Community*, 472 n. 3.

[60]Cf. 2:17, 4:2, 7:12, 8:21. Epictetus *Disc.* 1.14.1-6 also speaks of the philosopher understanding that everything is done in God's sight (ἐφορᾶται ὑπὸ τοῦ θεοῦ), but there the reason is not a sense of accountability before God, but because one's soul is by nature part and portion of the divine Being. Paul may be reflecting on the tradition of Deut 19:17 (19:15 will be quoted in 2 Cor 13:1) which says that when one is accused of wrongdoing, the parties are to appear "before the Lord" (ἔναντι κυρίου) so that false testimony can be revealed. Paul is claiming that his testimony is given before God; God will reveal truth and falsehood. See Fitzgerald, "Paul and Ancient Epistolary Theorists," 199.

[61]Witherington, *Conflict & Community*, 374, 468.

[62]Martin, *2 Corinthians*, 479.

[63]Note Hermogenes *On Stases*, 401: "Generally speaking, epilogues are developed from the same heads as introductions and they have the same force . . . ."

and thus also with an explanation for why the Corinthians should see Paul as one whom the Lord will find δόκιμος.

Paul's position has also been strengthened by the *ethos* of the eschatological roles in which he presented himself in 11:1-12:18.[64] Here in the *peroratio*, Paul continues to strengthen his position by casting himself in an active role. In 12:20-21, Paul lists some of the charges that he himself might have to make against the Corinthians; if such a case needs to be brought, the witnesses are now ready (13:1-2). The Corinthians must realize that just as Paul speaks ἐν Χριστῷ (12:19), so too Christ speaks in Paul (13:3). To come as one shaped by the cross is to come as one marked by weakness. "The character of Christ speaking through an apostle is determined by the character of the Christ who speaks,"[65] and Christ remains the crucified one. Paradoxically this also brings the power of God (13:4a), and it is this power that will accompany Paul when he comes.[66]

Paul continues to turn the tables on the Corinthians in 13:5-10.[67] There, it is they who must be examined, it is their status as δόκιμοι that is in question. Paul's own reference to speaking κατέναντι θεοῦ should call the Corinthians to recognize where they too stand in relation to God's judgment.[68] Paul closes the letter with one more reference to the authority

---

[64]Paul's presence, even through a letter, can convey eschatological power (1 Cor 5:3-5). See Robert W. Funk, "The Apostolic Parousia: Form and Significance," in *Christian History and Interpretation: Studies Presented to John Knox*, ed. W. R. Farmer, C. F. D. Moule, and R. R. Niebuhr (Cambridge: Cambridge University, 1967), 249-68.

[65]James D. G. Dunn, *Jesus and the Spirit. A Study of the Religious and Charismatic Experience of Jesus and the First Christians as Reflected in the New Testament* (London: SCM Press, 1975), 330-31. See also Murphy-O'Connor, *Theology*, 133.

[66]εἰς ὑμᾶς in v. 4 refers to the time when Paul will arrive in Corinth, and thus we should understand ζήσομεν not as looking forward to Christ's Parousia at the End, but looking ahead to Paul's upcoming arrival at Corinth. So Leivestad, "Meekness and Gentleness," 162-63; Plummer, *Second Epistle*, 375; Furnish, *II Corinthians*, 571; Martin, *2 Corinthians*, 477. Contra Eduard Schweizer, "Dying and Rising With Christ," *NTS* 14 (1967-68): 2.

[67]Note how Dio Chrysostom, having been criticized for the price of grain, places his hearers on the defensive and holds before them the danger of judgment from the proconsuls in *Or.* 46.14: "And let no one imagine that it is in anger over my own position that I have said these things rather than in fear for yours, lest possibly you may some day be accused of being violent and lawless."

[68]Hay, "Shaping of Theology," 152.

the Lord has given to him, recalling again the language in Jeremiah about God's action of building and demolishing. Thus in the end Paul is not content, as he seemed to be in 11:1-12:18, to have the Corinthians be a kind of jury (even while remembering that God is the ultimate judge).[69]

> Paul n'entendait pas se tenir devant ses fidèles en attitude d'accusé, car ils ne sont pas ses juges (cf. 1 Cor. 4:3). Tout ce qu'il a dit lui-même n'etait destiné qu'à reveiller leurs sentiments endormis et à les premunir contre les séducteurs. . . . et il a parlé dans l'esprit du Christ, sous le regard de Dieu, seulement pour remplir son devoir d'apôtre (cf. 11:17).[70]

Paul's coming to Corinth will not be as a defendant, but as prosecutor,[71] or even as judge.[72] Paul's arrival anticipates the coming judgment of God.[73] Paul brings the eschatological crisis into the present of the Corinthians, because in him and in his weakness the Corinthians *can* see Christ crucified, and in him they *can* hear Christ speaking (13:3). It is they who may find themselves not δόκιμοι in the Lord's judgment (10:18), but ἀδόκιμοι (13:5). If they are found to be so when Paul arrives, that judgment will be anticipated in the present through him, and the community will experience authority expressed in demolition (13:10).[74] The game is up, and it is not Paul's position as apostle but the Corinthians' identity as a people δόκιμος to God that is in jeopardy.

---

[69]Witherington, *Conflict & Community*, 392.

[70]Ernest Berhard Allo, *Saint Paul. Seconde épître aux Corinthiens* (Paris: Etudes Bibliques, 1937), 330.

[71]See Fitzgerald, "Paul, the Ancient Epistolary Theorists," 199.

[72]Ernst Käsemann, "Sentences of Holy Law in the New Testament," in *New Testament Questions of Today* (Philadelphia: Fortress, 1969), 75; Witherington, *Conflict & Community*, 334 n. 25, 469 n. 13.

[73]Rogahn, "Function," 112.

[74]See Bultmann, *Second Letter*, 243; Young and Ford, *Meaning and Truth*, 71.

SUMMARY AND CONCLUSION

This study set out to investigate the argumentative strategy that Paul uses in 2 Corinthians 10-13 to counter the practice of apostolic evaluation being carried out in Corinth, and our specific question was whether or not there was anything that gave Paul's various arguments cohesiveness, particularly comparing them with what Paul had said in 1 Corinthians 1-4. We set out to use rhetorical analysis as a tool to understand Paul's argumentative strategy. This study has claimed not only that 2 Corinthians 10-13 can be analyzed profitably according to ancient rhetorical practice, but that such an analysis helps us to notice the argumentative strategy and to differentiate the various steps that Paul uses in his attempt to move his audience to a new position.

Chapter 1 described the renewal of rhetorical analysis in the discipline of biblical studies in recent years, and advocated the methodology laid out by George Kennedy which pays particular attention to the practices and expectations which are preserved in the rhetorical handbooks and works of late western antiquity. Chapter 1 also showed that *stasis* theory is an important part of rhetorical strategy, and has largely been ignored by modern biblical scholarship.

Chapter 2 took up the first two steps in our rhetorical analysis: a defense of 2 Corinthians 10-13 as a rhetorical unit, and a description of the rhetorical situation which prompted these chapters. Along with a review of traditional arguments regarding the compositional unity of 2 Corinthians, we also critiqued more recent rhetorical analyses which have claimed that these chapters form a fitting, logical, and appropriate ending to the argumentation of 2 Corinthians as a whole. Our analysis challenged those conclusions, and argued that 2 Corinthians 10-13 is best read as a separate rhetorical work, chronologically placed between 1 Corinthians and 2 Corinthians 1-9.

Chapter 2 then took up a description of the rhetorical situation which Paul seeks to address through this letter. Attention was focused on three main factors which became important in the Corinthians' evaluation of Paul; each of these factors had roots in behaviors already addressed in 1 Corinthians, and each of them affected the social status of both Paul and the Corinthians: 1) Paul's deliberate choice not to engage in the kind of rhetorical activity that was valued by society and expected by the Corinthians. 2) Paul's insistence on financial self-support. 3) The comparison being made between Paul and his rivals at Corinth. We concluded that Paul's rivals in 2 Cor 10-13 are probably Jewish Christian missionaries who had adopted the style and standards of hellenistic society, and who found in the Corinthians an audience that was eager to model church and apostolate after the pattern of competition between various teachers and philosophers practiced in Greco-Roman society.

Chapter 3 took up an analysis of the rhetorical arrangement of 2 Corinthians 10-13. Other studies have discussed only particular aspects of rhetoric in these chapters, or have attempted to fit 2 Corinthians 10-13 into a larger rhetorical unit of the whole of 2 Corinthians. Our study found that these chapters proceed in close agreement with the practice reflected in the rhetorical handbooks: 10:1-6 was analyzed as the *exordium*; 10:7-11 as the *propositio*; 10:12-18 as the *narratio*; 11:1-12:18 as the *probatio* (in three separate arguments: 11:1-15 dealing with the issue of who truly belongs to Christ, 11:16-12:13 dealing with Paul's boasting as a fool and in the Lord, 12:14-18 dealing with Paul's return to Corinth and his consistency regarding the collection for Jerusalem); 12:19-13:10 as the *peroratio*.

With that rhetorical analysis as a foundation, chapter 4 turned to examine the issues of rhetorical species and *stasis* as important considerations in understanding the argumentative strategy of this work. Recent scholarship has treated the issue of rhetorical species too mechanically, and thus has failed to recognize how the species of rhetoric can and does change according to the author's purpose and the developing needs and opportunities that arise in the course of the argumentation. Thus we saw that Paul begins this letter as a piece of deliberative rhetoric, urging the Corinthians to obedience. Since his own authority is under question, Paul moves on in chapter 11 and the first part of chapter 12 to engage in what must be considered judicial rhetoric, even though Paul considers it inappropriate to place his ministry under the approval or disapproval of the Corinthians. Throughout this argument, by means of irony and parody, Paul seeks to move the hearers to realize that their criteria are not proper, and have been brought to an end by the cross. With that established, Paul can return at 12:19 to deliberative rhetoric, again urging the Corinthians to examine themselves and return to a proper relationship with their apostle.

We also noted how recent scholarship has ignored the issue of rhetorical *stasis*, and we noted a shift in the primary *stases* of 2 Cor 10-13 which parallels the shift in species, and which clarifies the strategy of Paul in this letter. By examining the passages which our rhetorical analysis identified as pivotal, and which present us with Paul's perception of the points where he and the Corinthians are parting ways, we identified three primary *stases*.

In 10:1-18, Paul argues from the *stasis* of jurisdiction. The Corinthians have no authority to stand in judgment over his apostolic ministry so that they might reject it in favor of another that they would prefer. Paul supports this position by developing a strong sense of his *ethos* as one who is and will be engaged in spiritual battle on God's side, and as the one who was sent to Corinth as none other has been. Finally, the position is secured when Paul shows that such evaluations as the Corinthians want to do are based on the wrong standards: boasting must be only ἐν κυρίῳ, and judgment belongs to the Lord alone. This position, and the eschatological perspective which informs it, we found to be consistent with Paul's position in 1 Cor 1-4.

In 11:1, we found a shift in the *stasis* of the argument which corresponds with the shift in species. Paul sees that he will have to move onto the playing field chosen by the Corinthians; though they have no right to judge, he will for a time treat them as a jury. However, he attacks the entire situation by arguing on the *stasis* of quality that their whole scheme of evaluation has been brought to an end by God's eschatological action on the cross. Since it is the κύριος who must commend, Paul shows them that the nature of apostolic ministry must be derived from the nature of the κύριος on whom the proclamation is centered: Christ crucified.[1] God has worked salvation through the weakness of the cross, and God continues to work with divine power through the weakness of apostolic ministry. In the apostle whose life continues to display God's decision to work through human weakness, the eschatological power of God has infiltrated the present.

> The experienced tension between the Old and New Ages does not mean that the New is struggling to emerge out of the Old but that the intrusion of the New challenges the Old during the temporary overlap.[2]

Paul strengthens this position by adopting several eschatological roles for himself throughout this argument: father of the eschatological bride,

---

[1]"Paul's understanding of the apostolate, the Christian life, and indeed of the change in the cosmos itself, takes its structure from his understanding of the cross." Gaventa, "Apostle and Church," 192.

[2]Leander E. Keck, "Paul as Thinker," *Int* 47 (1993): 31.

opponent of Satan and his servants, one who has already been caught up out of this age.

Finally, at 12:19 we found another shift not only in species, but also in *stasis*. If Paul's argument so far has been successful, by this point he has led his audience to see that their enterprise of comparison and judgment has been turned on its head by God. The old-age ways of evaluation are now invalid, rendered ineffective by the cross; Paul has applied the pattern of Jesus' death and resurrection to apostolic ministry, and under its power the criteria of the Corinthians must give way.[3]

Paul is now able to return to the *stasis* which he preferred in 1 Cor 1-4 and 2 Cor 10, that of jurisdiction. Paul again warns his people that they do not have the right to stand in judgment over his apostolic ministry, and now he presents himself as the judge who will bring to them an anticipation of the eschatological judgment of God. Paul can do this because the Christ who was crucified in weakness and now lives by the power of God is the one who is speaking in him (2 Cor 13:3-4).

Though Paul has had to adjust his strategy to the difficulties presented to him in Corinth and must argue (for a time) as though they have the right to judge his ministry as their apostle, there is a fundamental consistency which underlies his argumentation. The consistent core in all of Paul's rhetoric around this issue, whether argued on the *stasis* of jurisdiction or of quality, is that the cross of Christ has become paradigmatic for apostolic ministry and for the church.

The eschatological crisis which the cross has brought upon the world is at the heart of Paul's argument in 1 Cor 1-4 and 2 Cor 10. God's action has shown the world's judgment to be worthless, part of a dying and doomed age. The Corinthians' view of God's power, and their placing of confidence (their boasting), must be shaped accordingly. Likewise, it is God's radical action on the cross that has turned the enterprise of apostolic competition and evaluation on its head. It deserves only irony and parody. The standards of the Corinthians, which are simply the standards of society smuggled into the church, have met their end at the cross. From now on, boasting will be in weakness, because it is through the weakness of the cross that God has chosen to reveal power. When in the final section of this letter Paul returns to the position that the Corinthians will not be the judges over him, it is again the eschatological

---

[3]Kraftchick, "Death in Us," 162, 164; Witherington, *Conflict & Community*, 298.

event of the cross that stands at the center of the argument.[4] It is the power of the Crucified which is at work in Paul, and Paul will be coming to Corinth with that power.

It has been claimed that the argument between Paul and his rivals in 2 Corinthians 10-13 was not over theology.

> Paul is at odds with his opponents not so much because they are offering "another gospel" (11:4), but because they do not accept his vision of ministry, that is, its cruciform, Christlike, and servant shape.[5]

However, to say that Paul's concern for a cruciform ministry is not a theological issue is to miss the point, just as it misses the point to credit Paul's emphasis on weakness to his frustration in Athens[6] or to his isolation from earlier missionary support,[7] or to summarize the difference between Paul and his rivals at Corinth as Paul's impression that they worked from self-serving motives.[8]

For Paul, the Corinthians' failure to understand that the life of the church and the apostolic ministry must continue to be shaped by the eschatological event of the cross struck at the very heart of the gospel. It is not that the Corinthian rivals rejected the cross as an event.[9] Paul is able

---

[4]It is only at this point that the cross becomes an explicit part of the discourse (13:4), but the determinative nature of the cross has been presumed from 10:1 onward. See Hay, "Shaping of Theology," 150-51; contra Max Alain Chevallier, "L'Argumentation de Paul dans II Corinthiens 10 à 13," *RHPR* 70 (1990): 12-15. Since Paul has chosen to build much of his early argumentation on irony and parody, he has waited until the end, when his approach is more straightforward, to bring the cross out into the open.

[5]Witherington, *Conflict & Community*, 442. A similar conclusion is reached by Sumney, *Identifying Paul's Opponents*. Talbert, *Reading Corinthians*, 117 sees more clearly that although it may be difficult to define the theological issue at stake, it is sufficiently serious for Paul to label the interlopers as preachers of "another gospel," a point that Witherington seems to pass over too lightly.

[6]Black, *Paul, Apostle of Weakness*, 101.

[7]Martin, *2 Corinthians*, lix. See Martin's more adequate analysis on pp. lx-lxi regarding the role of the cross in Paul's apostolic practice.

[8]Talbert, *Reading Corinthians*, 130.

[9]Morna Hooker, *Not Ashamed of the Gospel. New Testament Interpretations of the Death of Christ* (Grand Rapids: Eerdmans, 1994), 14 says "though the Corinthians played down the shame and scandal of the cross, they did not go so far as to deny that Christ had died."

to speak of the crucified Christ, and assume that the image will be accepted. But they did not embody the scandal of the cross in the life of the church or in the model of apostolic ministry.[10]

> What the Corinthians were in danger of forgetting was the implication
> of the manner of Jesus' death for their own way of life.[11]

Paul insists that it is the cross which must remain the paradigm for faith and ministry. The cross

> is not a station on the road to glory or a temporary diversion quickly to
> be passed over in a retelling of the story of Christ . . . . Rather the cross
> is the *esse* of Christian existence.[12]

The cross cannot be bypassed, because it is there rather than through what the world identifies as strength that God has chosen to save. Nor can it be dismissed by illegitimately anticipating the eschatological life of the resurrection; faith must be lived in the present, and until the Parousia the cross remains *the* criterion for the church's faith and mission.[13] It is insufficient to claim that life is found *after* death, or *after* the cross; rather, Paul insists, the heart of the gospel is that life is found *in the midst of* weakness, suffering, and death.[14] At stake is nothing less than the place of the cross in the ongoing life of the church, and in its understanding of how God has chosen to be known—theological stakes indeed!

Paul will not let the cross go. Since the cross is God's eschatological action which has judged the world, and since we continue to live on this side of the eschaton, we continue to know God only through the cross.

---

[10]Gaventa, "Apostle and Church," 191 states that both sides in the debate spoke of Jesus' death and resurrection, but for Paul it was the death that figured most prominently in the present conduct of ministry.

[11]Hooker, *Not Ashamed*, 14.

[12]Martin, *2 Corinthians*, lx-lxi.

[13]J. Louis Martyn, "Epistemology at the Turn of the Ages: 2 Corinthians 5:16," in *Christian History and Interpretation: Studies Presented to John Knox*, ed. W. R. Farmer, C. F. D. Moule, and R. R. Niebuhr (Cambridge: Cambridge University, 1967), 269-87.

[14]Roetzel, "As Dying," 9. Ernst Käsemann, "For and Against a Theology of Resurrection," 67: "If the cross is simply the gloomy entrance to heaven, the final and utmost obstacle to triumph, the Christian message does not fundamentally differ from what can be said by competing religions."

Thus with regard to the evaluations going on at Corinth, "the only test of the validity of any ministry is whether it conveys the word of Christ to his people,"[15] and that remains a word of the cross. Paul ties his own ministry with the message that he has been called to proclaim in an "indissoluble unity,"[16] so that the latter is translated into the former.[17] By doing so, Paul incurred what could only be judged by the criteria used in Corinth as shame.[18] Paul's opponents in Corinth were unwilling to see that the cross brought an end to old structures built on power, beauty and eloquence.

Thus Paul's task in this letter is to convince his people to abandon a view of faith, the church, and ministry that is supported by the standards and values of the society around them, and to accept a model that will mean the end of such values and quests for them: a cruciform model. Did Paul's rhetoric succeed? If our analysis of the order of these letters is correct, then the relative peace and reconciliation reflected in 2 Cor 1-9 is an indication that it did. Perhaps the fact that these letters were preserved at all is an indication that Paul's authority was restored at Corinth.[19] Another indication may be that the churches of Achaia do share in Paul's collection for the saints at Jerusalem (Rom 15:26).

If Paul's argument proved persuasive, it is in part because he had not yet completely lost the church at Corinth.[20] He built much of his argument on his own role as their apostle and their willingness to believe that he had a role in God's eschatological power active among them. He also succeeds because he not only argues for his own acceptance; in the process he demolishes the social criteria used in Corinth as well as the theological position of his critics.[21]

Whatever success Paul had with this letter appears to have been short-lived. By the end of the first century, the community is again fractured and in at least partial rebellion against its leaders, so that

---

[15]Barrett, *Second Epistle*, 335.

[16]Martin, *2 Corinthians*, lxiii.

[17]Thus Paul, explaining his ministry, speaks more of his own suffering in 2 Corinthians than he does in any of his other letters (1:4-10; 4:7-12, 16-17; 6:4-10; 7:5; 11:23-29; 12:7-10). See Murphy-O'Connor, *Theology*, 143.

[18]See Lincoln, "Paul the Visionary," 373; Marshall, *Enmity*, 402.

[19]Meeks, *First Urban Christians*, 137.

[20]See Hay, "Shaping of Theology," 150.

[21]Betz, "Problem of Rhetoric," 42.

Clement must reprimand them and remind them to read again what Paul had written.[22] Corinth does not easily embrace the cross.

Perhaps we should ask whether Paul's words can fare any better today. Are Paul's words about "power in weakness" simply an excuse to allow unqualified people to exercise authority in the church?[23] Can Paul's claim to be above the scrutiny and judgment of his congregation be tolerated in a day when the church suffers the pain of clergy misconduct in many forms? Do Paul's words only support irresponsible work and shoddy homiletics in the guise of ministry that has dismissed the importance of power, eloquence and beauty?

It is the consistent core of Paul's arguments that this study has identified which will guide a proper hearing of Paul's words. Throughout these dealings with Corinth, Paul has pointed to how God has fundamentally changed the world and marked the church with the cross. Paul is always aware not that he is beyond judgment, but that he is under the scrutiny and answerable to the judgment of God. It is the Lord who will or will not commend, and that Lord is the Crucified One. Paul remains answerable to the cross. The church today probably cannot and should not tolerate one who would claim authority in the way that Paul did in Corinth. Ministers must be answerable to congregations and church structures. Above all, they are responsible to embody the word of the cross for the people they serve. The church always seems to be tempted to simply adopt and reflect the values and criteria of the surrounding society as the means by which the church evaluates its ministries and ministers. The church cannot ignore Paul's call to life shaped by the criterion of the cross; it remains to be seen whether or not the church will hear it. Paul's arguments may or may not have succeeded in Corinth; the church still needs to listen.

---

[22]1 Clement 47. Clement apparently only knows about 1 Corinthians, and his comments may indicate that Corinth has failed to deal with Paul's words as carrying authority for them.

[23]Young and Ford, *Meaning and Truth*, 160.

SELECTED BIBLIOGRAPHY

REFERENCE WORKS

Balz, Horst, and Gerhard Schneider. *Exegetical Dictionary of the New Testament.* 3 vols. Grand Rapids: Eerdmans, 1990-93.
S.v. "ἐπιείκεια," by Heinz Giesen. 2:26.
S.v. "κανών," by Alexander Sand. 2:249.

Bauer, Walter A. *A Greek-English Lexicon of the New Testament and Other Early Christian Literature.* Trans., adapted, and augmented by William F. Arndt, F. Wilbur Gingrich, and Frederick W. Danker. 2d ed. Chicago: University of Chicago, 1979.

Blass, F., and A. Debrunner. *A Greek Grammar of the New Testament and Other Early Christian Literature.* Trans. and rev. by Robert W. Funk. Chicago: University of Chicago, 1961.

Brown, F., S. R. Driver and C. A. Briggs. *A Hebrew and English Lexicon of the Old Testament.* Oxford: Clarendon, 1972.

Buttrick, George Arthur, and Keith Crim, eds. *The Interpreter's Dictionary of the Bible.* 5 vols. Nashville: Abingdon, 1962, 1976.
S.v. "Corinthians, Second," by S. MacLean Gilmour. 1:692-98.
S.v. "Corinthians, Second Letter to the," by Dieter Georgi. Sup.:183-86.
S.v. "Rhetoric and Oratory," by Frederick C. Grant. 4:75-77.

Denis, Albert-Marie, ed. *Concordance grecque des pseudépigraphes d'Ancien Testament.* Louvain: Université Catholique de Louvain, 1987.

Gramcord. The Gramcord Institute. Vancouver, Wash.

Hammond, N. G. L., and H. H. Scullard, eds. *The Oxford Classical Dictionary.* 2d ed. Oxford: Clarendon, 1970.
S.v. "Education," by Frederick A. G. Beck. 369-72.
S.v. "Isocrates," by George Law Cawkwell. 554-55.

Hatch, Edwin, and Henry A. Redpath. *A Concordance to the Septuagint and Other Greek Versions of the Old Testament.* 3 vols. Oxford: Clarendon, 1897; reprint, Grand Rapids: Baker, 1983.

Kittel, Gerhard, ed. *Theological Dictionary of the New Testament.* 10 vols. Trans. G. W. Bromiley. Grand Rapids: Eerdmans, 1964-76. S.v. "ἀπόστολος," by Karl H. Rengstorf. 1:407-445. S.v. "κανών," by Hermann Wolfgang Beyer. 3:596-602. S.v. "καυχάομαι," by Rudolf Bultmann. 3:645-53. S.v. "ταπεινός," by Walter Grundmann. 8:1-26.

Lanham, Richard. *A Handlist of Rhetorical Terms.* Berkeley: University of California, 1968.

Liddell, Henry George, and Robert Scott. *A Greek-English Lexicon.* 9th ed. Rev. by Henry Stuart Jones and Roderick McKenzie. Oxford: Clarendon, 1968.

Moule, C. F. D. *An Idiom Book of New Testament Greek.* 2d ed. Cambridge: Cambridge University, 1959.

Moulton, J. H., W. F. Howard, and N. Turner. *A Grammar of New Testament Greek.* 4 vols. Edinburgh: T & T Clark, 1906-76.

Smyth, Herbert Weir. *Greek Grammar.* Rev. by Gordon M. Massing. Cambridge: Harvard University, 1956.

ANCIENT TEXTS AND TRANSLATIONS

The Apostolic Fathers. 2 vols. Trans. K. Lake. Loeb Classical Library. New York: Putnam's Sons, 1912-13.

Die apostolischen Väter. 3 Auflage. Ed. F. X. Funk and K. Bihlmeyer. Tübingen: Mohr, 1970.

Apuleius. *Metamorphoses.* 2 vols. Trans. J. Arthur Hanson. Loeb Classical Library. Cambridge: Harvard University, 1989.

Aristotle. *The Art of Rhetoric.* Trans. John Henry Freese. Loeb Classical Library. Cambridge: Harvard University, 1926.

_____. *The Politics.* Trans. H. Rackham. Loeb Classical Library. Cambridge: Harvard University, 1932; reprint ed., 1950.

_____. *Topica.* Trans. E. S. Forster. Loeb Classical Library. Cambridge: Harvard University, 1960.

Augustine. *On Christian Doctrine.* Indianapolis: Bobbs-Merrill, 1958.

Biblia Hebraica Stuttgartensia. Ed. K. Elliger, W. Rudolph, et al. Stuttgart: Deutsche Bibelgesellschaft, 1983.

Cicero. *Brutus, Orator.* Trans. G. L. Hendrickson and H. M. Hubbell. Loeb Classical Library. Cambridge: Harvard University, 1939.

_____. *De Inventione, De Optimo, Genere Oratorum, Topica.* Trans. H. M. Hubbell. Loeb Classical Library. Cambridge: Harvard University, 1949.

_____. *The Letters to Atticus.* 3 vols. Trans. E. O. Winstedt. Loeb Classical Library. Cambridge: Harvard University, 1912-18.

_____. *The Letters to His Friends.* 4 vols. Trans. W. Glynn Williams, M. Cary, and Mary Henderson. Loeb Classical Library. Cambridge: Harvard University, 1927-72.

_____. *De Oratore, De Fato, Paradoxa Stoicorum, De Partitione Oratoria.* 2 vols. Trans. E. W. Sutton and H. Rackham. Loeb Classical Library. Cambridge: Harvard University, 1942.

[_____]. *Rhetorica ad Herennium.* Trans. Harry Caplan. Loeb Classical Library. Cambridge: Harvard University, 1954.

The Cynic Epistles. A Study Edition. Ed. Abraham J. Malherbe. Missoula, Mont.: Scholars, 1977.

Demetrius. *On Style.* Trans. W. Hamilton Fyfe and W. Rhys Roberts. Loeb Classical Library. In Aristotle vol. 23, *The Poetics.* Cambridge: Harvard University, 1932.

Demosthenes. 7 vols. Trans. C. A. Vince and J. H. Vince. Loeb
Classical Library. Cambridge: Harvard University, 1926-49.

Dio Chrysostom. *Orations.* Trans. J. W. Cohoon and H. L. Crosby. 5
vols. Loeb Classical Library. Cambridge: Harvard University,
1932-51.

Diogenes Laertius. *The Lives of Eminent Philosophers.* 2 vols. Trans.
R. D. Hicks. Loeb Classical Library. Cambridge: Harvard
University, 1925.

Epictetus. *The Discourses as Reported by Arrian, The Manual, and
Fragments.* Trans. A. W. Oldfather. Loeb Classical Library. 2
vols. Cambridge: Harvard University, 1926-28.

Hermogenes. *On Stases.* Trans. with introduction and notes by Raymond
E. Nadeau. *Speech Monographs* 31 (1964): 361-424.

_____. *Hermogenis Opera.* Ed. H. Rabe. Rhetores Graeci VI.
Lipsiae: Teubner, 1913.

Homer. *The Iliad.* 2 vols. Trans. A. T. Murray. Loeb Classical Library.
Cambridge: Harvard University, 1924.

_____. *The Odyssey.* 2 vols. Trans. A. T. Murray. Loeb Classical
Library. Cambridge: Harvard University, 1953.

Irenaeus. "Against Heresies." In *The Ante-Nicene Fathers*, vol. 1, trans.
and ed. Alexander Roberts and James Donaldson, 309-567. New
York: Christian Literature Company, 1885.

Isocrates. 3 vols. Trans. George Norlin and Larue Van Hook. Loeb
Classical Library. Cambridge: Harvard University, 1928-45.

Josephus. 9 vols. Trans. H. St. J. Thackeray, R. Marcus, and L. H.
Feldman. Loeb Classical Library. Cambridge: Harvard University,
1956-65.

Juvenal. *The Satires.* Trans. G. G. Ramsay. Loeb Classical Library.
New York: G. P. Putnam's Sons, 1918.

Longinus. *On the Sublime.* Trans. W. H. Fyfe. Loeb Classical Library. In Aristotle vol. 23, *The Poetics.* Cambridge: Harvard University, 1927.

Lucian of Samosata. 8 vols. Trans. A. M. Harmon and M. D. Macleod. Loeb Classical Library. Cambridge: Harvard University, 1913-67.

Marcus Aurelius. *The Communings With Himself of Marcus Aurelius Antoninus, Emperor of Rome, together with His Speeches and Sayings.* Trans. C. R. Haines. Loeb Classical Library. Cambridge: Harvard University, 1930.

Martial. *Epigrams.* Loeb Classical Library. Cambridge: Harvard University, 1943.

New Testament Apocrypha. 2 vols. Ed. E. Hennecke, W. Schneemelcher, R. McL. Wilson. Philadelphia: Westminster, 1963, 1965.

Novum Testamentum Graece. 27th ed. Rev. and ed. K. Aland et al. Stuttgart: Deutsche Bibelgesellschaft, 1993.

The Old Testament Pseudepigrapha. 2 vols. Ed. J. H. Charlesworth. Garden City, N.Y.: Doubleday, 1983-85.

The Oxyrhynchus Papyri. Ed. B. P. Grenfell, A. S. Hunt, et al. London: Egypt Exploration Fund, 1898-.

Philo. 12 vols. Trans. F. H. Colson, G. H. Whitaker, et al. Loeb Classical Library. Cambridge: Harvard University, 1929-53.

Philostratus. *The Life of Apollonius of Tyana.* 2 vols. Trans. F. C. Conybeare. Loeb Classical Library. Cambridge: Harvard University, 1912.

_____. *The Lives of the Sophists.* Trans. W. C. Wright. Loeb Classical Library. New York: Putnam's Sons, 1922.

Plato. 12 vols. Trans. H. N. Fowler, W. R. M. Lamb, et al. Loeb Classical Library. Cambridge: Harvard University, 1914-35.

_____. *The Collected Dialogues.*   Ed. Edith Hamilton and Huntington Cairns. Princeton: Princeton University, 1961.

Pliny. *Letters, Panegyricus.* 2 vols. Trans. B. Radice. Loeb Classical Library. Cambridge: Harvard University, 1969.

Plutarch. *Lives.* 11 vols. Trans. B. Perrin. Loeb Classical Library. Cambridge: Harvard University, 1914-26.

_____. "On Praising Oneself Inoffensively." In *Plutarch's Moralia*, Vol. 7, 110-167. Trans. Phillip H. De Lacy and Benedict Einerson. Loeb Classical Library. Cambridge: Harvard University, 1959.

Polybius. *The Histories.* 6 vols. Trans. W. R. Paton. Loeb Classical Library. Cambridge: Harvard University, 1922-27.

Quintilian. *Institutio Oratoria.* Trans. H. E. Butler. Loeb Classical Library. 4 vols. Cambridge: Harvard University, 1920-22.

Seneca. *Ad Lucilium Epistulae Morales.* 3 vols. Trans. R. M. Gummere. Loeb Classical Library. New York: Putnam's Sons, 1918-25; rev. ed. 1943, 1953.

_____. *Moral Essays.* 3 vols. Trans. John W. Basore. Loeb Classical Library. Cambridge: Harvard University, 1928-35.

Seneca the Elder. *Controversiae, Suasoriae.* Trans. M. Winterbottom. 2 vols. Loeb Classical Library. Cambridge: Harvard University, 1974.

Septuaginta. Ed. A. Rohlfs. Stuttgart: Deutsche Bibelgesellschaft, 1935.

Sparks, H. F. D., ed. *The Apocryphal Old Testament.* Oxford: Oxford University, 1984.

Suetonius. *The Lives of the Caesars.* 2 vols. Trans. J. C. Rolfe. Loeb Classical Library. Cambridge: Harvard University, 1914.

Tacitus. "A Dialog on Oratory." In *Tacitus. Agricola, Germania, Dialogus*. Trans. M. Hutton and William Peterson. Loeb Classical Library. Cambridge: Harvard University, 1914; rev. ed. 1970.

Tacitus. *The Histories and the Annals*. 4 vols. Trans. C. H. Moore and J. Jackson. Loeb Classical Library. Cambridge: Harvard University, 1925-37.

Tertullian. "On Modesty." In *The Ante-Nicene Fathers*, vol. 4, trans. S. Thelwall, ed. Alexander Roberts and James Donaldson, 74-101. New York: Christian Literature Company, 1885.

Xenophon. 7 vols. Trans. Carleton L. Brownson et al. Loeb Classical Library. Cambridge: Harvard University, 1918-68.

COMMENTARIES ON 2 CORINTHIANS

Allo, Ernest Berhard. *Saint Paul. Seconde épître aux Corinthiens*. Paris: Gabalda, 1956.

Arrington, French L. *The Ministry of Reconciliation: A Study of 2 Corinthians*. Grand Rapids: Baker, 1980.

Barrett, C. K. *A Commentary on the Second Epistle to the Corinthians*. New York: Harper & Row, 1973; reprint, Peabody, Mass.: Hendrickson, 1987.

Best, Ernest. *Second Corinthians*. Interpretation Commentaries. Louisville: John Knox, 1987.

Bruce, F. F. *1 & 2 Corinthians*. London: Marshall, Morgan & Scott, 1971.

Bultmann, Rudolf. *The Second Letter to the Corinthians*. Göttingen: Vandenheock & Ruprecht, 1976; reprint ed., Minneapolis: Augsburg, 1985.

Carrez, Maurice. *La deuxième épître de Saint Paul aux Corinthiens*. Geneva: Labor et Fides, 1986.

Carson, D. A. *From Triumphalism to Maturity: An Exposition of II Corinthians 10-13*. Grand Rapids: Baker, 1984.

Danker, Frederick. *II Corinthians*. Augsburg Commentary on the New Testament. Minneapolis: Augsburg, 1989.

Filson, Floyd V. "The Second Epistle to the Corinthians." In *The Interpreter's Bible* 10:265-425. Ed. G. Buttrick et al. Nashville: Abingdon, 1953.

Furnish, Victor Paul. *II Corinthians*. The Anchor Bible. Garden City: Doubleday, 1984.

Goudge, Henry L. *The Second Epistle to the Corinthians*. London: Methuen & Co., 1927.

Hanson, R. P. C. *2 Corinthians*. Torch Bible Commentaries. London: SCM Press, 1967.

Harris, Murray J. "2 Corinthians." In *The Expositor's Bible Commentary*. 10:301-406. Ed. F. E. Gaebelein. Grand Rapids: Zondervan, 1976.

Heinrici, Carl F. G. *Das zweite Sendschreiben des Apostels Paulus an die Korinther*. Berlin: Hertz, 1887.

Héring, Jean. *The Second Epistle of St. Paul to the Corinthians*. Trans. A. W. Heathcote and P. J. Allcock. London: Epworth, 1967.

Hughes, Philip E. *Paul's Second Epistle to the Corinthians*. NICNT. Grand Rapids: Eerdmans, 1962.

John Chrysostom. *The Homilies of Saint John Chrysostom Archbishop of Constantinople, on the Epistles of Paul to the Corinthians*. The Nicene and Post-Nicene Fathers, Vol. 12. New York: Christian Literature Company, 1889.

Kennedy, J. H. *The Second and Third Epistles of St. Paul to the Corinthians*. London: Methuen, 1900.

Kruse, C. G. *The Second Epistle of Paul to the Corinthians: An Introduction and Commentary.* Tyndale New Testament Commentaries. Grand Rapids: Eerdmans, 1987.

Lang, Friedrich. *Die Briefe an die Korinther.* Göttingen: Vandenhoeck & Ruprecht, 1986.

Lietzmann, Hans. *An die Korinther I, II.* With supplement by W. G. Kümmel. Tübingen: Mohr, 1969.

Martin, Ralph P. *2 Corinthians.* Word Biblical Commentary. Waco, Tex.: Word, 1986.

Menzies, Allan. *The Second Epistle of the Apostle Paul to the Corinthians.* London: Macmillan & Co., 1912.

Pfitzner, Victor C. *Strength in Weakness: A Commentary on 2 Corinthians.* Adelaide: Lutheran Publishing House, 1992.

Plummer, Alfred. *A Critical and Exegetical Commentary on the Second Epistle of Paul to the Corinthians.* ICC. Edinburgh: T & T Clark, 1915.

Strachen, Robert H. *The Second Epistle of Paul to the Corinthians.* New York: Harper & Brothers, 1935.

Talbert, Charles. *Reading Corinthians: A Literary and Theological Commentary on 1 and 2 Corinthians.* New York: Crossroads, 1987.

Tasker, R. V. G. *The Second Epistle to the Corinthians.* Grand Rapids: Eerdmans, 1958.

Wendland, Heinz Dietrich. *Die Briefe an die Korinther.* 15th ed. Göttingen: Vandenhoeck & Ruprecht, 1980.

Windisch, Hans. *Der zweite Korintherbrief.* Göttingen: Vandenhoeck and Ruprecht, 1924. Reprint ed. G. Strecker, 1970.

Witherington, Ben III.   *Conflict and Community in Corinth: A Socio-Rhetorical Commentary on 1 and 2 Corinthians.* Grand Rapids: Eerdmans, 1995.

Wolff, Christian. *Der zweite Brief des Paulus an die Korinther.* Berlin: Evangelische Verlagsanstalt, 1989.

OTHER MONOGRAPHS AND ARTICLES

Achtemeier, Paul J. "Omne Verbum Sonat: The New Testament and the Oral Environment of Late Western Antiquity." *JBL* 109 (1990): 3-27.

Aletti, J. N.   "La dispositio rhétorique dans le épîtres pauliniennes: proposition de méthode." *NTS* 38 (1992): 385-401.

Allo, Ernest Berhard. "Le defaut d'eloquence et de 'style oral' de Saint Paul." *RSPT* 23 (1934): 29-39.

Armstrong, A. Hillary, ed. *Cambridge History of Later Greek and Early Medieval Philosophy.* London: Cambridge University, 1967.

_____. "Greek Philosophy from the Age of Cicero to Plotinus." In *The Crucible of Christianity: Judaism, Hellenism and the Historical Background to the Christian Faith*, ed. Arnold Toynbee, 209-14. New York: World, 1969.

Aune, David E.   *The New Testament in Its Literary Environment.* Philadelphia: Westminster, 1987.

_____.   *Prophecy in Early Christianity and the Ancient Mediterranean World.* Grand Rapids: Eerdmans, 1983.

Bahr, Gordon J. "Paul and Letter Writing in the First Century." *CBQ* 28 (1966): 465-77.

_____. "The Subscriptions in the Pauline Letters." *JBL* 87 (1968): 27-41.

Baird, William. "Visions, Revelation and Ministry: Reflections on 2 Corinthians 12:1-5 and Galatians 1:11-17." *JBL* 104 (1985): 651-62.

Barré, Michael L. "Paul as 'Eschatological Person:' A New Look at 2 Corinthians 11:29." *CBQ* 37 (1975): 500-26.

_____. "Qumran and the Weakness of Paul." *CBQ* 42 (1980): 216-27.

Barrett, C. K. "Cephas and Corinth." Chap. in *Essays on Paul*. Philadelphia: Westminster, 1982.

_____. "Christianity at Corinth." Chap. in *Essays on Paul*. Philadelphia: Westminster, 1982.

_____. *The First Epistle to the Corinthians*. New York: Harper & Row, 1968; reprint, Peabody, Mass.: Hendrickson, 1987.

_____. "Paul's Opponents in Second Corinthians." *NTS* 17 (1971): 233-54.

_____. "ψευδαπόστολοι (2 Cor 11:13)." Chap. in *Essays on Paul*. Philadelphia: Westminster, 1982.

Bassler, Jouette. "Perspectives from Paul, 1: Money and Mission; 2: The Great Collection." Chap. in *God and Mammon: Asking for Money in the New Testament*. Nashville: Abingdon, 1991.

Bates, W. H. "The Integrity of 2 Corinthians." *NTS* 12 (1965-66): 50-69.

Batey, Richard. "Paul's Interaction with the Corinthians." *JBL* 84 (1965): 139-46.

Baumgarten, Siegmund Jakob. *Auslegung der beiden Briefe St. Pauli an die Corinther*. Halle: Gebauer, 1761.

Baur, Ferdinand C. *Paul: His Life and Work*. 2 vols. Rev. A. Menzies. London: Williams and Norgate, 1875-76.

Baur, Karl Ludwig. *Rhetoricae Paulinae, vel Quid oratorium sit in oratione Pauli.* 2 vols. Halae: Impensis Orphanotrophei, 1782.

Beaudean, William. *Paul's Theology of Preaching.* Macon, Ga.: Mercer University, 1988.

Berger, Klaus. "Hellenistiche Gattungen im Neuen Testament." In *Austieg und Niedergang der Römischen Welt* 2.25.2, ed. Hildegard Temorini and Wolfgang Haase, 1031-432. Berlin: de Gruyter, 1984.

_____. "Rhetorical Criticism, New Form Criticism, and New Testament Hermeneutics." In *Rhetoric and the New Testament: Essays from the 1992 Heidelberg Conference*, ed. Stanley Porter and Thomas Olbricht, 390-96. JSNT Sup. 90. Sheffield: JSOT, 1993.

Betz, Hans Dieter. *Der Apostel Paulus und die sokratische Tradition, Eine exegetische Untersuchung zu einer "Apologie" 2 Korinther 10-13.* Beiträge zur historischen Theologie 45. Tübingen: Mohr-Siebeck, 1972.

_____. *Galatians.* Hermeneia Commentary. Philadelphia: Fortress, 1979.

_____. *Paul's Apology: II Cor. 10-13 and the Socratic Tradition.* Berkeley: Center for Hermeneutical Studies, 1975.

_____. "The Problem of Rhetoric and Theology According to the Apostle Paul." In *L'Apôtre Paul: Personalité, style et conception du ministère*, ed. A. Vanhoye, 16-48. Leuven: Leuven University, 1986.

_____. *2 Corinthians 8 & 9. A Commentary on Two Administrative Letters of the Apostle Paul.* Hermeneia Commentary. Philadelphia: Fortress, 1985.

Bitzer, Lloyd F. "The Rhetorical Situation." *Philosophy and Rhetoric* 1 (1968): 1-14.

Bjerkelund, Carl J. *Parakalo: Form, Funktion und Sinn der parakalo-Sätze in den paulinischen Briefen.* Oslo: Universitetsforlaget, 1967.

Black, C. Clifton III. "Keeping Up With Recent Studies: Rhetorical Criticism and Biblical Interpretation." *ExpTim* 100 (1989): 252-58.

_____. "Rhetorical Questions: The New Testament, Classical Rhetoric, and Current Interpretation." *Dialog* 29 (1990): 62-63, 68-71.

Black, David Alan. *Paul, Apostle of Weakness. Astheneia and Its Cognates in the Pauline Literature.* New York: Lang, 1984.

Blass, Friedrich Wilhelm. *Die Rhythmen der asianischen und römischen Kunstprosa.* Leipzig: Diechert, 1905.

Bonner, Stanley F. *Education in Ancient Rome.* London: Methuen, 1970.

_____. *Roman Declamation in the Late Republic and Early Empire.* Liverpool: University of Liverpool, 1949.

Boomershine, Thomas E. "Epistemology at the Turn of the Ages in Paul, Jesus and Mark: Rhetoric and Dialectic in Apocalyptic and the New Testament." In *Apocalyptic and the New Testament*, ed. J. Marcus and M. Soards, 147-67. Sheffield: JSOT Press, 1989.

Bornkamm, Günther. "Faith and Reason in Paul." Chap. in *Early Christian Experience.* New York: Harper & Row, 1969.

_____. "The History of the So-Called Second Letter to the Corinthians." *NTS* 8 (1962): 258-64.

_____. *Paul.* New York: Harper & Row, 1971.

Botha, Pieter J. J. "Greco-Roman Literacy as Setting for New Testament Writings." *Neot* 26 (1992): 195-215.

_____. "The Verbal Art of the Pauline Letters: Rhetoric, Performance and Presence." In *Rhetoric and the New Testament:*

Essays from the 1992 Heidelberg Conference, ed. Stanley Porter and Thomas Olbricht, 409-28. JSNT Sup. 90. Sheffield: JSOT, 1993.

Bouwsma, William J. *Calvinism as Theologia Rhetorica.* Ed. Wilhelm Wuellner. Berkeley: University of California, 1987.

Bowersock, G. W. *Greek Sophists in the Roman Empire.* Oxford: Clarendon, 1969.

Braet, Antione. "The Classical Doctrine of Status and the Rhetorical Theory of Argumentation." *Philosophy and Rhetoric* 20 (1987): 79-93.

Bruce, F. F. *Paul, Apostle of the Heart Set Free.* Grand Rapids: Eerdmans, 1977.

Buck, C. H. "The Collection for the Saints." *HTR* 43 (1950): 1-29.

Bultmann, Rudolf. *Exegetische Probleme des zweiten Korintherbriefes.* Uppsala: Wretmans, 1947.

_____. "The Significance of the Historical Jesus for the Theology of Paul." Chap. in *Faith and Understanding.* London: SCM Press, 1969.

_____. *Der Stil der paulinischen Predigt und die kynischstoische Diatribe.* Göttingen: Vandenhoeck & Ruprecht, 1910.

Caird, George B. "Everything to Everyone: The Theology of the Corinthian Epistles." *Int* 13 (1959): 387-99.

Cambier, Jules. "Le critère paulinien de l'apostolat en 2 Cor 12,6s." *Biblica* 43 (1962): 481-518.

Carrez, Maurice. "Réalité christologique et référence apostolique de l'apôtre Paul en présence d'une église divisée (2 Cor 10-13)." In *L'Apôtre Paul: Personalité, style et conception du ministère*, ed. A. Vanhoye, 163-83. Leuven: Leuven University, 1986.

Carroll, John T., and Joel B. Green. *The Death of Jesus in Early Christianity.* Peabody, Mass.: Hendrickson, 1995.

Chadwick, Henry. *The Enigma of St. Paul.* London: Athlone, 1969.

Chevallier, Max Alain. "L'argumentation de Paul dans II Corinthiens 10 à 13." *RHPR* 70 (1990): 3-15.

Chow, John K. *Patronage and Power. A Study of Social Networks in Corinth.* JSNT Sup. 75. Sheffield: JSOT Press, 1992.

Clark, D. L. *Rhetoric in Greco-Roman Education.* New York: Columbia University, 1957.

Clarke, Andrew D. *Secular & Christian Leadership in Corinth: A Socio-Historical and Exegetical Study of 1 Corinthians 1-6.* Leiden: Brill, 1993.

Clarke, M. L. *Higher Education in the Ancient World.* London: Routledge & Kegan Paul, 1971.

_____. *Rhetoric at Rome.* London: Cohen and West, 1953.

Classen, C. J. "St. Paul's Epistles and Ancient Greek and Roman Rhetoric." *Rhetorica* 10 (1992): 319-44.

Collins, John J. "Chiasmus, the 'ABA' Pattern and the Text of Paul." In *Analytica* 17, 575-84. Rome: Pontifical Biblical Institute, 1963.

Conley, Thomas M. *Philon Rhetor. A Study of Rhetoric and Exegesis: Protocol of the Forty-Seventh Colloquy.* Berkeley: Center for Hermeneutical Studies in Hellenistic & Modern Culture, 1984.

Conzelmann, Hans. *1 Corinthians.* Hermeneia Commentary. Trans. James W. Leitch. Philadelphia: Fortress, 1975.

Corbett, Edward. *Classical Rhetoric for the Modern Student.* Oxford: Oxford University, 1965.

Corrington, Gail Paterson. *The Divine Man: His Origin & Function in Hellenistic Popular Religion.* Frankfurt: Peter Lang, 1986.

Cousar, Charles B. *A Theology of the Cross. The Death of Jesus in the Pauline Letters.* Minneapolis: Fortress, 1990.

Crafton, Jeffrey. *The Agency of the Apostle: A Dramatistic Analysis of Paul's Response to Conflict in 2 Corinthians.* JSNT Sup. 51. Sheffield: JSOT Press, 1991.

Culpepper, R. Alan. *Anatomy of the Fourth Gospel: A Study in Literary Design.* Philadelphia: Fortress, 1983.

Danker, Frederick. *Benefactor: Epigraphic Study of a Greco-Roman and New Testament Semantic Field.* St. Louis: Clayton Publishing, 1982.

_____. "Paul's Debt to the 'De Corona' of Demosthenes: A Study of Rhetorical Techniques in Second Corinthians." In *Persuasive Artistry: Essays in New Testament Rhetoric in Honor of George A. Kennedy,* ed. Duane F. Watson, 262-80. Sheffield: Sheffield Academic Press, 1991.

Daube, David. "Rabbinic Methods of Interpretation and Hellenistic Rhetoric." *HUCA* 22 (1949): 239-64.

Deissmann, Adolf. *Light from the Ancient East: The New Testament Illustrated by Recently Discovered Texts of the Greco-Roman World.* Trans. L. R. M. Strachan. London: Hodder & Stoughton, 1927.

_____. *Paul: A Study in Social and Religious History.* 2d ed. Trans. W. Wilson. London: Hodder & Stoughton, 1926.

Dewey, Arthur J. "A Matter of Honor: A Social-Historical Analysis of 2 Corinthians 10." *HTR* 78 (1985): 209-17.

Dill, Samuel. "The Philosophic Missionary." Chap. in *Roman Society from Nero to Marcus Aurelius.* London: Macmillan & Co., 1937.

Dodd, C. H. *The Apostolic Preaching and Its Development*. New York: Harper & Row, 1965.

Doty, William G. "The Classification of Epistolary Literature." *CBQ* 31 (1969): 183-99.

_____. *Letters in Primitive Christianity*. Philadelphia: Fortress, 1973.

Doughty, Darrell J. "The Presence and Future of Salvation in Corinth." *ZNW* 66 (1975): 61-90.

Downing, F. Gerald. "Cynics and Christians." *NTS* 30 (1984): 584-93.

Drescher, Richard. "Der zweite Korintherbrief und die Vorgänge in Korinth seit Abfassung des ersten Korintherbriefs." *TSK* 70 (1897): 43-111.

Dunn, James D. G. *Jesus and the Spirit. A Study of the Religious and Charismatic Experience of Jesus and the First Christians as Reflected in the New Testament*. London: SCM Press, 1975.

Eagleton, Terry. *Literary Theory: An Introduction*. Minneapolis, Minn.: University of Minnesota, 1983.

Ellingworth, Paul. "Grammar, Meaning and Verse Divisions in 2 Cor 11:16-29." *BT* 43 (1992): 245-46.

Elliott, John H. "Patronage and Clientism in Early Christian Society: A Short Reading Guide." *Forum* 3 (1987): 39-48.

Ellis, E. Earle. "Christ Crucified." In *Reconciliation and Hope. New Testament Essays in Atonement and Eschatology Presented to L. L. Morris*, ed. Robert Banks, 69-75. Exeter: Paternoster Press, 1974.

_____. "Paul and His Opponents." Chap. in *Prophecy and Hermeneutic in Early Christianity*. Grand Rapids: Eerdmans, 1978.

_____. "Paul and His Opponents: Trends in Research." In *Christianity, Judaism and Other Greco-Roman Cults: Studies for*

Morton Smith at Sixty, Part 1, ed. Jacob Neusner, 264-98. Leiden: Brill, 1975.

_____. *Paul and His Recent Interpreters*. Grand Rapids: Eerdmans, 1961.

_____. *Pauline Theology: Ministry and Society*. Grand Rapids: Eerdmans, 1989.

Elsom, Helen. "The New Testament and Greco-Roman Writing." In *The Literary Guide to the Bible*, ed. R. Alter and F. Kermode, 561-78. Cambridge: Harvard University, 1987.

Fantham, Elaine. "Imitation and Decline: Rhetorical Theory and Practice in the First Century after Christ." *Classical Philology* 73 (1978): 102-16.

Fitzgerald, John T. *Cracks in an Earthen Vessel: An Examination of the Catalogues of Hardships in the Corinthian Correspondence*. SBLDS 99. Atlanta: Scholars, 1988.

_____. "Paul, the Ancient Epistolary Theorists, and 2 Corinthians 10-13." In *Greeks, Romans and Christians*, ed. David L. Balch, Everett Ferguson and Wayne A. Meeks, 190-200. Minneapolis: Fortress, 1990.

Forbes, Christopher. "Comparison, Self-Praise, & Irony: Paul's Boasting and the Conventions of Hellenistic Rhetoric." *NTS* 32 (1986): 1-30.

_____. "Unaccustomed As I Am: St. Paul the Public Speaker in Corinth." *Buried History* 19 (1983): 11-16.

Fredrickson, David E. "Freedom of Speech in the Pauline Epistles." Unpublished paper presented at 1993 Society of Biblical Literature meeting.

Fridrichsen, Anton. "Zum Stil des paulinischen Peristasenkatalogs, 2 Cor 11:23ff." *Symbolae Osloenses* 7 (1928): 25-29.

Friedrich, Gerhard. "Die Gegner des Paulus im 2 Korintherbrief." In *Abraham unser Vater*, ed. O. Betz, M. Hengel and P. Schmidt, 181-215. Leiden: Brill, 1963.

Fuchs, Eric. "La Faiblese, glorie de l'apostolat selon Paul. Étude sur 2 Corinthiens 10-13." *ETR* 55 (1980): 231-53.

Funk, Robert W. "The Apostolic Parousia: Form and Significance." In *Christian History and Interpretation: Studies Presented to John Knox*, ed. W. R. Farmer, C. F. D. Moule and R. R. Niebuhr, 249-68. Cambridge: Cambridge University, 1967.

_____. *Language, Hermeneutic, and Word of God: The Problem of Language in the New Testament and Contemporary Theology.* New York: Harper & Row, 1966.

Gager, John G. "Functional Diversity in Paul's Use of End-Time Language." *JBL* 89 (1970): 325-37.

Gamble, Harry. "The Redaction of the Pauline Letters and the Formation of the Pauline Corpus." *JBL* 94 (1975): 403-18.

Garland, David E. "Paul's Apostolic Authority: The Power of Christ Sustaining Weakness (2 Corinthians 10-13)." *RevExp* 86 (1989): 371-89.

Garnsey, Peter. *Social Status and Legal Privilege in the Roman Empire.* Oxford: Clarendon, 1970.

Garrett, Susan R. "The God of This World and the Affliction of Paul: 2 Cor 4:1-12." In *Greeks, Romans, and Christians: Essays in Honor of Abraham J. Malherbe*, ed. D. L. Balch, E. Ferguson, and W. A. Meeks, 99-117. Minneapolis: Fortress, 1990.

Gaventa, Beverly Roberts. "Apostle and Church in 2 Corinthians: A Response to David M. Hay and Steven J. Kraftchick." In *Pauline Theology II: 1 & 2 Corinthians*, ed. David M. Hay, 182-99. Minneapolis: Fortress, 1993.

Georgi, Dieter. "Forms of Religious Propoganda." In *Jesus in His Time*, ed. Hans Jürgen Schultz, 124-31. Philadelphia: Fortress, 1971.

_____. *The Opponents of Paul in Second Corinthians*. Philadelphia: Fortress, 1986.

_____. *Remembering the Poor: The History of Paul's Collection for Jerusalem*. Nashville: Abingdon, 1992.

_____. "Socioeconomic Reasons for the 'Divine Man' as a Propogandistic Pattern." In *Aspects of Religious Propoganda in Judaism and Early Christianity*, ed. Elisabeth Schüssler Fiorenza, 27-42. Notre Dame: University of Notre Dame, 1976.

Gill, David W. J. "In Search of the Social Elite in the Corinthian Church." *TynB* 44 (1993): 323-37.

Gitay, Yegoshua. *Prophecy and Persuasion: A Study of Isaiah 40-48*. Forum Theologiae Linguisticae 14. Ed. Erhardt Güttgemanns. Bonn: Linguistica Biblica, 1981.

Glasswell, M. E. "Some Issues of Church and Society in the Light of Paul's Eschatology." In *Paul and Paulinism: Essays in Honour of C. K. Barrett*, ed. M. Hooker, 310-19. London: SPCK, 1982.

Goguel, Maurice. *Introduction au Nouveau Testament. IV/2: Les Épîtres pauliniennes*. Paris: Leroux, 1926.

Grant, Robert M. "Work and Occupation." Chap. in *Early Christianity and Society*. San Francisco: Harper & Row, 1977.

Gunther, John J. *St. Paul's Opponents and Their Background: A Study of Apocalyptic and Jewish Sectarian Teachings*. Leiden: Brill, 1973.

Guthrie, D. *New Testament Introduction*. 3d ed. Chicago: Inter-Varsity Press, 1970.

Güttgemanns, Erhardt. *Der leidende Apostel und sein Herr*. Göttingen: Vandenhoeck & Ruprecht, 1966.

Hafemann, Scott. "Self-Commendation and Apostolic Legitimacy in 2 Corinthians." *NTS* 36 (1990): 66-88.

Hall, Robert G. "The Rhetorical Outline for Galatians: A Reconsideration." *JBL* 106 (1987): 277-87.

Hamerton-Kelly, Robert G. "Paul's Hermeneutic of the Cross." *Dialog* 32 (1993): 247-54.

Hanson, Anthony Tyrrell. *The Paradox of the Cross in the Thought of St. Paul.* JSNT Sup. 17. Sheffield: Sheffield Academic Press, 1987.

Harada, Makoto. "Paul's Weakness: A Study in Pauline Polemics (2 Cor 10-13)." Ph.D. diss., Boston University, 1968.

Harrisville, Roy A. "A Critique of Current Biblical Criticism." *Word and World* 15 (1995): 206-13.

Harvey, A. E. "Forty Strokes Save One: Social Aspects of Judaizing and Apostasy." Chap. in *Alternate Approaches to New Testament Study.* London: SPCK, 1985.

Hausrath, Adolf. *Der Vier-Capitelbrief des Paulus an die Korinther.* Heidelberg: Bassermann, 1870.

Hay, David M. "Paul's Indifference to Authority." *JBL* 88 (1969): 36-44.

_____. "The Shaping of Theology in 2 Corinthians: Convictions, Doubts, and Warrants." Chap. in *Pauline Theology Vol. II: 1 & 2 Corinthians.* Minneapolis: Fortress, 1993.

_____, ed. *Pauline Theology, Vol. II: 1 and 2 Corinthians.* Minneapolis: Fortress, 1993.

Heinrici, Carl F. G. "Zum Hellenismus des Paulus." Chap. in *Der zweite Brief an die Korinther, mit einem Anhang.* Göttingen: Vandenhoeck & Ruprecht, 1900.

Hengel, Martin. *Judaism and Hellenism. Studies in their Encounter in Palestine during the Early Hellenistic Period.* Trans. John Bowden. Philadelphia: Fortress, 1974.

_____. *The Pre-Christian Paul.* London: SCM Press, 1991.

Hester, James D. "Placing the Blame: The Presence of Epideictic in Galatians." In *Persuasive Artistry: Essays in New Testament Rhetoric in Honor of George A. Kennedy,* ed. Duane F. Watson, 281-307. Sheffield: Sheffield Academic Press, 1991.

_____. "Rhetorical Structure of Galatians 1:1-2:14." *JBL* 103 (1984): 223-33.

_____. "The Use and Influence of Rhetoric in Galatians." *TZ* 42 (1986): 386-408.

Hickling, Colin J. A. "Is the Second Epistle to the Corinthians a Source for Early Christian History?" *ZNW* 66 (1975): 284-87.

Hock, Ronald F. "Simon the Shoemaker as the Ideal Cynic." *GRBS* 17 (1976): 41-53.

_____. *The Social Context of Paul's Ministry: Tentmaking and Apostleship.* Philadelphia: Fortress, 1980.

Hodgson, Robert. "Paul the Apostle and First Century Tribulation Lists." *ZNW* 74 (1983): 59-80.

Holladay, Carl. *Theios Aner in Hellenistic Judaism: A Critique of the Use of This Category in New Testament Christology.* SBLDS 40. Missoula: Scholars, 1977.

Holland, Glenn. "Speaking Like a Fool: Irony in 2 Corinthians 10-13." In *Rhetoric and the New Testament: Essays from the 1992 Heidelberg Conference,* ed. Stanley Porter and Thomas Olbricht, 250-64. JSNT Sup. 90. Sheffield: JSOT, 1993.

Holmberg, Bengt. *Paul and Power: The Structure of Authority in the Primitive Church as Reflected in the Pauline Epistles.* Philadelphia: Fortress, 1980.

Hooker, Morna D. *Not Ashamed of the Gospel. New Testament Interpretations of the Death of Christ.* Grand Rapids: Eerdmans, 1994.

Horsley, G. H. R, ed. *New Documents Illustrating Early Christianity.* New Ryde: Macquarrie University, 1981-87.

Horsley, Richard. "How Can Some of You Say There Is No Resurrection of the Dead? Spiritual Elitism in Corinth." *NovT* 20 (1978): 203-40.

_____. "Pneumatikos versus Psychikos: Distinction of Status Among the Corinthians." *HTR* 69 (1976): 269-88.

_____. "Wisdom of Word and Words of Wisdom in Corinth." *CBQ* 39: 224-39.

Hughes, F. W. *Early Christian Rhetoric and 2 Thessalonians.* JSNT Sup. 30. Sheffield: JSOT, 1989.

Humphries, Raymond. "Paul's Rhetoric of Argumentation in 1 Cor 1-4." Ph.D. diss., Graduate Theological Union, 1979.

Hydahl, N. "Die Frage nach der literarischen Einheit des zweiten Korintherbriefes." *ZNW* 64 (1973): 289-306.

Jennrick, Walter A. "Classical Rhetoric in the New Testament." *Classical Journal* 44 (1948): 30-32.

Jervell, Jacob. "The Signs of an Apostle: Paul's Miracles." Chap. in *The Unknown Paul.* Minneapolis: Augsburg, 1984.

Judge, E. A. "Cultural Conformity and Innovation in Paul: Some Clues from Contemporary Documents." *TynB* 35 (1984): 3-24.

_____. "The Early Christians as a Scholastic Community: Part II." *JRH* 1 (1960-61): 125-27.

_____. "Paul's Boasting in Relation to Contemporary Professional Practice." *AusBR* 16 (1968): 37-50.

_____. "The Reaction Against Classical Education in the New Testament." *Evangelical Review of Theology* 9 (1985): 166-74.

_____. "The Social Identity of the First Christians: A Question of Method in Religious History." *JRH* 11 (1980): 201-17.

_____. *The Social Pattern of Christian Groups in the First Century.* London: Tyndale, 1960.

_____. "St. Paul and Classical Society." *JAC* 15 (1972): 19-36.

_____. "St. Paul and Socrates." *Interchange: Papers on Biblical and Current Questions* 13 (1973): 106-16.

Käsemann, Ernst. "For and Against a Theology of Resurrection: I & II Corinthians." Chap. in *Jesus Means Freedom.* Philadelphia: Fortress, 1969.

_____. "Die Legitimität des Apostels: Eine Untersuchung zu II Kor. 10-13." *ZNW* 41 (1942): 33-71.

_____. "On the Subject of Primitive Christian Apocalyptic." Chap. in *New Testament Questions of Today.* Philadelphia: Fortress, 1969.

_____. "The Saving Significance of the Death of Jesus in Paul." Chap. in *Perspectives on Paul.* Philadelphia: Fortress, 1971.

_____. "Sentences of Holy Law in the New Testament." Chap. in *New Testament Questions of Today.* Philadelphia: Fortress, 1969.

Kaster, R. A. "Notes on 'Primary' and 'Secondary' Schools in Late Antiquity." *TAPA* 113 (1983): 323-46.

Keck, Leander E. "Paul as Thinker." *Int* 47 (1993): 27-38.

Kee, Doyle. "Who Were the 'Super-Apostles' of 2 Cor 10-13?" *Restoration Quarterly* 23 (1980): 65-76.

Kennedy, George A. *The Art of Persuasion in Greece.* Princeton: Princeton University, 1963.

_____. *The Art of Rhetoric in the Roman World: 300 B.C. - A.D. 300.* Princeton: Princeton University, 1972.

_____. *Classical Rhetoric and Its Secular Tradition from Ancient to Modern Times.* Chapel Hill: University of North Carolina, 1980.

_____. *New Testament Interpretation Through Rhetorical Criticism.* Chapel Hill: University of North Carolina, 1984.

_____. *Quintilian.* New York: Twayne Publishers, 1969.

_____. "Truth and Rhetoric in the Pauline Epistles." In *The Bible as Rhetoric*, ed. M. Warner, 195-202. London: Routledge, 1990.

Kessler, Martin. "An Introduction to Rhetorical Criticism." *Semitics* 7 (1980): 1-27.

_____. "A Methodological Setting for Rhetorical Criticism." *Semitics* 4 (1974): 22-36.

Kingsbury, Jack Dean. "The 'Divine Man' as the Key to Mark's Christology—The End of an Era?" *Int* 35 (1981): 243-57.

Koester, Helmut. *Introduction to the New Testament.* 2 vols. Philadelphia: Fortress, 1982.

Kraftchick, Steven J. "Death in Us, Life in You: The Apostolic Medium." In *Pauline Theology, Volume II: 1 & 2 Corinthians*, ed. David M. Hay, 156-81. Minneapolis: Fortress, 1993.

Krenkel, Max. *Beiträge zur Aufhellung der Geschichte und der Briefe des Apostels Paulus.* 2d ed. Braunschweig: Schwetschke, 1895.

Kruse, C. G. "The Relationship between the Opposition to Paul Reflected in 2 Corinthians 1-7 and 10-13." *EvQ* 61 (1989): 195-202.

Kümmel, Werner Georg. *Introduction to the New Testament*. Nashville: Abingdon, 1975.

Lake, Kirsopp. *The Earlier Epistles of St. Paul*. London: Rivington's, 1927.

Lambrecht, Jan. "Rhetorical Criticism and the New Testament." *Bijdragen: Tidjschrift voor Philosophia en Theologie* 50 (1989): 239-53.

Lampe, Geoffrey. "Church Discipline and the Interpretations of the Epistles to the Corinthians." In *Christian History and Interpretation: Studies Presented to John Knox*, ed. W. R. Farmer, C. F. D. Moule, and R. R. Niebuhr, 337-61. Cambridge: Cambridge University, 1967.

Lampe, Peter. "Theological Wisdom and the 'Word About the Cross:' The Rhetorical Scheme of 1 Corinthians 1-4." *Int* 44 (1990): 117-31.

Lane, William L. "Covenant: Key to Paul's Conflict with Corinth." *TynB* 33 (1982): 3-29.

Lausberg, Heinrich. *Handbuch der literarischen Rhetorik*. Munich: Heubner, 1960.

Leivestad, Ragnar. "The Meekness and Gentleness of Christ: 2 Cor. 10:1." *NTS* 12 (1966): 156-64.

Lincoln, Andrew T. "Paul the Visionary: The Setting and Significance of the Rapture to Paradise in 2 Corinthians 12:1-10." *NTS* 25 (1979): 204-20.

_____. "2 Corinthians, the Heavenly House and the Third Heaven." Chap. in *Paradise Now and Not Yet: Studies in the Role of the*

Heavenly Dimension in Paul's Thought with Special Reference to his Eschatology. Cambridge: Cambridge University, 1981.

Litfin, A. D. "St. Paul's Theology of Proclamation: An Investigation of 1 Corinthians 1-4 in the Light of Greco-Roman Rhetoric." Ph.D. diss., Oxford University, 1983.

Longenecker, Richard N. *Galatians.* Word Biblical Commentary. Dallas, Tex.: Word, 1990.

Loubser, J. A. "A New Look at Paradox and Irony in 2 Corinthians 10-13." *Neot* 26 (1992): 507-21.

Lund, N. *Chiasmus in the New Testament.* Chapel Hill: University of North Carolina, 1942.

Lundy, Susan Ruth and Wayne N. Thompson. "Pliny, A Neglected Roman Rhetorician." *The Quarterly Journal of Speech* 66 (1980): 407-17.

Luther, Martin. *Lectures on Galatians, 1535, Chapters 1-4.* Luther's Works, Vol. 26. Ed. Jaroslav Pelikan. St. Louis: Concordia, 1963.

Lyons, George. *Pauline Autobiography: Toward a New Understanding.* SBLDS 73. Atlanta: Scholars, 1985.

Machalet, Christian. "Paulus und seine Gegner: Eine Untersuchung zu den Korintherbriefen." In *Theokratia: Jahrbuch des Inst. Judaicum Delitzschianum II*, ed. W. Dietrich et al., 183-203. Leiden: Brill, 1970-72.

Mack, Burton. *Rhetoric and the New Testament.* GBS. Philadelphia: Fortress, 1990.

Malherbe, Abraham J. *Ancient Epistolary Theorists.* Atlanta: Scholars, 1988.

_____. "Antisthenes and Odysseus, and Paul at War." *HTR* 76 (1983): 143-74.

_____. "The Corinthian Collection." *Restoration Quarterly* 3 (1959): 221-33.

_____. "Exhortation in First Thessalonians." *NovT* 25 (1983): 238-56.

_____. *Paul and the Popular Philosophers*. Minneapolis: Fortress, 1989.

_____. "Paul: Hellenistic Philosopher or Christian Pastor?" *ATR* 68 (1986): 3-13.

_____. "A Physical Description of Paul." In *Christians Among Jews and Gentiles*, ed. George W. E. Nickelsburg and George W. MacRae, 170-75. Philadelphia: Fortress, 1986.

_____. "Seneca on Paul as Letter Writer." In *The Future of Early Christianity*, ed. B. A. Pearson, 414-21. Minneapolis: Fortress, 1983.

_____. *Social Aspects of Early Christianity*. Philadelphia: Fortress, 1983.

Malina, Bruce J. *The New Testament World: Insights from Cultural Anthropology*. Louisville: John Knox, 1981.

Manson, Thomas W. "The Corinthian Correspondence." Chap. in *Studies in the Gospels and Epistles*. Manchester: Manchester University, 1962.

Marguerat, Daniel "2 Corinthiens 10-13: Paul et l'expérience de Deiu." *ETR* 63 (1988): 497-519.

Marrou, Henri. *A History of Education in Antiquity*. Madison, Wisc.: University of Wisconsin, 1982.

Marshall, Peter. *Enmity in Corinth: Social Conventions in Paul's Relations with the Corinthians*. Tübingen: Mohr, 1987.

_____. "Invective: Paul and His Enemies in Corinth." In *Perspectives on Language and Text*, ed. E. Conrad and E. Newing, 359-73. Winona Lake, Ind.: Eisenbrauns, 1987.

Martin, Dale B. *The Corinthian Body.* New Haven: Yale University, 1995.

_____. *Slavery as Salvation: The Metaphor of Slavery in Pauline Christianity.* New Haven: Yale University, 1990.

Martin, Ralph P. "The Opponents of Paul in 2 Corinthians: An Old Issue Revisited." Chap. in *Tradition and Interpretation in the New Testament.* Grand Rapids: Eerdmans, 1987.

_____. "The Setting of 2 Corinthians." *TynB* 37 (1986): 3-19.

Martin, Troy. "Apostasy to Paganism: The Rhetorical Stasis of The Galatian Controversy." *JBL* 114 (1995): 437-61.

Martyn, J. Louis. "Epistemology at the Turn of the Ages: 2 Corinthians 5:16". In *Christian History and Interpretation: Studies Presented to John Knox*, ed. W. R. Farmer, C. F. D. Moule, and R. R. Niebuhr, 269-87. Cambridge: Cambridge University, 1967.

McCant, Jerry W. "Paul's Thorn of Rejected Apostleship." *NTS* 34 (1988): 550-72.

McClelland, S. E. "Super-Apostles, Servants of Christ, Servants of Satan: A Response." *JSNT* 14 (1982): 82-87.

Meeks, Wayne A. *The First Urban Christians: The Social World of the Apostle Paul.* New Haven: Yale University, 1983.

_____. "Social Functions of Apocalyptic Language in Pauline Christianity." In *Apocalypticism in the Mediterranean World*, ed. D. Hellholm, 687-705. Tübingen: Mohr, 1983.

Melanchthon, Philipp. "Commentarii in epistolem ad Romanos." Wittenberg, 1532. Ed. Rolf Schäfer. In *Melanchthon's Werke in Auswahl* 5. Gütersloh: Mohn, 1965.

Metzger, Bruce M. *A Textual Commentary on the Greek New Testament.* New York: United Bible Societies, 1971.

Meynet, R. "Histoire de 'l'analyse rhétorique' en exégèse biblique." *Rhetorica* 8 (1990): 291-312.

Minear, Paul S. "Some Pauline Thoughts on Dying: A Study of 2 Corinthians." In *From Faith to Faith: Essays in Honor of Donald G. Miller on His Seventieth Birthday*, ed. D. Y. Hadidian, 91-106. Pittsburgh: Pickwick, 1979.

Mitchell, Margaret M. *Paul and the Rhetoric of Reconciliation.* Tübingen: Mohr, 1991.

Mott, Stephen C. "The Power of Giving and Receiving: Reciprocity in Hellenistic Benevolence." In *Current Issues in Biblical and Patristic Interpretation: Studies in Honor of Merrill C. Tenney*, ed. G. F. Hawthorne, 60-72. Grand Rapids: Eerdmans, 1975.

Muilenburg, James. "Form Criticism and Beyond." *JBL* 88 (1969): 1-18.

Mullins, T. Y. "Paul's Thorn in the Flesh." *JBL* 76 (1957): 299-303.

Munck, Johannes. *Paul and the Salvation of Mankind.* Trans. F. Clarke. Richmond: John Knox, 1959.

Murphy, James. *A Synoptic History of Classical Rhetoric.* New York: Random House, 1972.

Murphy-O'Connor, Jerome. "Another Jesus (2 Cor 11:4)." *RB* 97 (1990): 238-51.

_____. "Co-Authorship in the Corinthian Correspondence." *RB* 100 (1993): 562-79.

_____. "The Date of 2 Corinthians 10-13." *AusBR* 39 (1991): 31-43.

_____. *St. Paul's Corinth: Texts and Archaeology.* Wilmington, Del.: Michael Glazier, 1983.

_____. *The Theology of the Second Letter to the Corinthians.* Cambridge: Cambridge University, 1991.

Nadeau, Ray. "Classical Systems of Stases in Greek: Hermagoras to Hermogenes." *GRBS* 2 (1959): 51-71.

Nickle, Keith. *The Collection: A Study in Paul's Strategy.* London: SCM Press, 1966.

Nisbet, P. "The Thorn in the Flesh." *ExpTim* 80 (1969): 126.

Nock, A. D. *Conversion.* Oxford: Oxford University, 1933.

_____. *St. Paul.* New York: Harper & Brothers, 1938.

Norden, Eduard. *Die Antike Kunstprosa vom VI Jahrhundert v. Chr. bis in die Zeit der Renaissance.* 3d ed., 1898; reprint ed., Stuttgart: Teubner, 1958.

O'Brien, Peter Thomas. *Introductory Thanksgivings in the Letters of Paul.* Leiden: Brill, 1977.

O'Collins, Gerald G. "Power Made Perfect in Weakness: 2 Cor 12:9-10." *CBQ* 33 (1971): 528-37.

Olson, Stanley N. "Confidence Expressions in Paul: Epistolary Conventions and the Purpose of 2 Corinthians." Ph.D. diss., Yale University, 1976.

_____. "Epistolary Uses of Expressions of Self-Confidence." *JBL* 103 (1984): 585-97.

_____. "Pauline Expressions of Confidence in his Addressees." *CBQ* 47 (1985): 282-95.

Oostendorp, Derk William. *Another Jesus: A Gospel of Jewish-Christian Superiority in 2 Corinthians.* Kampen: J. H. Kok, 1967.

Park, David M. "Paul's σκόλοψ τῇ σαρκί: Thorn or Stake?" *NovT* 22 (1980): 179-83.

Patrick, Dale. *Rhetoric and Biblical Interpretation*. Sheffield: Almond, 1990.

Perelman, Chaim. *The New Rhetoric and the Humanities. Essays on Rhetoric and Its Applications*. Dordrecht: Reidel, 1979.

_____ and L. Olbrechts-Tyteca. *The New Rhetoric: A Treatise on Argumentation*. Trans. J. Wilkinson and P. Weaver. Notre Dame: Notre Dame University, 1969.

Peterson, Norman. *Literary Criticism for New Testament Critics*. GBS. Philadelphia: Fortress, 1978.

Plank, Karl A. *Paul and the Irony of Affliction*. Atlanta: Scholars, 1987.

Pogoloff, Stephen Mark. "Isocrates and Contemporary Hermeneutics." In *Persuasive Artistry: Studies in New Testament Rhetoric in Honor of George A. Kennedy*, ed. Duane F. Watson, 338-62. Sheffield: Sheffield Academic Press, 1991.

_____. *Logos and Sophia: The Rhetorical Situation of First Corinthians*. SBLDS 134. Atlanta: Scholars, 1992.

Porter, Stanley. "The Theoretical Justification for Application of Rhetorical Categories to Pauline Epistolary Literature." In *Rhetoric and the New Testament: Essays from the 1992 Heidelberg Conference*, ed. Stanley Porter and Thomas Olbricht, 100-122. JSNT Sup. 90. Sheffield: JSOT, 1993.

Price, James L. "Aspects of Paul's Theology and Their Bearing on Literary Problems of Second Corinthians." In *Studies in the History and Text of the New Testament: Festschrift for K. W. Clark*, ed. B. D. Daniels and M. J. Suggs, 95-106. Grand Rapids: Eerdmans, 1967.

Price, Robert M. "Punished in Paradise (An Exegetical Theory on 2 Corinthians 12:1-10)." *JSNT* 7 (1980): 33-40.

Puskas, Charles B. *The Letters of Paul: An Introduction.* Collegeville, Minn.: Liturgical Press, 1993.

Räisänen, Heikki. *Paul and the Law.* 2d ed. Tübingen: Mohr, 1987.

Raymond, James C. "Enthymemes, Examples, and Rhetorical Method." In *Essays in Classical Rhetoric and Modern Discourse,* ed. Robert J. Connerset et al., 140-51. Edwardsville, Ill.: South Illinois, 1984.

Reed, Jeffrey T. "Using Ancient Rhetorical Categories to Interpret Paul's Letters: A Question of Genre." In *Rhetoric and the New Testament: Essays from the 1992 Heidelberg Conference,* ed. Stanley Porter and Thomas Olbricht, 292-324. JSNT Sup. 90. Sheffield: JSOT, 1993.

Reumann, John. "St. Paul's Use of Irony." *LQ* 7 (1955): 140-45.

Rhoads, David, and Donald Michie. *Mark as Story: An Introduction to the Narrative of a Gospel.* Philadelphia: Fortress, 1982.

Robbins, Vernon, and John H. Patton. "Rhetorical and Biblical Criticism." *Quarterly Journal of Speech* 66 (1980): 32-50.

Roetzel, Calvin. "As Dying, and Behold We Live: Death and Resurrection in Paul's Theology." *Int* 46 (1992): 5-18.

_____. *Judgment in the Community: A Study of the Relationship Between Eschatology and Ecclesiology in Paul.* Leiden: Brill, 1972.

Rogahn, Kenneth. "The Function of Future-Eschatological Statements in the Pauline Epistles." Ph.D. diss., Princeton, 1975.

Rowland, C. *The Open Heaven. A Study of Apocalyptic in Judaism and Early Christianity.* London: SPCK, 1982.

Royaards, Hermannus Joannes. *Disputatio inauguralis De altera Pauli ad Corinthios epistola, et observanda in illa apostoli indole et oratione.* Trajecti ad Rhenum: J. Altheer, 1818.

Ruegg, U. "Paul et la rhetorique ancienne." *Bulletin du centre protestant d'etudes* 35 (1983): 5-35.

Russell, D. A. *Greek Declamation.* Cambridge: Cambridge University, 1983.

Saake, Helmut. "Paulus als Ekstatiker. Pneumatologische Beobachtungen zu 2 Kor 12, 1-10." *Bib* 53 (1972): 404-10.

Saller, R. P. *Personal Patronage under the Empire.* Cambridge: Cambridge University, 1982.

Sampley, J. Paul. "Before God I Do Not Lie (Gal. 1:20): Paul's Self-Defense in the Light of Roman Legal Praxis." *NTS* 23 (1977): 477-82.

_____. "Paul, His Opponents in 2 Corinthians 10-13, and the Rhetorical Handbooks." In *The Social World of Formative Christianity and Judaism*, ed. Jacob Neusner, Peder Borgen, Ernest S. Frerichs and Richard Horsley, 162-77. Philadelphia: Fortress, 1988.

Savage, T. B. "Power Through Weakness: An Historical and Exegetical Examination of Paul's Understanding of the Ministry in 2 Corinthians." Ph.D. diss., Cambridge University, 1986.

Schäfer, R. "Melanchthon's Hermeneutik im Römerbrief-Kommentar von 1532." *ZTK* 60 (1963): 216-35.

Schmithals, Walter. *Gnosticism in Corinth: An Investigation of the Letters to the Corinthians.* Trans. John E. Steely. Nashville: Abingdon, 1971.

_____. *The Office of Apostle in the Early Church.* Nashville: Abingdon, 1969.

Schnackenburg, Rudolf. "Apostles Before and During Paul's Time." In *Apostolic History and the Gospel*, ed. W. W. Gasque and R. P. Martin, 287-303. Grand Rapids: Eerdmans, 1970.

Schneider, N. *Die rhetorische Eigenart der paulinischen Antithese.* Tübingen: Mohr, 1970.

Schöllgen, G. "Was wissen wir über die Sozialstruktur der paulinischen Gemeinde?" *NTS* 34 (1988): 71-82.

Schrage, Wolfgang. "Leid, Kreuz und Eschaton: Die Peristasenkataloge als Merkmale paulinischer theologia crucis und Eschatologie." *EvT* 34 (1974): 141-75.

Schubert, Paul. *Form and Function of the Pauline Thanksgivings.* Berlin: Töpelmann, 1939.

Schutz, John Howard. *Paul and the Anatomy of Apostolic Authority.* Cambridge: Cambridge University, 1975.

Schweizer, Eduard. "Dying and Rising With Christ." *NTS* 14 (1967-68): 1-11.

Semler, Johann S. *Paraphrasis II. Epistolae ad Corinthos.* Halle, 1776.

Sevenster, Jan N. *Paul and Seneca.* Leiden: Brill, 1961.

Smith, Morton. "On the History of the 'Divine Man'." In *Paganisme, Judaisme, Christianisme,* ed. F. F. Bruce, 335-45. Paris: Éditions E. De Boccard, 1978.

_____. "Prolegomena to a Discussion of Aretalogies, Divine Men, the Gospels & Jesus." *JBL* 90 (1971): 174-99.

Smith, N. G. "The Thorn that Stayed. An Exposition of 2 Cor 12:7-9." *Int* 13 (1959): 409-16.

Smith, William A. *Ancient Education.* New York: Philosophical Library, 1955.

Snyman, Andreas H. "On Studying the Figures (Schemata) in the New Testament." *Bib* 69 (1988): 93-107.

Spencer, Aida Besançon. *Paul's Literary Style: A Stylistic and Historical Comparison of II Corinthians 11:16-12:13, Romans 8:9-39 and Philippians 3:2-4:13*. Jackson, Mo.: Evangelical Theological Society, 1984.

_____. "The Wise Fool (and the Foolish Wise)." *NovT* 23 (1981): 349-60.

Spittler, Russell P. "The Limits of Ecstasy: An Exegesis of 2 Corinthians 12:1-10." In *Current Issues in Biblical and Patristic Interpretation in Honor of Merrill C. Tenney*, ed. G. F. Hawthorne, 259-66. Grand Rapids: Eerdmans, 1975.

Stambaugh, John E. and David L. Balch. *The New Testament in Its Social Environment*. Philadelphia: Westminster, 1986.

Stamps, Dennis L. "Rethinking the Rhetorical Situation: The Entextualization of the Situation in New Testament Epistles." In *Rhetoric and the New Testament: Essays from the 1992 Heidelberg Conference*, ed. Stanley Porter and Thomas Olbricht, 193-210. JSNT Sup. 90. Sheffield: JSOT, 1993.

_____. "Rhetorical Criticism and the Rhetoric of New Testament Criticism." *Journal of Literature and Theology* 6 (1992): 268-79.

Standaert, Beno. "La rhetorique ancienne dans saint Paul." In *L'Apôtre Paul: Personalité, style et conception du ministère*, ed. A. Vanhoye, 78-92. Leuven: Leuven University, 1986.

Stephenson, Alan M. G. "A Defense of the Integrity of 2 Corinthians." Chap. in *The Authorship and Integrity of the New Testament*. London: SPCK, 1965.

Stevenson, T. R. "The Ideal Benefactor and the Father Analogy in Greek and Roman Thought." *Classical Quarterly* 42 (1992): 421-36.

Stirewalt, M. Luther. "Paul's Evaluation of Letter Writing." In *Search the Scriptures: New Testament Studies in Honor of Raymond T. Stamm*, ed. J. M. Myers, O. Reimherr, and H. N. Bream, 179-96. Leiden: Brill, 1969.

Stowers, Stanley K. *The Diatribe and Paul's Letter to the Romans.* SBLDS 57. Chico, Calif.: Scholars, 1981.

_____. *Letter Writing in Greco-Roman Antiquity.* Philadelphia: Westminster, 1986.

_____. "Paul on the Use and Abuse of Reason." In *Greeks, Romans and Christians: Essays in Honor of Abraham J. Malherbe*, 253-86. Minneapolis: Fortress, 1990.

_____. "Social Status, Public Speaking and Private Teaching: The Circumstances of Paul's Preaching Activity." *NovT* 26 (1984): 59-82.

Strecker, Georg. "Die Legitimität des paulinischen Apostolates nach 2 Korinther 10-13." *NTS* 38 (1992): 566-86.

Sumney, Jerry L. *Identifying Paul's Opponents: The Question of Method in 2 Corinthians.* JSNT Sup. 40. Sheffield: JSOT Press, 1990.

Tabor, James D. *Things Unutterable: Paul's Ascent to Paradise in its Greco-Roman, Judaic, and Early Christian Contexts.* Studies in Judaism. Lanham, Md.: University Press of America, 1986.

Taylor, N. H. "The Composition and Chronology of Second Corinthians." *JSNT* 44 (1991): 67-87.

Theissen, Gerd. *The Social Setting of Pauline Christianity: Essays on Corinth.* Philadelphia: Fortress, 1982.

Thiele, Georg. *Hermagoras: Ein Beitrag zur Geschichte der Rhetorik.* Strassburg: Trubner, 1893.

Thierry, Johannes Jacobus. "Der Dorn im Fleische (2 Kor 12:7-9)." *NovT* 5 (1962): 301-10.

Thiselton, Anthony C. "Realized Eschatology in Corinth." *NTS* 24 (1977-78): 510-26.

Thrall, Margaret E. "Super-Apostles, Servants of Christ, Servants of Satan." *JSNT* 6 (1980): 42-57.

Tiede, David L. *The Charismatic Figure as Miracle Worker.* Missoula, Mont.: Scholars, 1972.

Travis, Stephen H. *Paul's Boasting in 2 Corinthians 10-12.* Studia Evangelica VI. Berlin: Akademic Verlag, 1973.

Van Unnik, Willem C. "First Century A.D. Literary Culture and Early Christian Literature." *NedTTs* 25 (1971): 28-43.

Vielhauer, Philipp. *Geschichte der urchristlichen Literatur.* Berlin: de Gruyter, 1975.

Voelz, James W. "The Language of the New Testament." In *Austieg und Niedergang der Römischen Welt* 2.25.2, ed. Hildegard Temorini and Wolfgang Haase, 893-977. Berlin: Walter de Gruyter, 1984.

Von Campenhausen, Hans. "Apostolic Authority and the Freedom of the Congregation in the Thought of Paul." Chap. in *Ecclesiastical Authority and Spiritual Power in the Church of the First Three Centuries.* London: Adam & Charles Black, 1969.

Watson, Duane F. "1 Corinthians 10:23-11:1 in the Light of Greco-Roman Rhetoric: The Role of Rhetorical Questions." *JBL* 108 (1989): 301-18.

_____. "1 John 2:12-14 as Distributio, Conduplicatio, and Expolitio: A Rhetorical Understanding." *JSNT* 35 (1989): 97-110.

_____. *Invention, Arrangement, and Style: Rhetorical Criticism of Jude and 2 Peter.* SBLDS 104. Atlanta: Scholars, 1988.

_____. "The New Testament and Greco-Roman Rhetoric: A Bibliographical Update." *Journal of the Evangelical Theological Society* 33 (1990): 513-24.

_____. "The New Testament and Greco-Roman Rhetoric: A Bibliography." *Journal of the Evangelical Theological Society* 31 (1988): 465-72.

_____. "A Rhetorical Analysis of Philippians and Its Implications for the Unity Question." *NovT* 30 (1988): 57-88.

_____, and Alan Hauser. *Rhetorical Criticism of the Bible: A Comprehensive Bibliography With Notes on History and Method.* Leiden: Brill, 1994.

Watson, Francis. "2 Corinthians 10-13 and Paul's Painful Letter to the Corinthians." *JTS* 35 (1984): 324-46.

Webb, William J. *Returning Home: New Covenant and Sacred Exodus as the Contextual Framework for 2 Corinthians.* JSNT Sup. 85. Sheffield: JSOT, 1993.

Weiss, Johannes. "Beiträge zur paulinischen Rhetorik." In *Theologische Studien, Bernhard Weiss zu seinem 70 Geburtstag dargebracht,* 165-247. Göttingen: Vandenhoeck & Ruprecht, 1910.

_____. *Das Urchristentum.* Göttingen: Vandenhoeck & Ruprecht, 1917. Translation: *The History of Primitive Christianity.* Trans. by "four friends." Ed. F. C. Grant. New York: Wilson-Erickson, 1937.

Wettstein, Johann Jacob. Η ΚΑΙΝΗ ΔΙΑΘΗΚΗ. *Novum Testamentum Graecum.* 2 vols. Amsterdam: Ex officina Dommeriana, 1751, 1752.

White, John L. *Light from Ancient Letters.* Philadelphia: Fortress, 1986.

_____. "St. Paul and the Apostolic Letter Tradition." *CBQ* 45 (1983): 433-44.

Wilckins, Ulrich. *Weisheit und Torheit. Eine exegetisch-religionsgeschichtliche Untersuchung zu 1 Kor. 1 und 2.* Tübingen: Mohr, 1959.

Wilder, Amos. *The Language of the Gospel: Early Christian Rhetoric.* New York: Harper & Row, 1964.

Wiles, Maurice. *The Divine Apostle: The Interpretation of St. Paul's Epistles in the Early Church.* Cambridge: Cambridge University, 1967.

Wilke, Christian Gottlob. *Die neutestamentliche Rhetorik: Ein Seitenstück zur Grammatik des neutestamentlichen Sprachidioms.* Dresden: Arnold, 1843.

Winter, Bruce. "Are Philo and Paul Among the Sophists? A Hellenistic Jewish and Christian Response to a First Century Movement." Ph.D. diss., Macquarrie University, 1988.

Wire, Antoinette Clark. *Corinthian Women Prophets: A Reconstruction Through Paul's Rhetoric.* Minneapolis: Fortress, 1990.

Woods, Laurie. "Opposition to a Man and His Message: Paul's 'Thorn in the Flesh' (2 Cor 12:7)." *AusBR* 39 (1991): 44-53.

Wuellner, Wilhelm. "Biblical Exegesis in the Light of the History and Historicity of Rhetoric and the Nature of the Rhetoric of Religion." In *Rhetoric and the New Testament: Essays from the 1992 Heidelberg Conference,* ed. Stanley Porter and Thomas Olbricht, 492-513. JSNT Sup. 90. Sheffield: JSOT, 1993.

_____. "Greek Rhetoric and Pauline Argumentation." In *Early Christian Literature and the Classical Intellectual Tradition: In Honorem Robert M. Grant,* ed. R. Schoedel and Robert Wilken, 177-88. Paris: Beauchesne, 1979.

_____. "Paul as Pastor: The Function of Rhetorical Questions in First Corinthians." In *L'Apôtre Paul: Personnalité, style et conception du ministère,* ed. A. Vanhoye, 49-77. Leuven: Leuven University, 1986.

_____. "Paul's Rhetoric of Argumentation in Romans: An Alternative to the Donfried-Karris Debate over Romans." In *The*

Romans Debate (Revised and Expanded), ed. Karl P. Donfried, 128-46. Peabody, Mass.: Hendrickson, 1991.

_____. "Where is Rhetorical Criticism Taking Us?" *CBQ* 49 (1987): 448-63.

Young, Francis and David F. Ford. *Meaning and Truth in 2 Corinthians.* Grand Rapids: Eerdmans, 1988.

Zmijewski, Josef. *Der Stil der paulinischen "Narrenrede." Analyse der Sprachgestaltung in 2 Kor 11,1-12,10 als Beitrag zur Methodik von Stiluntersuchungen neutestamentlicher Texte.* Cologne: Hanstein, 1978.